D1738902

The Text of
Genesis 1–11

בראשית

4QGen[h(title)]

The Text of Genesis 1–11

Textual Studies and Critical Edition

Ronald S. Hendel

New York   Oxford
Oxford University Press
1998

Oxford University Press

Oxford   New York
Athens   Auckland   Bangkok   Bogota   Bombay
Buenos Aires   Calcutta   Cape Town   Dar es Salaam
Delhi   Florence   Hong Kong   Istanbul   Karachi
Kuala Lumpur   Madras   Madrid   Melbourne
Mexico City   Nairobi   Paris   Singapore
Taipei   Tokyo   Toronto   Warsaw

and associated companies in
Berlin   Ibadan

Copyright © 1998 by Ronald S. Hendel

Published by Oxford University Press, Inc.
198 Madison Avenue, New York, New York 10016

Oxford is a registered trademark of Oxford University Press

Library of Congress Cataloging-in-Publication Data
Hendel, Ronald S.
The text of Genesis 1–11 : textual studies and critical edition /
Ronald S. Hendel
p.   cm.
Includes bibliographical references and indexes.
ISBN 0-19-511961-4
1. Bible. O.T. Genesis I–XI—Criticism, Textual.   I. Title.
BS1235.2.H3595   1998
222'.110446—dc21   97-27791

1 3 5 7 9 8 6 4 2

Printed in the United States of America
on acid-free paper

For Frank

who taught me the pleasures of the text

Preface

The frontispiece to this book is a fragment of the oldest preserved title page or dust jacket (*page de gard*) of Genesis, 4QGen[h(title)]. The alert reader will note that the word בראשית has suffered a scribal error: the א is missing. This mistake, motivated by the phonetic quiescence of א in the speech of this period, is fairly common in the Qumran scrolls (Qimron 1986: 25–26; cf. several instances in the retelling of Genesis 1 in 4QJub[a]; DJD 13, 13–14). This earliest evidence for the Hebrew title of Genesis provides a striking example of the vicissitudes of ancient texts and is an apt reminder of the simple necessity of textual criticism of the Hebrew Bible.

This work began as preparation for a commentary on Genesis 1–11 but soon grew to its own proportions. To comment on a biblical book involves, among other things, ascertaining what the text is. This leads necessarily to an examination of the extant textual evidence. If one chooses to comment on a particular biblical manuscript, such as the Aleppo Codex (as represented in the HUBP) or the St. Petersburg Codex (as represented in *BHS*), one needs a rationale for having made such a choice and for not engaging with the other textual evidence. With the ongoing publication of the Qumran biblical texts, it has become increasingly difficult for a biblical scholar to be a Masoretic fundamentalist. In other words, to comment on a biblical text requires making serious text-critical decisions, whether or not one acknowledges having made those decisions. These issues concerning the biblical text are central to the very possibility of biblical commentary in the post-Qumran age.

One of the chief contentions of this work is that the field of textual criticism of the Hebrew Bible is sufficiently mature—in terms of both the adequacy of method and the amount of reliable data—to warrant the production of fully critical texts and editions. As in comparable fields of text-oriented scholarship, the study of the versions and manuscripts ought naturally to lead to this end. I hope to show that in the case of Genesis, and by extension the other books of the Torah, such an aim is viable and pragmatic, even if by necessity never perfectly achieved. Wallace Stevens's observation that "the imperfect is our paradise" holds true for textual criticism as it does for our other forms of life.

In the course of my research I have had the benefit of the criticism and advice of several remarkable scholars: Frank Moore Cross, David Noel Freedman, Baruch Halpern, and Emanuel Tov. The resulting work is far better for their attentions, though, of course, they are not culpable for the outcome. I also wish to thank the graduate students in my 1993 textual criticism seminar at UCLA, Robert Cole, Roger Good, and Raju Kunjummen, for their dedication and acuity. James Davila was kind enough to make available to me in advance of publication his fine edition of the 4QGenesis fragments, now available in DJD 12. My thanks also to the Institute of Microfilmed Hebrew Manuscripts at the Hebrew University, Jerusalem, and the Ancient Biblical Manuscript Center, Claremont, California, for providing me microfilms of important Masoretic manuscripts.

My work on this project was supported in part by a fellowship from the National Endowment for the Humanities for the academic year 1991–92. I am grateful to this noble and embattled institution.

This book is dedicated to Frank Cross, my teacher, mentor, and friend since freshman year. The Mishnah ʾAbot rightly counsels: "Get yourself a teacher." I count myself fortunate to have had such a one.

Finally, my thanks and love to Ann, who doesn't have to read this book either, and to Eddie and Natty, who sensibly prefer books with more pictures and fewer words.

R. S. H.
January 7, 1998

Contents

Abbreviations and Symbols

TEXTS AND EDITIONS

Major Versions (see §1.4 for sigla for the prehistory of the major versions)

G Septuagint (G^A = Codex Alexandrinus; G^{911} = Berlin Papyrus)

Cited from J. W. Wevers, ed., *Genesis. Septuaginta: Vetus Testamentum Graecum Auctoritate Academiae Scientiarum Gottingensis editum 1.* Göttingen: Vandenhoeck & Ruprecht, 1974.

M Masoretic text (M^K = *kĕtîb*; M^Q = *qĕrê*)

Cited from collation of major Masoretic texts (see §7.4).

Q Qumran

1QGen cited from D. Barthélemy and J. T. Milik, *Qumran Cave I.* DJD 1. Oxford: Clarendon, 1955: 49-50.

6QpaleoGen cited from M. Baillet, J. T. Milik, and R. de Vaux, eds., *Les 'petites grottes' de Qumrân.* DJD 3. Oxford: Clarendon, 1962: 105-6.

$4QGen^{b-k}$ cited from *editio princeps* by J. R. Davila in E. Ulrich, F. M. Cross, et al., eds., *Qumran Cave 4, Vol. VII: Genesis to Numbers.* DJD 12. Oxford: Clarendon, 1994: 31-78. See also Davila 1989.

$4QCommGen^a$ (= 4Q252) cited from G. Brooke, et al., eds., *Qumran Cave 4, Vol. XVII: Parabiblical Texts, Part 3.* DJD 22. Oxford: Clarendon, 1996: 185-207. See also Lim 1992 and 1993.

S Samaritan text

Cited from L. F. Giron Blanc, ed., *Pentateuco Hebreo-Samaritano: Genesis. Edición crítica sobre la base de Manuscritos inéditos.* TE 15. Madrid: Instituto Arias Montano, 1976.

Minor Versions

Syr Syriac Peshiṭta

Cited from Peshiṭta Institute, *The Old Testament in Syriac. Vol. 1: Genesis-Exodus.* Leiden: Brill, 1977.

Tg^O Targum Onqelos

Cited from A. Sperber, ed., *The Bible in Aramaic. Vol. I: The Pentateuch according to Targum Onqelos.* Leiden: Brill, 1959.

Tg^P　Palestinian Targums　(Tg^N = Neofiti;　Tg^J = Pseudo-Jonathan)

Cited from A. Díez Macho, ed., *Biblia Polyglotta Matritensia, Series IV: Targum Palaestinense in Pentateuchum. Vol. 1: Genesis*. Madrid: Consejo Superior de Investigaciones Cientificas, 1988.

Vg　Latin Vulgate

Cited from H. Quentin, ed., *Biblia Sacra iuxta Latinam Vulgatam versionem. Vol. I: Genesis*. Rome: Typis polyglottis Vaticanis, 1926. Also cited from the *editio minor*: R. Weber, ed., *Biblica Sacra iuxta Vulgatam versionem*. 3d ed. Stuttgart: Deutsche Bibelgesellschaft, 1983.

Masoretic Manuscripts and Related Materials

A　Aleppo Codex　(ca. 925 C.E.)

Text no longer extant for Genesis. Details cited from textual notes of M. D. Cassuto, published in Ofer 1989.

bA　Ben Asher
bN　Ben Naphtali

From Mishael Ben Uzziel, *Kitāb al-Khilaf*; cited from Lipschütz 1962.

C3　Cairo Pentateuch Codex　(ca. 10th century C.E.)

MS Gottheil 18. Cited from microfilm, Jewish National and University Library, Jerusalem (photographed by the Institute of Microfilmed Hebrew Manuscripts, 1981); see Penkower 1988.

L　St. Petersburg (formerly Leningrad) Codex (ca. 1009 C.E.)

MS Firkovitch B19a. Cited from microfilm, Ancient Biblical Manuscript Center, Claremont, California (photographed by Bruce and Kenneth Zuckerman, 1993); see now D. N. Freedman, et al., eds., *The Leningrad Codex: A Facsimile Edition*. Grand Rapids: Eerdmans, 1997. Also transcribed in *BHS* and Dotan 1973.

S　Damascus Pentateuch Codex　(ca. 10th century C.E.)

MS 24 ° 5702, Jewish National and University Library, Jerusalem (formerly MS Sassoon 507). Text extant from Gen 9:26. Cited from facsimile edition, D. S. Loewinger, ed., *Early Hebrew Manuscripts in Facsimile, Vol. 1: The Damascus Pentateuch, Part I*. Copenhagen: Rosenkilde and Bagger, 1978. Also cited from microfilm, Ancient Biblical Manuscript Center, Claremont, California.

V　Venice edition　(Second Rabbinic Bible, 1524-25)

Edited by Jacob ben Ḥayyim from several MSS. Cited from facsimile edition, M. H. Goshen-Gottstein, ed., *Biblia Rabbinica: A Reprint of the 1525 Venice Edition*. 2 vols. Jerusalem: Makor, 1972.

Ancillary Sources

Ant   *Jewish Antiquities*, by Flavius Josephus

Cited from H. S. J. Thackeray, ed. and trans., *Josephus. Vol. 4.* LCL 242. Cambridge: Harvard University, 1930.

Jub   *Jubilees*

Cited from J. C. VanderKam, ed. and trans., *The Book of Jubilees.* 2 vols. CSC 510-11. Louvain: Peeters, 1989.

11QJub and 11QJub^M cited from VanderKam 1977.

LAB   *Biblical Antiquities (Liber Antiquitatum Biblicarum)*, by Pseudo-Philo

Cited from D. J. Harrington and J. Cazeaux, ed. and trans., *Pseudo-Philon: Les Antiquités Bibliques.* Vol. 1. SC 229. Paris: Cerf, 1976. Also Harrington, trans., "Pseudo-Philo," in J. H. Charlesworth, ed., *The Old Testament Pseudepigrapha.* Vol. 2. Garden City, NY: Doubleday, 1985: 297-377.

OTHER SIGLA (primarily in textual notes)

]	separator in textual note: primary reading to left, secondary reading(s) with comment to right
+	plus
∩	haplography
*	reconstructed reading
< >	diagnostic conjecture
[ ]	restoration in lacuna of Qumran text
˙	uncertain letter in Qumran text
#	fragmentary reading in Qumran text
1°	first (second, etc.) occurrence in a verse
→	changed to
§	chapter and section of this book or another reference work
‖	separator between textual notes in Apparatus II
cf	compare
fin	final
init	initial
mg	variant reading written in margin (only Tg^N)
ms(s)	manuscript(s); when superscripted, ms(s) cited in apparatus of critical edition
mult	multiple occurrences
om	omitted
pm	first hand (*prima manus*)
prps	perhaps
sim	similarly
v(v)	verse(s)

PERIODICALS, REFERENCE WORKS, SERIES

AB	Anchor Bible
ABD	*The Anchor Bible Dictionary*, ed. D. N. Freedman. 6 vols. New York: Doubleday, 1992.
AnBib	Analecta biblica
AOAT	Alter Orient und Altes Testament
ArB	Aramaic Bible
BASOR	*Bulletin of the American Schools of Oriental Research*
BDB	F. Brown, S. R. Driver, and C. A. Briggs, *Hebrew and English Lexicon of the Old Testament*. Oxford: Clarendon, 1907.
BHS	*Biblia Hebraica Stuttgartensia*, eds. K. Elliger and W. Rudolph. Stuttgart: Deutsche Bibelgesellschaft, 1977. Genesis edited by O. Eissfeldt, 1969.
Bib	*Biblica*
BibOr	Biblica et Orientalia
BIOSCS	*Bulletin of the International Organization for Septuagint and Cognate Studies*
BN	*Biblische Notizen*
BR	*Bible Review*
BZAW	Beihefte zur Zeitschrift für die alttestamentliche Wissenschaft
CBQ	*Catholic Biblical Quarterly*
CRINT	Compendia Rerum Iudaicarum ad Novum Testamentum
CSC	Corpus Scriptorum Christianorum Orientalium
CTS	College Theology Society Resources in Religion
DJD	Discoveries in the Judaean Desert
DSD	*Dead Sea Discoveries*
EB	*Encyclopaedia Britannica*. 15th ed. Chicago, 1992.
EJ	*Encyclopedia Judaica*. 16 vols. Jerusalem: Keter, 1971.
GKB	W. Gesenius, E. Kautzsch, and G. Bergsträsser, *Hebräische Grammatik*. 2 vols. 29th ed. Leipzig: Hinrichs, 1918-29. Reprint, Hildesheim: Olms, 1962.
GKC	W. Gesenius and E. Kautzsch, *Gesenius' Hebrew Grammar*. 2d ed. Oxford: Clarendon, 1910. Trans. A. E. Cowley of *Hebräische Grammatik*, 28th ed., 1909.
HDB	*A Dictionary of the Bible*, ed. J. Hastings. 5 vols. New York: Scribner's, 1899-1904.
HKAT	Handkommentar zum Alten Testament
HSM	Harvard Semitic Monographs
HSS	Harvard Semitic Studies
HTR	*Harvard Theological Review*
HUBP	Hebrew University Bible Project
HUCA	*Hebrew Union College Annual*
HTR	*Harvard Theological Review*

ICC	International Critical Commentary
IEJ	*Israel Exploration Journal*
JBL	*Journal of Biblical Literature*
JJS	*Journal of Jewish Studies*
JM	P. Joüon and T. Muraoka, *A Grammar of Biblical Hebrew*. 2 vols. Rome: Pontifical Biblical Institute, 1991. Rev. and trans. of Joüon, *Grammaire de l'hébreu biblique*, 1923.
JNSL	*Journal of Northwest Semitic Languages*
JQR	*Jewish Quarterly Review*
JR	*Journal of Religion*
JSOT	*Journal for the Study of the Old Testament*
JSOTSup	Supplement series, *JSOT*
JSS	*Journal of Semitic Studies*
JSSM	Journal of Semitic Studies Monograph
JTS	*Journal of Theological Studies*
LCL	Loeb Classical Library
MPI	Monographs of the Peshiṭta Institute, Leiden
MS	Masoretic Studies
MSU	Mitteilungen des Septuaginta-Unternehmens
NAB	*The New American Bible*, eds. L. F. Hartman, et al. Nashville: Nelson, 1971. Genesis prepared by D. N. Freedman.
OBO	Orbis Biblicus et Orientalis
OECS	Oxford Early Christian Studies
OTS	Oudtestamentische Studiën
QH	Quaderni di *Henoch*
RevQ	*Revue de Qumran*
SBLDS	Society of Biblical Literature Dissertation Series
SC	Sources chrétiennes
ScrHier	Scripta hierosolymitana
SCS	Septuagint and Cognate Studies
ST	*Studia Theologica*
STDJ	Studies on the Texts of the Desert of Judah
TE	Textos y Estudios 'Cardenal Cisneros' de la Biblia Poliglota Matritense
TT	*Theologisch Tijdschrift*
VT	*Vetus Testamentum*
VTSup	Supplements to *Vetus Testamentum*
WBC	Word Biblical Commentary
WC	Westminster Commentaries
WMANT	Wissenschaftliche Monographien zum Alten und Neuen Testament
ZAH	*Zeitschrift für Althebraistik*
ZAW	*Zeitschrift für die Alttestamentliche Wissenschaft*

Part I

Textual Studies

ואנשי כנסת הגדולה שהחזירו התורה
לישנה מצאו מחלוקות בספרים

And the men of the great synagogue,
who restored the Torah to its ancient state,
found divergences among the texts.

David Qimḥi
Introduction to Commentary on Joshua

CHAPTER ONE

Theory, Method, Tools

1.1 THE NECESSITY OF TEXTUAL CRITICISM

The task of textual criticism begins with a recognition of the validity of
Heraclitus' maxim in the transmission of texts: πάντα ῥεῖ, "all things flow." All
texts transmitted by scribes, as by other means, change over time. The changes
are, in varying proportions, conscious or accidental. Textual criticism involves
isolating these changes, recording and analyzing them, correcting them when
possible, and producing critical texts and editions. In essence, the textual critic
attempts to reverse the accumulated flow of textual change or entropy, with the
goal of reconstituting a better text.

The textual critic of the Hebrew Bible is helped immensely by the recent production of comprehensive introductions to the field, particularly the works by
Tov (1981 and 1992a) and McCarter (1986). Most of the theoretical and methodological issues relevant to the task are handled splendidly by these scholars. In
a time of rebirth for textual criticism in the post-Qumran era (see Goshen-
Gottstein 1983), a number of issues require further thought and refinement.
None is more important than clarifying the theoretical and practical necessity of
textual criticism.

Many biblical scholars currently eschew the practice of textual criticism, for
the most part because of a misconception of the grounds for the task. Careful
reflection on the nature of the biblical text will clarify the necessity of the task.
To recall Housman's barb on the text-critical obtuseness of his time: "Three
minutes' thought would suffice to find it out; but thought is irksome and three
minutes is a long time" (1961a: 56). A few minutes may not be too much to ask
for the possibility of textual criticism of the Hebrew Bible.

The grounds for textual criticism of this text involve the very concept of the
Hebrew Bible and, correspondingly, the concept of any written text. Consider,
for example, any specific text of the Hebrew Bible, such as *BHS* or another

3

modern printed edition. While *BHS* is certainly *a* text of the Hebrew Bible, it cannot be maintained that it is *the* text, nor is it in any coherent sense the *final* text. This edition consists of a transcription, with critical apparatus, of a single codex, the famous one in the state library in St. Petersburg (L), which identifies itself as having been copied from good Ben Asher manuscripts around 1009 C.E. If one uses another printed edition of the Hebrew Bible, in all likelihood it descends from the Second Rabbinic Bible (V), compiled by Jacob Ben Ḥayyim from various Masoretic manuscripts and printed in Venice in 1524–25. In hundreds of details of spelling, vocalization, and Masoretic marginalia, L and V differ. Clearly, both are texts of the Hebrew Bible, and just as clearly they are different texts, neither being *the* text. To use one such text without acknowledging other important texts and manuscripts is either a sign of romantic involvement with a single text or a sign of ignorance of the fact of textual multiplicity. To adopt a single manuscript as *the* Hebrew Bible or *the* Masoretic text is tantamount to, as Wilamowitz remarked in the study of Greek texts, "idolizing one manuscript as the sole source of grace" (apud Maas 1958: 52).

A recent important translation of the Hebrew Bible illustrates this textual situation. The Jewish Publication Society published in 1985 the completed version of its new translation, which was created by a committee that included over the years a number of distinguished biblical scholars, including Orlinsky, Ginsberg, Speiser, Greenberg, and Greenfield. These scholars collaborated on what the subtitle calls "the new JPS translation according to the traditional Hebrew text." The manuscript or edition used as the traditional text is not identified (see p. xvii). In fact, the translators did not limit themselves to a single manuscript or edition, to Masoretic texts, or solely to Hebrew texts. In explanatory notes throughout, G and other versions, major and minor, are mentioned prominently, and in a number of places the G reading is adopted in the text of the translation. For this admirable translation, the "traditional text" consists of a multiplicity of texts. I cite this textual condition not as a criticism but as a virtue of this work. This distinguished group chose not to confine themselves to a single manuscript or edition but made use of a wide range of textual data, even though their stated aim is to translate the "traditional Hebrew text." This is a perspicuous example of the necessity of textual criticism of the Hebrew Bible. To translate a single manuscript as "the traditional Hebrew text," in the judgment of the JPS committee, would have been a breach of trust, an act of bad faith. No single manuscript or text represents in itself the Hebrew Bible.

What, then, is the text of the Hebrew Bible? For the textual critic, as Kenney notes, "a text is not a concrete artifact, like a pot or a statue, but an abstract concept or idea" (1992: 614). What we have are texts, editions, translations, and fragments. Each of these preserves a version of the text, and each version has been affected by the vicissitudes of time and transmission. The fundamental hypothesis of the textual critic is that by collating and analyzing the extant textual data a better or earlier or more original reading can at times be determined. This hypothesis holds that textual change can be reversed, at least in part. The textual critic works *toward* the idea of the text, while conscious of the fact that the text in its plenitude can never be realized. The more data and the better methods available to the critic, the better the chance of finding a solution to a particular problem, but the end of textual criticism is never at hand. Textual criticism is a process, a dialogue, rather than a completed task. A critical text, if done properly, is a better text, but it is not *the* text in itself. Hence, for both practical and theoretical reasons, we may say that the nonexistence of *the* biblical text provides textual criticism with its justification.

Literary critics, among others, ought to be aware of this textual condition when reading the Hebrew Bible. Ironically, literary critics in the biblical field are generally the most resistant to text-critical issues. Those who attempt to read the text with insight are too often blind to the problem of the very concept of the biblical text. Tanselle aptly laments the lack of such textual awareness in literary criticism generally (see also McGann 1991): "Various theories of literature have arisen from the premise that the *meaning* of verbal statements is indeterminate; but such theories remain superficial unless they confront the indeterminacy of the *texts* of those statements" (1989: 24). Attending to some problems addressed in reader-response theory, he notes:

> One's response to a work is obviously conditioned by the text of it one encounters. . . . Those persons wishing simply to have an aesthetic object to respond to and analyze may not be willing to consider other texts of the work . . . but if they see, as they must, that their responses would be different if the text were different, they cannot avoid questioning the text. . . . The act of interpreting the work is inseparable from the act of questioning the text. (1989: 32)

Reflection on the theoretical constituency of the biblical text, along with cognizance of the textual differences among the extant texts, should make biblical scholars more sensitive to the necessity of textual criticism. Indeed, textual study in all its forms may be enhanced by closing the illusory gap between what used to be called lower and higher criticism.

Tov rightly emphasizes that "M and the biblical text are *not* identical concepts" (1992a: xxxviii). Awareness of this difference, and the difference that it makes, provides the grounds for textual criticism.

1.2 TYPES OF TEXT-CRITICAL DECISIONS

For the most part, the work of the textual critic consists of identifying and adjudicating among variant readings. The kinds of variants and the problems involving variants in translation documents have been expertly analyzed by Tov (1981: 73–250). The textual critic also faces an obligation to analyze textual problems where variant readings do not exist. This latter task has been evaluated differently by biblical textual critics: some regard it as a necessary part of textual criticism (Cross 1979: 50–54; McCarter 1986: 74–75; Deist 1988: 205; Tov 1992a: 351–69); others eschew it (Barthélemy 1982: *74–*77; Goshen-Gottstein 1992a: 206). With these disagreements in mind, I propose to outline some distinctions among types of textual decisions. These differences concern methodological limits in the presence or absence of textual variants. The following distinctions may help to clarify the nature of textual judgments under different evidential circumstances.

In my experience, there are four distinguishable types of text-critical decisions. These are ideal types in Weber's sense of the term; in practice, there may be some overlap among them. The proximate goal in each case is the archetype, defined as the "earliest inferable textual state" (Kenney 1992: 616), and the original is the ideal or theoretical goal (on the relationship between the archetype and the original, see §7.1–2). In the approximate order of their frequency, the four types are as follows:

1. Adjudicating among variants to determine which is plausibly the archetype.
2. Reconstructing the archetype on the basis of the variants where none of the variants is plausibly the archetype.
3. Reconstructing the archetype in the absence of textual variants.
4. Adopting a diagnostic conjecture in the absence of textual variants.

For those who eschew textual emendation in any form, only type 1 is permissible. Types 2, 3, and 4 concern the varying possibilities of textual criticism as "the art of removing error" (from Housman's definition of textual criticism; 1961b: 131) where the archetype is more elusive.

The following examples from Genesis 1–11 illustrate the methodological conditions for each of the four types of text-critical decision.

1) Gen 10:4 רדנים S (רודנים) G (Ρόδιοι) cf 1 Chron 1:7 (רודנים) [רדנים M; דורנים Syr

In this reading, there are three significant variants, bracketing as textually insignificant the differences in orthography (see §7.3). Two variants are distributed among M, S, and G, and a third is found in Syr (the other minor versions agree with M; see §1.3). The variations among these readings derive from a graphic confusion between ר and ד, a common category of scribal error. In fact, of the four possible permutations of the two letters, three are realized among the texts: רד (S G), דד (M), and דר (Syr); the only not realized is רר, a combination that is phonetically unlikely.

The key question for the textual critic faced by variant readings is *utrum in alterum abiturum erat?*, "which reading is the more liable to have been corrupted into the other?" (West 1973: 51–53; McCarter 1986: 72). To answer this question, one must imagine and weigh the possible arguments for and against the primacy or secondary origin of each variant.

In this verse, as in all such cases, consideration of the context is essential. Genesis 10:4 lists the sons of יון, "Ionia." The reading shared by S and G and reflected in 1 Chron 1:7 (M and G), רדנים, "Rhodes," fits the requirement of context and is followed by most commentators. The M reading, דדנים, is plausibly secondary, influenced by the more common toponym, דדן, "Dedan," which occurs three verses later (Gen 10:7). Dedan is an Arabian toponym and tribe (cf. Gen 25:3; Jer 25:23, 49:8). The M reading is understandable as the result of a graphic error influenced by anticipation. The Syr reading, דורנים, is anomalous, with no obvious referent; it may have been influenced by Aramaic דורא, "village."

To argue for the priority of the M reading, one would want to find a referent for M's דדנים in Ionia. Dodona, an old inland cult site, has sometimes been proposed (see Dillmann's apt criticism of this view; 1897: 337). But the reference to איי, "islands," in the following verse makes רדנים a far more plausible reading. Lipiński notes that contacts between Rhodes and the Near East are attested regularly beginning in the 14th century B.C.E. (1990: 53).

In cases where there is a sound argument for the primacy of one variant and the secondary origin of the others, it is unnecessary and methodologically unsound to propose an unattested reading. Proposals such as that of *BHS* (ad loc.) "prp ודנים (Danuna Δαναοι)" have little to recommend them.

In Gen 10:4, the archetypal reading is most plausibly רדנים, preserved in S, G, and the Genesis text used by the Chronicler. This instance of graphic error was noted by Jonah ibn Janaḥ and Rashi in the 11th century (Greenspahn 1987: 249) and by many others since. The archetypal reading was corrupted in M and further in Syr. A parallel situation occurs in Ezek 27:15 with רדן (G) versus דדן (M); note there also a contextual reference to איים, "islands."

In type 1, where the textual critic adjudicates among variant readings, absolute certainty is not attainable. The criteria for a sound decision are juridical: one examines and weighs the evidence and considers the possible textual histories. The textual critic is the arbiter among the imagined claims among the variants, weighing the claims for primacy against the countervailing arguments for scribal change. As in the comparable case of law, the best argument with regard to evidence, reason, and precedent should prevail.

An additional methodological principle provides a check on the possible abuse of this procedure. Where the arguments for the primacy of one or another variant are of roughly equal weight, or where the critic has good reason to be skeptical of the various claims to primacy, I have chosen, as a default value, to adopt the reading of M. This principle is a conservative one, causing the critic to err more frequently in favor of M than the other versions. One useful effect of this principle is that a decision in favor of a non-M variant is understood to have been made for good reason. This default principle serves both as a check on potential excesses and as a sign to readers that the differences from M in the critical text are not the result of the editor's whim.

2) Gen 5:19   *שנה מאות תשע* [שנה מאות שמנה M G (ετη οκτακοσια); חמש
         S מאות ושבע שנה ושמנים

In some instances, none of the variants is plausibly the archetype; that is, none is liable to have been corrupted into the other. In this reading from the chronology of the antediluvian patriarchs, the major versions disagree on the years Jared lived after the birth of his son Enoch: M and G read 800, and S reads 785. According to the textual analysis advanced in chapter 4, it appears that the archetypal chronology has been altered in the textual traditions ancestral to M, S, and G. To prevent Jared from living through the flood (he was not on the ark), the proto-M and proto-G textual traditions have reduced his remaining years after the birth of Enoch by 100, and the proto-S tradition has reduced this figure by 115. In proto-G, this adjustment has been made consistently for all of the antediluvian patriarchs from Adam to Lamech, so the archetype is easily ascertained by adding 100 to the G figure of 800. In proto-M and proto-S, adjustments have been made only for Jared, Methuselah, and Lamech, the three patriarchs who, according to the archetypal chronology, lived through the flood. This textual "scandal" in the archetype provides sufficient motive for the secondary adjustments in the proto-M, proto-G, and proto-S textual traditions.

In this type of text-critical decision, the archetype has not survived among the extant variants. The archetype can, however, plausibly be reconstructed by a careful analysis of the relationships among the variants. A kind of triangulation is required, yielding a reliable reconstruction of the archetype. But the reconstruction has a different status than in those cases where no variants exist. The reconstruction of the archetype is indeed an emendation (i.e., it is an unattested reading), but its adoption has a greater degree of certainty than cases where no clear textual history is possible. Sound judgment is necessary, and certainty is of a lesser degree than in type 1.

3) Gen 9:7 *ורדו cf G^{mss} (και κατακυριευσατε)] ורבו M S G (και πληθυνεσθε)

In some instances, there are no obvious variants, but a reconstructed archetype can be ascertained with some confidence. The textual problem in Gen 9:7 has long been noted and may have been corrected as early as the G textual groups *b* and *d* (see the first apparatus of Wevers's edition, ad loc.). It is possible, however, that Wevers has misidentified the G reading here and that the *b* and *d* groups preserve the authentic G reading (on ancient readings in these groups and the possible Lucianic affinity of *d*, see Wevers 1974: 228).

In this instance, many commentators have preferred a Hebrew reading of ורדו, "and rule." The basis for this judgment is the obvious literary relationship between Gen 9:7 and Gen 1:27 (note the sequence of verbs in Gen 1:28: פרו ורבו ורדו . . .). In light of the redundancy of ורבו in Gen 9:7 (ורבו occurs three words previously), this literary relationship make ורדו a plausible reconstruction, even in the absence of clear textual variants. The secondary reading ורבו in Gen 9:7 is easily explicable as an assimilation by reminiscence of the previous ורבו.

In this type of text-critical decision, the reconstruction of the archetype is dependent solely on good arguments and good judgment, without the benefit of variants. Its certainty is of a lesser degree than type 1 and is comparable to that of type 2.

4) Gen 4:22 <אבי כל> cf Tg^{OJ}] om M S G

The least degree of certainty obtains where a textual problem is detectable but a clear solution not ascertainable. Genesis 4:22 is a good example, where the sequence תובל קין לטש כל חרש yields no sense. The translations, ancient and modern, attempt to make some sense of the verse, generally drawing on the preceding expressions of occupation for Tubal-Cain's brothers (vv 20–21), each introduced by הוא היה אבי כל or הוא היה אבי (see §3.2). There lacks, however, a cogent text-critical argument for reconstructing the archetype. In this class of textual situations, the textual critic may propose or adopt a "diagnostic conjecture" (Maas 1958: 53–54; West 1973: 58). A diagnostic conjecture is an educated guess, sometimes no more than a filler or place-marker for a corrupt text.

This class of problem can lead the textual critic into "the treacherous marsh-land of intuition, *inneres Sprachgefühl*," as Goshen-Gottstein colorfully cautions (1983: 398 n. 117). Many conjectures of this type have contaminated the practice of biblical textual criticism over the last century, and the scholar should be wary of them. Nonetheless, when recognized as "mere" conjecture, these blunt emendations have a place in textual criticism. Indeed, as West (1973: 59) and Tov (1992a: 353–54) point out, a number of past diagnostic conjectures has been proven to be authentic variants by subsequent manuscript discoveries.

In the apparatus to the critical text in chapter 8, reconstructions of types 2 and 3 are marked by an asterisk, *x. Diagnostic conjectures are indicated in the apparatus and the critical text by angled brackets, < x >.

Textual criticism is a field in which there is an obvious need for sound methodological principles. The essence of the task is to weigh not only the facts but also the arguments surrounding the facts. Such judgments require reason, intuition, and experience. Textual criticism is, as Tov notes, "the art of defining the problems and finding arguments for and against the originality of readings. Indeed, the quintessence of textual evaluation is the formulation and weighing of these arguments" (1992a: 309–10).

1.3 MAJOR AND MINOR VERSIONS

An important methodological issue is the distinction of value among the manuscripts. Such distinctions inevitably affect judgments on the merits of individual readings. This is the problem of "external criteria" (see Tov 1992a: 298–302; McCarter 1986: 71–72). Although primary readings may be preserved in any textual source, it is clear that some texts are, in their aggregate of readings, more valuable than others. Tov characterizes M, S, G, and Q as "the major textual witnesses" (1981: 272) because they are earliest and best sources for ancient readings. In this work, I refer to these four sources as the major versions, using the term *version* in a descriptive sense following Talmon (1975: 382 n. 3). The next best set of sources are the early translations stemming from the Common Era: Tgs, Syr, and Vg. I refer to these three sources as the minor versions.

The distinction between the major and minor versions is appropriate for a number of reasons. Chronologically, the major versions arose prior to the establishment of the rabbinic-M text as the canonical text of rabbinic Judaism. In contrast, the minor versions arose after this historic event, and they each bear its imprint (see §6.3). In addition, the variant readings in the minor versions possess a relatively greater degree of indeterminacy because of the more pronounced exegetical *Tendenzen* in these texts. While Tov and McCarter are correct to stress that authentic variants are of value no matter what their source, in practice it is much more difficult to distinguish the authentic variants from the pseudo-variants in Tgs, Syr, and Vg.

Because of the greater indeterminacy in the readings of the minor versions, I adopt in this work the following working principle. The readings of the minor versions are used primarily as corroborating evidence for readings in the major versions. This conservative principle represents, in my experience, an accommodation of theory to practice. Although I may lose some authentic variants by adopting this procedure, it provides a useful check on promiscuous emendation (note the frequent appeal to the minor versions without support from the major versions in *BHS*). As with the principle of adopting the M reading where adjudication among the variants is inconclusive (see §1.2), this principle does not eliminate errors in judgment but rather makes the aggregate of errors more likely to be conservative (i.e., toward the major versions).

In this work, I adopt a corresponding stylistic convention concerning the difference between the major and minor versions. The testimony of a minor version is listed only where its reading diverges from M. This convention serves to reduce the clutter of textual notes and apparatus with no loss of textual information.

1.4 TERMS FOR THE PREHISTORY OF M, S, AND G

In addition to sigla for manuscripts and editions (see Abbreviations and Symbols), the textual critic needs appropriate terms to refer to the various phases in the textual histories of the manuscript traditions. In the case of the Hebrew Bible, there is no consensus on the terms to be used and the historical entities to which the terms refer, particularly for M.

There is a general consensus, however, on the utility of distinguishing between three phases in the textual history of M (see Tov 1992a: 29–36; Goshen-Gottstein 1967: 244–50). These three phases have as their points of departure the following textual events:

1. The literary and editorial completion of the original text for each biblical book (see Tov 1992a: 164–80 and §7.1–2).
2. The establishment of a canonical text for each biblical book in Pharisaic/Rabbinic Judaism.
3. The production of the classical Masoretic codices by the Tiberian Masoretes.

There is much that we do not know about the circumstances of these three turn-
ing points, but, even so, they are important moments in the history of M.

   Scholars differ on appropriate terms for these phases in the textual history of
M. Barthélemy uses the terms pre-Massoretic, proto-Massoretic, and Massoretic
(1992: iv–v). Cross advocates the terms proto-Rabbinic, Rabbinic, and Massoretic (1979: 39–40; 1992: 7–11). Tov refers to phases 1 and 2 as proto-
Masoretic and to phase 3 as Masoretic (1992a: 22–25). Although the termino-
logical issue is not important in itself, clarity and consistency are useful.

   In this work, I will use the following terms for the three phases in the history
of M: *proto-M* (phase 1); *rabbinic-M* (phase 2); and *M* (phase 3). Each of these
terms refers to a closely affiliated group of texts during a particular historical
span. This sequence allows for clarity of reference and also a measure of sym-
metry with the terms used for the other major versions. For G, it is necessary to
distinguish between proto-G (the textual tradition of the Hebrew *Vorlage* of G)
and G. For S, it is important to distinguish between proto-S (the textual tradition
of the text adopted by the Samaritans) and S. References to individual readings
in this work will rarely require attention to the historical phase denoted by the
term *rabbinic-M*. Hence most references will be to M or proto-M, S or proto-S,
G or proto-G.

   With regard to the prehistory of S, I have not followed Tov's suggestion that
"pre-S" is preferable to "proto-S" on the grounds that S is characterized by distinctive editorial changes in contrast to M and G (1992a: 81–82). Certainly the
transition from proto-S to S is characterized by a limited number of substitutions
and expansions (primarily involving references to Mt. Gerizim), but the transition from proto-G to G is also characterized by distinctive editorial change,
namely, translation into Greek. The circumstances of the transition from proto-
M to rabbinic-M is less clear, though it is plausible that the choice of texts was
deliberately limited to scrolls of a particular type of script and orthography (see
Cross 1992: 3–9). Each of the major versions, it would seem, was established by
editorial activity of one sort or another. Moreover, as has often been noted,
there is also a sociological parallelism among the three texts, in that each was
established in the context of a particular community—the Samaritans for S, the
Greek-speaking Jews of Alexandria for G; and the Pharisees/Rabbis for M. In
sum, there are enough similarities in the emergence of these texts to allow parallel terms for their prehistory.

   When citing M, I will follow the stylistic convention of DJD, in which
vowels and accents are unmarked. This reflects the historical practice for
Hebrew texts of phases 1 and 2 and Torah scrolls to the present. When citing G,

I will follow the similar convention in DJD (though not consistent there), in which accents and breathing marks are unmarked. This reflects the practice in the earliest Greek manuscripts, including the Septuagintal texts from Qumran and Naḥal Ḥever (see DJD 8 and 9).

1.5 TOOLS FOR THE TEXTUAL CRITICISM OF GENESIS

In his 1902 article, "Text of the Old Testament," Strack lamented the paucity of reliable data and tools for textual criticism: "We have no MSS of the Heb. OT from the first eight centuries of the Christian era, at least none whose date is certain. Unfortunately, moreover, we are as yet without critical editions . . . of the most important early Versions (LXX, Pesh., Targg.)" (1902: 726). To our benefit, Strack's lament has been ameliorated, sometimes spectacularly so, in the course of this century. The textual critic of Genesis now has available reliable editions of all the major and minor versions. (The editions of G and Vg feature fully critical texts; the others are diplomatic editions.) We also have the advantage of the discovery of Genesis texts from Qumran and other Dead Sea sites (Murabbaʿat, Naḥal Ḥever) dating from ca. 125 B.C.E. to ca. 125 C.E. The history of the M textual tradition has been the subject of an abundance of research, and better manuscripts in the M family have been discovered and published. Not least important, the procedures and goals of textual criticism have been codified in important works by Tov (1981, 1992a), McCarter (1986), and others (see esp. the contributions in Cross and Talmon 1975; Trebolle Barrera and Vegas Montaner 1992; Brooke and Lindars 1992).

The following is a selection of works of particular value in the study of the text of Genesis.

Commentaries and Reference Works

Dillmann (1897) and Skinner (1930) are invaluable; Gunkel (1910) is also helpful. Most other commentaries are inconsistent or superficial on textual matters. Spurrell (1896) and Barthelemy and colleagues (1973) are of limited use for textual criticism (on the latter's flaws, see Albrektson 1994).

Major Versions

M: Yeivin (1980), Tov (1992a: 22–79), and Barthélemy (1992: vii–cxvi) are essential. Goshen-Gottstein (1963, 1967, 1992a) provides the standard treatment of the textual history of M. For variants among the 10th to 12th century C.E. texts, Breuer (1976) provides a useful though incomplete collection. For variants in other manuscripts and printed editions, ca. 12th to 15th centuries C.E., see the apparatus in Ginsburg (1908). On the relative insignificance for textual criticism of the mass of medieval variants, with some possible exceptions, see Goshen-Gottstein (1967), Barthélemy (1992: xxxii–xlix), and Maori (1992).

G: Wevers (1974) is a useful though terse adjunct to his magisterial critical edition. His recent companion volume (1993; cf. Hendel 1995a) is helpful for style and language in G, though he consistently underestimates the text-critical value of G (see §2.1). Similar cautions apply to Rösel (1994) and Brown (1993; cf. Hendel 1994). Harl (1986) is very useful for exegetical matters. On all text-critical matters, Tov (1981) is essential.

S: The critical edition of Giron-Blanc replaces the old edition of von Gall. Also very useful is the parallel edition of M and S (from an 11th century manuscript) in Ṣadaqa and Ṣadaqa (1962). Purvis (1968), Waltke (1970; 1992), and Tov (1992a: 80–100) are reliable guides.

Q: The 4QGenesis fragments are ably edited by Davila in DJD 12. Text-critical commentary is available in Davila (1989, 1990, 1992).

Minor Versions

Tgs: The Madrid polyglot of the Palestinian Targums by Díez Macho is the most reliable and useful edition. Grossfeld (1988), McNamara (1992), and Maher (1992) are reliable guides to the rich exegesis in the Tgs. On the difficult task of discerning the history and relationships among the Tgs, see especially Alexander (1988a) and Kaufman (1994). On the Tgs in textual criticism, with some reference to Genesis, see Isenberg (1971) and Komlosh (1973).

Syr: The murky textual history of Syr Genesis has been explored in important studies by ter Haar Romeny (1995), Koster (1993), Dirksen (1992), Isenberg (1971), and Wernberg-Møller (1962). Brock (1979) and Maori (1995) are valuable on Jewish exegetical traditions in Syr.

Vg: On Jerome's textual sources and procedures, see Kedar (1988) and Kamesar (1993). Hayward (1995) provides text-critical commentary on Jerome's *Hebrew Questions on Genesis*.

Ancillary Sources

Jub: VanderKam's translation includes valuable text-critical notes. On textual affinities, see VanderKam (1977, 1988).

Ant: On the affinities of the Genesis text(s) used by Josephus, see especially Brock (1992a: 309, 328) and Fraenkel (1984).

LAB: Harrington's translation includes valuable text-critical notes. On textual affinities, see Harrington (1971).

CHAPTER TWO

M and G in Genesis 1:1 – 2:4

2.1 THE VALUE OF G IN GENESIS

A new era in the modern study of G began with the publication of "A New
Qumran Biblical Fragment related to the Original Hebrew underlying the Septuagint" (Cross 1953). This fragment, consisting of two columns from 4QSam[a],
demonstrated (in Cross's words) "the seriousness with which the LXX dealt with
the Hebrew text in their hands, and confirms most emphatically the usefulness of
the LXX for the establishment of a more nearly original Hebrew text" (1953:
25). Orlinsky clarified this newly gained perspective in a subsequent review of
the field of textual criticism:

> The LXX translation, no less than the MT itself, will have gained very considerable
> respect as a result of the Qumran discoveries in those circles where it has long—
> overlong—been necessary. And the LXX translators will no longer be blamed for
> dealing promiscuously with their Hebrew *Vorlagen*; it is to their *Vorlagen* that we
> shall have to go, and it is their *Vorlagen* that will have to be compared with the
> preserved MT. (1961: 121)

In recent years, other Qumran texts have been published that have clear
affinities to G, including (in the Pentateuch) 4QExod[b], 4QLev[d], and 4QDeut[q]
(published in DJD 12 and 14; see Tov 1992b). Numerous important studies have
refined our understanding of the history and text-critical value of G (see esp.
Tov 1981, 1988; and the recent reviews of the field in Tov 1992b; Hanhart
1992; Aejmelaeus 1987).

Unfortunately, in the study of Genesis, this new perspective on G has had
little practical effect. Most studies of the text of Genesis still blame the G translator for "dealing promiscuously" with M. A recent learned study by Wevers,
Notes on the Greek Text of Genesis, insists that G ought to be regarded primarily
as "an exegetical document" (1993: xx). Wevers assumes that M is the *Vorlage*
of G (Wevers aptly calls this a "prejudice" [1993: xiii]) and therefore infers that

any deviation from M reveals the Greek translator's exegesis. He states: "Through such details a picture of the attitudes, theological prejudices, even of the cultural environment of these Jewish translators gradually emerges" (1993: xxi). Other recent works on G of Genesis hold much the same view. Rösel's study of Genesis 1–11 bears its premise in its title: *Übersetzung als Vollendung der Auslegung* ("translation as the fulfillment of interpretation," a quote from H.-G. Gadamer). For Rösel, G is "directly comparable to the Targums" (1994: 254) as an early Jewish exegetical rendering of M (1994: 247–60). Cook's studies on Genesis also belong to this genre (1982, 1985, 1987). In the light of the present state of Septuagintal studies, the working assumption of these scholars—that G is a free translation of M—is an scholarly anachronism.

In the context of our current knowledge, any adequate method for approaching G of Genesis must acknowledge the conservative qualities of G as a translation document. Aejmelaeus aptly frames this issue:

> All in all, the scholar who wishes to attribute deliberate changes, harmonizations, completion of details and new accents to the translator is under the obligation to prove his thesis with weighty arguments and also to show why the divergences cannot have originated with the *Vorlage*. That the translator *may* have manipulated his original does not mean that he necessarily did so. All that is known of the translation techniques of the Septuagint points firmly enough in the opposite direction. (1987: 71)

The validity of this stance for Genesis has been demonstrated in Davila's recent studies of the 4QGenesis fragments. Davila concludes his analysis of the 4QGenesis variants in Genesis 1 as follows:

> The most important general implication of the new Qumran material presented in this study is that we must take the LXX of Genesis very seriously as a source for a Hebrew textual tradition alternate to the MT. We have strong reason to believe that the translators of Genesis treated their Vorlage with respect and rendered the Hebrew text before them into Greek with great care and minimal interpretation. (1990: 11)

These studies undermine the view that G of Genesis is primarily an exegesis of M. Rather, G is a literalistic translation of a Hebrew *Vorlage* that varied in many details from M (or, more properly, proto-M).

It is necessary to add, however, that even the most literal translation cannot help but be an interpretation. There are no semantically neutral translations of any linguistic text (see Steiner 1975). The key to understanding the nature of a translation document is attention to the kinds and degrees of interpretation operating in the work of translation. Recent studies of the translation technique in the G Pentateuch indicate that the translator of Genesis had a consistent technique, which may be described as a compromise between strict reproduction of all the details in the Hebrew and wavering attention to the demands of idiomatic Greek (Sollamo 1995: 81–94). The G translator tended to translate each Hebrew sense unit—and very often each lexical and grammatical unit—into a Greek equivalent. Brock aptly characterizes this translation style:

> As far as the individual words are concerned the translator draws—often with subtlety—on the vocabulary of contemporary Greek, but when faced with specifically Hebrew expressions (what Jerome called the language's ἰδιώματα) he hesitates between an idiomatic and a literal rendering. In the Pentateuch as a whole, and in Genesis in particular, it should be stressed that more often than not he chooses an idiomatic rendering, though not consistently so. (1972: 33)

The quality of this translation technique of greatest note for textual criticism is the tendency for one-to-one correspondence in G in Genesis. Whether the Greek equivalent is good Greek or translation Greek, the stability of this technique is the basis for careful retroversion of G readings to those of its Hebrew *Vorlage*.

A nuanced awareness of the relation between translation and interpretation in G of Genesis requires attention to the semantic possibilities available to the translator. Hanhart's studies have clarified the nature of this task:

> The LXX—and this is true for all the books translated—is *interpretation* only insofar as a decision is made between various possibilities of understanding which are already inherent in the formulation of the Hebrew *Vorlage* and thus given to the translator. Furthermore, the LXX is the *actualization* of the contemporary history of the translator only when the choice of the Greek equivalent is capable of doing justice both the the factuality and history of the original Hebrew witness and also to the contemporary history of the translator. The LXX is essentially *conservation*. (1992: 342–43)

The researcher needs to grasp that the G translator's interpretive scope was limited by the semantic possibilities of the source document. Only insofar as the source document could be rendered in multiple ways in the target language can the choices made be construed as revealing the translator's interpretive or cultural horizons.

The clearest locations of such interpretation are the obscure words and phrases in Hebrew. A paradigm example is the phrase תהו ובהו in Gen 1:2, an expression nearly untranslatable in any language ("unformed and void" in King James English; French has adopted the word "tohubohu"). By mapping the Greek-Hebrew equivalents (after Tov 1981: 75–76), we can see that G of Gen 1:2 is a literalistic, unit-by-unit translation, but some of the choices made may still be revealing:

η δε γη	=	וְהָאָרֶץ
ην	=	הָיְתָה
αορατος	=	תֹהוּ
και ακατασκευαστος	=	וָבֹהוּ
και σκοτος	=	וְחֹשֶׁךְ
επανω	=	עַל פְּנֵי
της αβυσσου	=	תְהוֹם
και πνευμα	=	וְרוּחַ
θεου	=	אֱלֹהִים
επεφερετο	=	מְרַחֶפֶת
πανω	=	עַל פְּנֵי
του υδατος	=	הַמָּיִם

Corresponding to תֹהוּ וָבֹהוּ, the G translator wrote αορατος και ακατασκευαστος, "unseen and unorganized." Scholars have noted that αορατος is a distinctive philosophical term in Greek, used by Plato to denote the "unseen" preexisting world of ideas (Sophist 246a–c; Theaetatus 155e; Timaeus 51a; see Hanhart 1992: 367; Harl 1986: 87; Rösel 1994: 31). This choice of a Greek equivalent expresses something of Platonic cosmology in biblical guise, perhaps joining the cosmologies of Plato and Moses, as was a commonplace in Hellenistic Jewish thought, particularly in Alexandria. Hence, we may have a glimpse of the Hellenistic conceptual world of the G translator via the translation of this obscure Hebrew phrase. Note that the phrase is rendered in two words joined with a conjunction, exactly like the Hebrew *Vorlage*. But within the constraints of a literal translation, something of contemporary Platonic cosmology may shine through.

As Hanhart stresses, exegesis in G is generally limited to the choice of the Greek equivalent. Occasionally, G softens the anthropomorphic realism of the Hebrew, as in Gen 2:7, where Yahweh breathes the breath of life εις το προσοπον αυτου, "into his face," corresponding to the Hebrew בְּאַפָּיו, "into his nose." Two instances of softening Yahweh's anthropomorphic emotions are found in Gen 6:6, where και ενεθυμηθη, "and he was concerned," renders וַיִּנָּחֶם, "and he was sorry"; and και διενοηθη, "and he meditated," renders וַיִּתְעַצֵּב אֶל לִבּוֹ, "and he grieved in his heart." Yet, in other places, blatant divine anthropomorphisms are rendered precisely in G, as in Gen 3:8, where Adam hears the noise of Yahweh's afternoon stroll through the Garden of Eden:

και ηκουσαν	=	וַיִּשְׁמְעוּ
την φωνην	=	אֶת קוֹל
κυριου του θεου	=	יהוה אֱלֹהִים
περιπατουντος	=	מִתְהַלֵּךְ
εν τω παραδεισω	=	בַּגָּן
το δειλινον	=	לְרוּחַ הַיּוֹם

Yahweh's "walking around," מתהלך, is precisely translated by Greek περιπατουντος. In such instances, we see the importance to the G translator of conserving the details of the Hebrew wording. Interpretation shines through only occasionally in the choice of Greek equivalents for this passage, as in the nice rendering of בגן, "in the garden," as εν τω παραδεισω, "in the paradise."

In our analysis of the variations between M and G in Gen 1:1–2:4, we will see that G closely translates the text of a Hebrew *Vorlage* that differed in numerous small instances from proto-M. The G *Vorlage* is characterized by considerably more harmonization than M. The harmonizations shared with S and those reflected in the minor versions confirm that the harmonizations occurred in the Hebrew scribal traditions and are not attributable to the G translator (see further §5.1–2). Even though the proto-G text used by the G translator was a relatively harmonized text, in some instances it preserves readings superior to M where M has been affected by scribal errors (see, e.g., at Gen 1:9 and 2:2). Some of the most striking divergences between M and G in Genesis are in Gen 1:1–2:4. Comparison in this text is therefore a useful point of entry into the respective traits of M and G in Genesis.

Wellhausen observed long ago that G of Genesis 1 is a more developed text than M, and he discerned that this development occurred in the Hebrew textual tradition: "The variants of the Septuagint are based on a systematic revision. These, however, had already been made in the Hebrew *Vorlage*" (1899: 184, see further §2.2 at Gen 1:9). The results of this study will corroborate his perception.

2.2 SIGNIFICANT TEXTUAL VARIANTS

Gen 1:6   למים M S G (και υδατος)] + ויהי כן G (και εγενετο ουτος)
Gen 1:7   ויהי כן M 4QGen^bg S] om G
Gen 1:20   השמים M 4QGen^bd S G (του ουρανου)] + ויהי כן G (και εγενετο ουτος)

The case of the repeated phrase ויהי כן, "and it was so," in the creation story takes us into the issue of harmonization in the biblical textual traditions. This phrase occurs six times in M (vv 7, 9, 11, 15, 24, 30), with one additional variation (v 3: ויהי אור); hence, the phrase occurs virtually seven times in M. In G, the phrase occurs seven times (vv 6, 9, 11, 15, 20, 24, 30), with the same additional variation in v 3, hence, virtually eight times. In M, the phrase occurs on five of the six days of creation, with the fifth day the exception. In G, the phrase occurs on all six days of creation. In both versions, the phrase occurs twice on the third day, once for each of the two acts of creation on that day, but only once on the sixth day, where the phrase is lacking in the creation of humans. The differences between M and G occur in vv 6, 7, and 20, involving the phrase's placement and daily distribution.

In vv 6–7, on the second day of creation, the phrase occurs in different places in M and G. This difference relates to the literary structure of the creation story, in which most of the acts of creation consist of a report of God's word (*Wortbericht*) + ויהי כן + a report of God's deed (*Tatbericht*). The account of the creation of sky on the second day includes the *Wortbericht* (v 6), introduced by ויאמר, "he said," and the *Tatbericht* (v 7), introduced by ויעש, "he made." In G, ויהי כן occurs in the expected location (end of v 6), between the *Wortbericht* and the *Tatbericht*. In M, the placement is anomalous (end of v 7): only here in Genesis 1 does the phrase ויהי כן occur after the *Tatbericht*.

The question faced by the textual critic is: Which reading, if any, is likely to be the archetypal or original text? Which is most liable to have been changed into the other? Because G conforms better to the overall structure of the story, it is possible that the G reading is original and that M has suffered some kind of scribal accident. There is, however, nothing in the context to motivate an accidental error in proto-M, nor is there any reason to suspect that the M reading is the result of intentional change. Conversely, it is possible that M preserves the original reading and that G is secondary. In this case, there is an obvious motive for the change in the proto-G textual tradition; as we have seen, the M reading is anomalous in context. It is plausible that a scribe in the proto-G tradition harmonized the placement of the phrase to conform with the pattern in the creation account as a whole. This act of textual harmonization yielded a more consistent and "perfect" text, as is the general motive for textual harmonization (see Tov 1985 and §5.1). On this explanation, the scribe had good motive for moving the phrase to its proper position between the *Wortbericht* and the *Tatbericht*. The M reading, unexpected as it is, plausibly preserves the original or archetypal text.

This argument for the primacy of the M reading and the harmonistic origin of the G reading accords with our understanding of the literary style of P. McEvenue has patiently traced the P narrative style, in which a tendency for structured organization and repetition is offset by consistent small variations within the pattern (1971: 185). Cassuto characterized this tendency in Genesis 1 as a general stylistic rule: "It is a basic principle of Biblical narrative prose not to repeat a statement in identical terms; with fine artistic sense, the narrator likes to alter the wording or to shorten it or to change the order of the words" (1961:

16). This style is evident in the variations on the pattern of *Wortbericht* + ויהי
כן + *Tatbericht*: the first day has the variation ויהי אור with no additional *Tatbericht*, the second day has ויהי כן after the *Tatbericht*, the fifth day lacks ויהי כן
(see on v 20), and the sixth day lacks a ויהי כן in the second (and final) act of
creation on that day. This stylistic tendency for variation within pattern is also
evident in the consistent variations of wording between the *Wortbericht* and *Tatbericht* for each act of creation after the first day. In sum, the argument for the
primacy of the M reading in vv 6–7 is consonant with the literary style of the
writer. This judgment agrees with Wellhausen's perception that in Genesis 1
"consistent conformity is not the principle of the original text" (1899: 184).

The analysis of the G reading of ויהי כן in v 20 follows the same reasoning.
There is no obvious motive, either accidental or intentional, for a scribe to omit
ויהי כן on the fifth day, so it is difficult to think that the M reading is secondary.
In contrast, there is good reason for a scribe to add the phrase here because such
a change would make this day of creation conform with the dominant pattern in
Genesis 1. The harmonizing impulse is good explanation for the plus in v 20
(G), as it is for the plus in v 6 (G). The M reading again is a departure from the
expected pattern. This is easily explained as a product of the P writer's style of
variation within repetition.

An additional reason to think that the absence of ויהי כן in v 20 is original
concerns the total number of repetitions of this phrase. The total in M is six,
though it is seven if one includes the variation ויהי אור in v 3. The presence of
the phrase in G of v 20 makes the total of the literal repetition of the phrase
seven, though it is eight if one includes the variation in v 3. If the ויהי כן in v 20
of proto-G is due to a harmonizing scribe, this might account for the literalistic
count of seven for the phrase in G (excluding in punctilious fashion the variation
in v 3), whereas the original text would have included the variation in the total
of seven. In both texts, seven is clearly a significant number in the literary structure of the seven days of creation (see Skinner 1930: 8–10; Cassuto 1961: 12–
15).

Although I have argued for the primacy of the M readings in vv 6, 7, and
20, it is possible to envisage another scenario argued by Tov (1985: 9–10).
When a phrase occurs in different places in different texts, it is possible that the
archetype lacked the phrase and that scribes in the different traditions inserted
the phrase independently. We would then have an instance of parallel attempts at
harmonization, yielding variant texts. Tov cites the variations in M and G in vv
6, 7, and 20 as an illustration of this scribal phenomenon and suggests that the
phrase was absent in all three verses of the original. Wellhausen proposed a

similar argument concerning these variants (1899: 184). This explanation is plausible and partially consonant with my explanation of the proto-G readings as an effect of scribal harmonization.

But the Wellhausen-Tov explanation has difficulty in explaining the M reading of the phrase in v 7 as a harmonization. As noted previously, the M phrase in v 7 is anomalous, giving rise to the harmonistic tendency to move it to v 6 (in G and followed by many modern commentators, e.g., Speiser 1964: 6; Schmidt 1973: 56; Westermann 1984: 78; *BHS* ad loc.). Yet to think that a harmonizing scribe in the proto-M tradition inserted the phrase in the wrong place undercuts the force of the explanation. Harmonizing pluses rarely yield a discordant text. I submit that this argument is less compelling than the previous argument that the M reading in v 7 is primary. In either analysis, however, the G readings in vv 6 and 20 derive from harmonizations in the proto-G scribal tradition and are not the free creation of the translator.

Gen 1:7   ויבדל M 4QGen$^{b\#g}$ S G (και διεχωρισεν)] + אלהים G (ο θεος)

The subject of the verb ויבדל, "he/it divided," is not specified in M of this verse, and G specifies the subject as אלהים, "God." In v 6, God says that the רקיע will function as the divider of the waters. The subject of the verb in v 7 of M is therefore ambiguous because one can as easily understand the subject to be the רקיע as God. The G reading is easily understood as an explicating plus, and there is no motive to think that the M reading is the result of an omission. In this case, the subject of the verb really is ambiguous, and commentators are divided on which should be inferred.

Gen 1:8   שמים M 4QGen$^{b\#g\#}$ S G (ουρανον)] + וירא אלהים כי טוב G (και ειδεν ο θεος οτι καλον)

The formula of divine approval occurs seven times in M, including a longer variation in the last repetition (vv 4, 10, 12, 18, 21, 25, 31). The formula is lacking for only one act of creation, the creation of sky on the second day. The G reading of v 8 contains the expected approval formula. While it is possible that proto-M lost this clause by a haplography triggered by homoioarkton (-וי ∩ וי-), it is more likely that the harmonizing tendency previously noted is responsible for this plus in proto-G.

In this explanation, the pattern of use for the approval formula, וירא אלהים כי טוב, is parallel to the pattern of use for the repeated phrase, ויהי כן. In each case, M has a total of seven repetitions, including one variation (the last and the first repetition, respectively). In contrast, G has seven repetitions of the precise phrase in each case and does not count the variation. The G readings reflect a strict sense of organization, characteristic of the sensibility of the harmonizing scribe, while the M readings display a preference for variation within repetition that is characteristic of P's literary style. This plus in G, parallel to the cases of vv 6–7 and 20, illustrates the nature of harmonization in the proto-G tradition.

Gen 1:9   מקוה 4QGen^h G (συναγωγην)] מקום 4QGen^b M S Jub 2:5 LAB 15:6

In Gen 1:9, there are two significant textual variations between M and G, for both of which 4QGenesis texts provide new evidence. In each case, *both* the M and G readings are attested at Qumran. An important implication of this new evidence concerns the text-critical value of G: in these cases, it is now clear that the G translator has accurately rendered a Hebrew *Vorlage* that differs from M. In this new circumstance, it is not sensible to take the position that the G translator changed the M text of v 9 in a manner coincidentally identical to the 4QGenesis readings (so Rösel 1994: 38–41).

Numerous scholars have noted that G συναγωγην, "gathering, collection," in v 9 corresponds to Hebrew מקוה and not מקום (e.g., Gunkel 1910: 107; Skinner 1930: 22; Speiser 1964: 6; Tov 1985: 21; Harl 1986: 90; *BHS* ad loc.). The data of the Hebrew-Greek equivalents clearly support this retroversion. Of the 47 places in Genesis where M reads מקום, "place," G translates with τοπος, "place," in 46 instances. The only exception is Gen 1:9. The consistency of the G translation of מקום in Genesis underscores the textual difference in this verse. The συναγωγην of G in v 9 is a precise translation of Hebrew מקוה, "gathering, collection." The correctness of this retroversion is now confirmed in 4QGen^h, which reads מקוה (noted in Skehan 1969: 89-90). Interestingly, G renders מקוה in the next verse (v 10) as συστηματα, "system, body," showing that the G translator is less consistent in rendering uncommon words.

Given our new respect for the variant preserved in G, the question remains: Which is the better reading? The graphic difference between the two words is slight, consisting of word-final ה versus final ם. The difference of meaning is also slight, "gathering" versus "place." A decisive argument for the preferred reading may be impossible, given the fine difference between the variants.

Davila has recently argued that the reading מקוה is secondary, either a mistake or a harmonization influenced by the occurrence of מקויהם in v 9b (see later). He reasons that "it is very difficult to explain why מקום would have been substituted for an original מקוה" (1990: 11). Although it is certainly possible that מקוה is secondary, it is not so difficult to explain why מקום may be secondary and מקוה the primary reading. A graphic confusion may account for this variation.

Graphic confusion of final ם and ה, while not commonplace, is attested in the biblical text, as demonstrated by the following examples:

Prov 20:16   נכריה M^Q
              נכרים M^K

1 Kings 14:31 אביה G (Aβιου)
              אבים M
              (sim 1 Kings 15:1,7,8 and 2 Chron 13:1–23)

Gen 18:21   הכצעקתה M S
              הכצעקתם G (ει κατα την κραυγην αυτων)
              (sim Severus Scroll; Siegel 1975: 19–20)

Delitzsch lists nearly two dozen cases of ה/ם confusion in the Hebrew Bible (1920: §122a, §129a). This count may be overly generous, but the previous examples are unambiguous and show the possibility of this graphic confusion in the square script. Included in Delitzsch's list is the variation in Gen 1:9, מקום/מקוה. In the light of these data, we cannot exclude the possibility of מקוה as original in Gen 1:9 and מקום the result of a simple graphic error.

If either מקום or מקוה might be mistaken for the other by graphic error, which is the more likely direction of change? Davila aptly notes that anticipation of מקויהם in 9b might motivate a misreading of מקום as מקוה in 9a. Yet another מקוה occurs in v 10. To frame an alternative suggestion, I would note that nouns and verbs from the root √קוה function as *Leitwörter* in the narrative in vv 9–10. If we take note of this stylistic trait, then מקוה is stylistically apt as the reading here. Moreover, the word מקוה is uncommon in Hebrew, whereas מקום is very common. It is a natural tendency for scribes to mistake an uncommon word for a common word, particularly when facilitated by graphic confusion. The reverse change, from a common word to an uncommon word, is far less frequent. If we heed this natural tendency in scribal traditions, then it is plausible that מקוה was lost in proto-M of v 9 (including the proto-M text, 4QGen^b) but preserved in proto-G and 4QGen^h. This argument may be the more compelling, in which case we should prefer the reading מקוה.

Gen 1:9   (ותרא) 4QGen$^{k\#}$ יקוו המים מתחת השמים אל מקויהם ותרא היבשה
           (היב[שה]) G (και συνηχθη το υδωρ το υποκατω του ουρανου εις τας συναγωγας αυτων και ωφθη η ξηρα) sim Jub 2:6] om M 4QGen^{bg} S

The long plus in G in the second half of v 9 is also supported by a 4QGenesis reading, as is the shorter text of M. Only the last two words of the plus, [ותרא היב[שה, are preserved in 4QGen^k. The verbal form in this phrase is most easily read as a converted imperfect (*waw* + short prefix form), hence "dry land appeared." This phrase, introducing the *Tatbericht* of this act of crea-

tion, differs from the corresponding phrase in the *Wortbericht*, ותראה היבשה (v
9a), in which the verbal form consists of *waw* + long prefix form, functioning
grammatically as a purpose/result clause: "so that dry land may appear" (on this
syntax, see Lambdin 1971: §107c; Waltke and O'Connor 1990: §34.6,
§39.9.2). It is very unlikely that a postexilic scribe would miswrite the long
prefix form in v 9a as a short prefix form, as the short form is virtually
moribund in Late Biblical Hebrew (Sáenz-Badillos 1993: 129; Qimron 1986:
81). Hence, it is unlikely that the 4QGen^k reading should be understood as an
erroneous writing of the *Wortbericht* of v 9a (pace Rösel 1994: 40).

The Qumran reading indicates the reliability of the G translation of its *Vorlage* of Genesis. The retroversion of the Greek (as previously) has been advo-
cated by many scholars (e.g., Gunkel 1910: 107; Skinner 1930: 22; *BHS* ad
loc.) and may be considered to be vindicated by 4QGen^k, albeit fragmentarily.
Well before the discovery of 4QGen^k, however, good reasons had been given for
understanding the G plus as a preservation of a Hebrew text. Wellhausen pointed
to the obvious Hebraism indicated by the lack of agreement between the plural
possessive pronoun, αυτων, and its governing noun, το υδωρ, which is singular
in Greek. The problem of grammatical discord is solved by noting that Hebrew
for "water," מים, is plural. The G reading reflects a Hebrew text with המים
governing the plural possessive pronoun (Wellhausen 1899: 184; Skinner 1930:
22; Tov 1985: 22). This is a case of a "syntactical Hebraism" (Tov 1988: 179),
demonstrating the effect of the Hebrew *Vorlage*.

Tov has strengthened the argument for a Hebrew original by noting the
literal, unit-by-unit Greek-Hebrew correspondences in v 9a, illustrating the
translation technique of the G translator of Genesis (1985: 21–22). He also notes
the differences in wording between vv 9a and 9b in G, showing that 9b has not
been constructed as a harmonization with its parallel by the G translator. Important in this regard are the Greek variations of συναγωγην (= מקוה; v 9a), τας
συναγωγας αυτων (v 9b), and συστηματα (= מקוה; v 10). Clearly the phrase in
v 9b is not a harmonization made on the basis of the Greek text of vv 9a or v 10
(a conclusion reached also by Schmidt 1973: 104). Tov concludes that this and
other "harmonizing changes and additions in ch. 1 derive from a Hebrew text
rather than the translator's harmonizing tendencies" (1985: 22).

These analyses of the G plus in v 9b as conserving a Hebrew text are compelling in themselves and are now confirmed by the partial preservation of this
reading in 4QGen^k. The text-critical task of adjudicating among the Hebrew
variants remains. Which reading is more likely to have given rise to the other?

It is possible that a harmonizing Hebrew scribe could have constructed a *Tat-*

bericht for v 9 where one was previously lacking. Yet Tov's arguments against understanding the plus as an inner-translational harmonization apply equally well to a possible origin in inner-Hebrew harmonization. Harmonizing pluses consistently mirror the wording of the parallel text. In this case, the variations in wording between v 9a (the *Wortbericht*) and v 9b (the *Tatbericht*) militate against this possibility (cf. G of vv 11–12, later, where the traits of secondary harmonization are apparent, the *Wortbericht* and *Tatbericht* having been precisely harmonized by a proto-G scribe). This style of variation within repetition is characteristic of the P writer and is unlikely to be the creation of a harmonizing scribe. Hence, the *Tatbericht* in v 9, as preserved in G and 4QGen[k] (and presumed in Jub), should be taken as the archetypal or original reading.

How might this sequence have been lost in proto-M? Davila plausibly suggests a haplography triggered by homoioarkton, as the scribe's eye jumped from ויקוו (v 9b) to ויקרא (v 10), both of which begin with the cluster ויק- (1990: 11). This is an attractive possibility, explaining the loss of the *Tatbericht* in proto-M by a simple scribal error. A somewhat more complicated possibility is that the scribe's eye jumped from היבשה at the end of v 9a to היבשה at the end of 9b, thereby omitting the *Tatbericht* of 9b. If in proto-M the ויהי כן was originally after the *Tatbericht*, as it is in v 7 (as noted previously), then a haplography by homoioteleuton would produce the short text of M.

To sum up the main points of the argument: (1) the G plus corresponds to a Hebrew reading which is partially preserved in 4QGen[k], (2) the longer reading is very likely the archetypal or original reading, and (3) proto-M (and other versions related to or influenced by proto-M) lost this reading by a haplography triggered by homoioarkton or homoioteleuton.

The absence of a *Tatbericht* for this act of creation in M is explicable as a textual error, which may now be remedied (as already in *NAB*; see Hartman et al. 1970: 328). God's creation of seas and dry land has its literary completion, long preserved in translation and in Qumran cave 4.

Gen 1:11 זרע M 4QGen[b] S G (σπερμα)] + למינהו G (κατα γενος και καθ´
ομοιοτητα) Syr
פרי 2° M 4QGen[b] S G (καρπον)] + למינו M 4QGen[b] S
בו M 4QGen[b] S G (εν αυτω)] + למינהו G (κατα γενος)

Gen 1:12 ועץ M S G (και ξυλον)] + פרי G (καρπιμον) Tg[P]
למינהו 2° M 4QGen[b] S G (κατα γενος)] + על הארץ G (επι της γης)

The creation of plants in vv 11–12 provides a paradigm example of harmonization in biblical scribal tradition. As we have seen, P's narrative style is characterized by variation within patterned repetition. This trait is consistently

manifested in the differences in wording between *Wortbericht* and *Tatbericht* in
the creation story. To harmonizing scribes, however, and to many pious interpreters, inconsistencies between God's commands and their outcome are impossible. Harmonizers, whether scribes or exegetes, try to clarify the precise correspondence between God's word and deed.

In the case of vv 11–12, the variations between the *Wortbericht* and the *Tatbericht* in M are uniformly eliminated in the G reading. A harmonizing scribe in
the proto-G tradition has made the text perfectly consistent by inserting four
harmonizing pluses in vv 11–12:

1. למינהו following זרע in v 11, based on זרע למינהו in v 12
2. למינהו following זרעו בו in v 11, based on זרעו בו למינהו in v 12
3. פרי following ועץ in v 12, based on ועץ פרי in v 11
4. על הארץ following זרעו בו למינהו in v 12, based on the newly expanded
   זרעו בו למינהו על הארץ in v 11 (change #2).

With these carefully placed insertions, the scribe has created an exact correspondence between God's command and its outcome. It is relatively easy to
conclude that the perfectly harmonized text in G is secondary to the character-
istically varied readings in M in these four places.

The only aspect of the G readings of vv 11–12 that derives solely from the
art of the G translator is the double translation of the first למינהו in each verse as
κατα γενος και καθ᾽ ομοιοτητα, "according to kind and according to likeness"
(see Harl 1986: 91; Wevers 1993: 6; Paradise 1986: 197). The second למינהו in
each verse is translated more simply as κατα γενος. Double translation of a
single Hebrew word is found occasionally in G of Genesis, as in Gen 3:14,
where גחנך is doubly translated as τω στηθει σου και τη κοιλια, "your breast
and belly." This sporadic translation technique apparently aims to express more
fully in Greek the semantics of the Hebrew word.

At one point in vv 11–12, M has a plus relative to G: the word למינו in v 11.
Gunkel correctly notes that the word is awkward in its context in M, breaking
up the phrase פרי אשר זרעו בו, "fruit with its seeds in it," which recurs in v 12.
It is probable that למינו is a scribal gloss in M (so Gunkel 1910: 108; Paradise
1986: 199; *BHS* ad loc.), perhaps a harmonistic insertion influenced by the
parallel phrase in v 12. If so, it is not a particularly elegant harmonization.

Gen 1:14 השמים M 4QGen^bk S G (του ουρανου)] + להאיר על הארץ S G (εις
φαυσιν της γης)

The G plus in v 14 is found also in S, indicating yet again that G accurately
reflects a Hebrew *Vorlage*. The number of harmonizing pluses shared by S and

G in Genesis 1–11 suggests a common history at some point in the proto-S and proto-G traditions (see §5.2 and §6.2). In the present context, the S reading is important primarily as testimony to the G translation technique in Genesis.

As in other instances, it is also possible to demonstrate from the Greek evidence that the G reading derives from a Hebrew text. Tov has shown that harmonizations typically repeat sequences verbatim from a parallel passage (1985: 20–22). Yet, the plus in G of v 14, εις φαυσιν της γης, differs from the parallel phrase in vv 15 and 17, ωστε φαινειν επι της γης, indicating that it is not the product of the translator's harmonization. In contrast, the Hebrew retroversion of G in v 14, להאיר על הארץ (= S), repeats verbatim the parallel phrase in vv 15 and 17, להאיר על הארץ. By this reasoning, we may conclude that the harmonized text in G of v 14 derives from a Hebrew text.

The secondary nature of this plus may be discerned by consideration of the literary context. The relevant portions of vv 15 and 17 read ברקיע השמים להאיר על הארץ. For v 14, M reads ברקיע השמים, to which a harmonizing scribe would naturally add להאיר על הארץ. But this harmonization of details disturbs the literary progression in these verses. Verses 14–15 relate the *Wortbericht* of this act of creation, in which two functions of the lights, להבדיל, "to divide," and להאיר, "to light," are commanded in two separate clauses. (In contrast, in the *Tatbericht* in vv 16–18, these two functions, along with למשל, "to rule," appear in a single clause.) The plus in G and S of v 14, mirroring the parallel phrase in vv 15 and 17, results in God uttering the phrase "to light up the earth" twice in the *Wortbericht* in identical language, thus needlessly repeating himself. The plus disturbs the discourse in the *Wortbericht* and fails to respect the literary variation between *Wortbericht* and *Tatbericht*. For these reasons, the longer reading is best viewed as a harmonization of details that ironically results in a disharmonious narrative.

Gen 1:27 בצלמו M S] om G

God's creation of humans in v 27 is often analyzed as poetry or parallelistic prose (e.g., Dillmann 1897: 83–84; Gunkel 1910: 112; Speiser 1964: 4; and most modern translations). The parallelism of the first two clauses, in which the textual variation occurs, is unambiguous:

ויברא אלהים את האדם בצלמו
בצלם אלהים ברא אתו

Each element in the first clause is echoed in form or syntax in the second clause. The structure of the parallelism may be schematized as: A B C D / D′ B A′ C′. The textual variant concerns the two words at the juncture of the two clauses,

בצלמו בצלם, "in his image, in the image (of)." In the prosody of the verse, the two successive words function as chiastic parallels.

Though it otherwise preserves the parallelistic style and syntax of the verse, G lacks an equivalent for Hebrew בצלמו. It is possible that the G reading preserves a better text and that the longer M reading is a secondary expansion (so *BHS* ad loc.). However, there is no obvious motivation for an expansion here, and it is not an easy case of dittography (note the suffix in בצלמו). Moreover, as we have noted, the word plays a stylistically definable role in the prosody of the passage. On these grounds, the M reading has the best claim to be the primary reading.

How may this reading have been lost in G? It is possible that the translator abridged the Hebrew text as "redundant" (so Lust 1991: 98; cf. Rösel 1994: 50). This is not very likely, given the translation technique of the G translator. It is far more likely that a text in the proto-G tradition suffered a haplography triggered by homoioarkton, the scribe's eye skipping from בצל- to בצל-, thereby accidentally simplifying the text (so Frankel 1841: 69). This is an easy scribal error and accords well with our understanding of the literary passage.

Gen 1:28 ויאמר להם אלהים M S] לאמר G (λεγων)

The difference between the M and G readings in this instance is relatively slight. Accordingly, it is difficult to find a clear argument for the primary reading. The M reading is somewhat awkward in the repetition of אלהים twice in two short clauses; hence, the shorter G reading may be preferred (so Skinner 1930: 33; Westermann 1984: 79). However, the exact correspondence of the G reading in the first part of the verse with the parallel passage in v 22, both reading ויברך אתם אלהים לאמר פרו ורבו ומלאו את, raises the suspicion that the G reading in v 28 has been harmonized with v 22. Wevers (1993: 16) and Rösel (1994: 51) regard the G reading as a harmonization made by the translator, but it is far more likely that the reading existed in proto-G, which had been affected by numerous secondary harmonizations.

Gen 1:28 ובכל הבהמה ובכל הארץ ובכל הרמש הרמש M S] ובכל חיה הרמשת G
(και παντων των κτηνων και πασης της γης και παντων των ερπετων των ερποντων)

The G reading in the second half of v 28 is easily explained as a harmonization with the parallel passage in v 26. As in G of vv 11–12 (noted previously), the *Tatbericht* (v 28) is harmonized with the antecedent *Wortbericht* (v 26).

The initial part of God's command is identical in both *Wortbericht* and *Tat-bericht* in M and G of vv 26 and 28: ורדו בדגת הים ובעף השמים, "rule over the fish of the sea and the birds of the sky." The rest of God's command, the speci-fication of land animals, is identical in the *Wortbericht* of M and G in v 26 but differs in the *Tatbericht* in v 28:

v 26 M = G   ובבהמה ובכל הארץ ובכל הרמש הרמש על הארץ
v 28 M   ובכל חיה הרמשת על הארץ
v 28 G   ובכל הבהמה ובכל הארץ ובכל הרמש הרמש על הארץ

From this comparison of *Wortbericht* and *Tatbericht*, one can see that M varies in the specification of land animals and that proto-G is identical in the two verses, with the minor exception of כל ה- before בהמה in v 28.

The reading preserved in G is a harmonization of *Wortbericht* and *Tatbericht* such that God's stated intention and his fulfillment of that intention are precisely equivalent. In contrast, the M reading reflects the characteristic style of variation within repetition in P. The harmonizing scribe in the proto-G tradition further expanded וב- to ובכל ה- in v 28 to make the mention of בהמה consistent with the other species in this sequence, all of which are modified by ובכל ה-. Ironically, in adding this last harmonizing detail, the scribe upset the perfect harmonization of *Wortbericht* and *Tatbericht*.

Gen 1:29 עשב זרע זרע M S G (χορτον σποριμον)] + מזריע? G (σπειρον)

For the עשב זרע זרע, "plants bearing seed," of M, the G equivalent is χορτον σποριμον σπειρον σπερμα, "seed-bearing plants bearing seed." It is pos-sible, as some have suggested, that σποριμον σπειρον is a double translation of the Hebrew participle זרע, in which case there is no textual variant (Harl 1986: 97; Wevers 1993: 17). It is perhaps more likely that the G text reflects a harmonizing plus based on the parallel passage in vv 11 and 12 (Rösel 1994: 51). The parallel passage, עשב מזריע זרע, χορτου σπειρον σπερμα, differs slightly from the phrase in v 29, particularly in its use of the Hiphil participle rather than the Qal participle. In the proto-G tradition, a scribe may have added the Hiphil participle to v 29 by a harmonistic impulse, yielding עשב זרע מזריע זרע, which the G reading reproduces. It is also possible that the G reading reflects a proto-G dittography of זרע, yielding עשב זרע זרע זרע. In either case, harmonizing plus or dittography, the G reading is most likely secondary, where-as the M reading preserves the stylistic variation of parallel passages character-istic of the original.

Gen 1:29 פרי M S G (καρπον)] + עץ M S

The M phrase, כל העץ אשר בו פרי עץ זרע זרע, "every tree in which there is fruit of the tree bearing seed," is obviously disturbed by the grammatical position of the second עץ, "(of the) tree." Although it is possible to view this phrase as merely awkward, it is plausibly a result of a scribal expansion. A scribe may have inserted the עץ after פרי by anticipation of the phrase (מ)פרי עץ in Gen 3:2 and 3:3, which also refers to God's command to humans concerning edible fruit. The expansion of the phrase in 1:29 may have been an accident, triggered by anticipation, or it may have resulted from an intentional harmonization. Accidental error is far more common than harmonization in the proto-M tradition (see chapter 3), so the balance of probability is with the former. In either case, the M reading is plausibly a secondary expansion, and the G reading, lacking the awkward עץ, may best preserve the archetypal or original reading (so Gunkel 1910: 114).

Gen 1:30 ולכל 3° M S G (και παντι)] + רמש G (ερπετω)

In the specification of creeping things in v 30, M reads ולכל רומש על הארץ, "and for everything that creeps on the earth," and G reads και παντι ερπετω ερποντι επι της γης, "and for every creeping thing that creeps on the earth." The G reading presumes the noun רמש preceding the participle רומש, as it does in the parallel phrases in vv 26 and 28 (G), ובכל הרמש הרמש על הארץ. The expanded phrase in G is therefore a likely product of scribal harmonization (so Skinner 1930: 34), whereas M preserves the variation of phrase in the original.

Gen 2:2   השׁשׁי S G (τη εκτη) Syr Jub 2:16] השׁביעי M

The most famous variant in the creation story concerns the day when God completed his work. The M reading, השׁביעי, "the seventh" day, is manifestly incorrect according to the narrative context. Defenders of M tend to translate the governing verb of the clause, ויכל, "(he) completed," as a pluperfect, "(he) had completed," but this tense value is very unlikely in this position (see esp. Dillmann 1897: 90; Skinner 1930: 37). The comparable examples adduced by Cassuto (1961: 61–62) and Wenham (1987: 35) are grammatically and logically sequential, not pluperfect, in Hebrew. Moreover, it is not clear that a pluperfect meaning fares any better for M ("God had completed on the seventh day the work that he had done"); one needs also to attribute an odd meaning to the preposition -ב ("by the seventh day," or the like). This multiplication of dubious grammatical arguments to make sense of M does not inspire confidence.

The reading shared by G, S, Syr, and Jub, הששי, "the sixth" day, is generally viewed as a secondary correction of a difficult original text (= M). As Skinner judiciously states, "*sixth* is so much the easier reading that one must hesitate to give it the preference" (1930: 37). Often, this secondary correction is attributed independently to scribes in each tradition. Even Tov comments, "It is impossible to determine whether the easier reading of the LXX was based on a variant הששי or whether the exegetical tendency developed independently in all three sources [G, S, and Syr]" (1981: 128). On this point, however, there is a good case against independent exegesis. All that we know about G of Genesis inspires confidence in the translator's intention to conserve the *Vorlage*, so a Hebrew reading, הששי, for proto-G is warranted (so Barr 1979: 11). Moreover, to posit that scribes or translators changed the text independently in three (or four) textual traditions is extremely unlikely, given our cognizance of the numerous shared readings in G, S, and Syr (see §5.2). It is far more parsimonious to view this shared reading as derived from a common root, as is probably the case in other instances. The variant shared by G, S, Syr, and Jub is most likely a single Hebrew reading, preserved in several branches of the stemmatic tree.

Having argued for the authenticity of this Hebrew variant, the question remains; Which is preferable on text-critical grounds? The M reading, as the *lectio difficilior*, may be preferred, and the reading preserved in G, S, Syr, and Jub regarded as a secondary exegetical revision. Yet, one hesitates to give preference to a reading that makes no sense. To consider the opposite possibility, how might a text reading הששי have given rise to a text reading השביעי? A plausible motive can be given for such a change.

The two clauses of v 2 contain strikingly similar sequences, parallelistic in style. Consider the graphic similarity of the two sequences from the word ביום:

v 2a   ביום הששי מלאכתו אשר עשה

v 2b   ביום השביעי מכל מלאכתו אשר עשה

With the exception of the stylistic variation of מכל in v 2b, the two sequences are identical but for the variation of הששי and השביעי. It is entirely possible that a scribe could have miswritten השביעי in place of הששי in the first clause, triggered by anticipation of the parallel in the second clause. This would be an accidental assimilation by anticipation. An intentional change of this kind in proto-M is far less likely. On this explanation, the reading הששי, which admittedly makes sense in its context, may have been altered to השביעי by a simple scribal error.

The weight of the respective arguments inclines toward the position that
הששי is the archetypal reading and probably original. (Note the nice numerical
parallelism of 6 / 7 / 7 in vv 2–3.) The reading השביעי is most plausibly a secondary change due to an accidental assimilation by anticipation.

Gen 2:4   אלה M S] זה ספר G (Αυτη η βιβλος)

The G reading corresponds to the parallel phrase in Gen 5:1, זה ספר תולדת
(Αυτη η βιβλος γενεσεως). It appears that a harmonizing scribe in the proto-G
tradition expanded the short Toledot formula in 2:4 to equal the longer form in
5:1, and that M preserves the original variation. Incidentally, the doubled self-
reference in G, Αυτη η βιβλος γενεσεως, "This is the book of genesis," is the
source of the Greek name for the book (already in Philo and a Greek fragment of
Jub 2:1; see Harl 1986: 32).

Gen 2:4   יהוה אלהים M S] אלהים G (ο θεος)

In Gen 2:4–3:24, M reads יהוה אלהים as the divine name 30 times. In the
first three instances (2:4, 5, 7), G reads אלהים. Only in 2:8 does G begin to read
יהוה אלהים. Thereafter, G reads יהוה אלהים (with M) 11 times and אלהים (contra
M) 5 times. In an additional three places (3:1, 3, 5), all in direct discourse, M
and G read אלהים. In sum, there are 15 agreements in divine name in M and G
in the Garden of Eden story and 8 disagreements, all replicating the disagree-
ment in Gen 2:4. What is one to make of this variation, which occurs just over
half the time in Gen 2:4–3:24?

The easiest solution draws on the tendency for scribal harmonizations in the
proto-G textual tradition. In Gen 1:1–2:3, the only divine name that occurs is
אלהים (over 35 times), and the shift in Gen 2:4 to יהוה אלהים is startling to any
reader. It is likely that a harmonizing scribe leveled through אלהים in 2:4, 5, 7
but then chose to alternate between יהוה אלהים (from the parent text) and אלהים,
with some preference given to יהוה אלהים. In this explanation, it is the shift in
divine names at the juncture of the two creation stories that poses a problem, and
a harmonizing scribe attempted to ameliorate this problem by blurring the transition from one name to another.

This explanation makes sense of the variants in the light of our understanding
of the textual characteristics of G and M. The opposite scenario—that G
preserves the original or archetypal readings and a scribe in the proto-M tradition altered them to make a dramatic break at Gen 2:4—has no obvious reason to
recommend it.

For fuller discussion of the problem of divine names, see §2.3.

Gen 2:4   ארץ ושמים M] שמים וארץ S Tg^N Syr Vg; את השמים ואת הארץ G (τον
ουρανον και την γην)

This G reading in 2:4b conforms to the order of the parallel phrase in v 4a
and 2:1, השמים והארץ, and in 1:1, את השמים ואת הארץ. Several minor versions
and S read similarly but, like M, lack the article. A harmonizing tendency
appears to be at work in this widespread reading, with M apparently preserving
the variation of the archetype or original. The desire to smooth over an
inconsistency in the text is sufficient motive to see the reading in G and the other
versions as a secondary harmonization. There is no motive for a scribe in the
proto-M tradition to create inconsistency where there was none; hence, the M
reading is to be preferred.

2.3 EXCURSUS: DIVINE NAMES IN G

In his work, *The Divine Names in Genesis*, Skinner noted generously that "every
Old Testament scholar is aware that the Mss. of the LXX simply teem with various readings of the divine names" (1914: 2). After considering the complexities
of the data, he concluded that the G variants are, for the most part, inner-Greek
corruptions "due to errors that have crept in during a long series of transcrip-
tions" (1914: 42). Hence, the G variants in the divine names have no text-
critical significance. In a recent reexamination of this problem, Harl comes to a
similar conclusion: "it is impossible to compare the two texts in the use of
divine names" (1986: 50).

A different argument has been advanced independently in recent studies by
Rösel and Wevers. In Rösel's view, the variation of divine names in G of
Genesis is due to the translator's desire to signify different aspects of God by the
terms κυριος, θεος, and κυριος ο θεος (1991: 374-77; 1994: 251-52). The
divine attributes signaled by these names are creator and ruler (for θεος), lord of
the chosen people (for κυριος), and creator of all people (for κυριος ο θεος). In
Rösel's theory, the G translator is a forerunner of Philo, for whom κυριος and
θεος were allegorical codes for God's sovereignty and his goodness, respectively
(e.g., *De Plantatione* 86; *De Abrahamo* 124). The classical rabbis developed a
different interpretation for the variation of divine names in the Bible: for them
יהוה and אלהים represent the attributes of compassion and justice, respectively
(e.g., *Gen. Rab.* 12.15 on Gen 2:4). The chief difference between the G translator and these later interpreters, according to Rösel's theory, is that the G translator deliberately revised the text of Genesis in order to embed in the text his
theology of divine names.

In a previous study of this issue, Wevers concluded: "there seems to be no pattern here of any kind. If this be the case, one can only assume a different parent text (or a careless translator)" (1985: 33). However, he seems to have changed his mind in his more recent *Notes on the Greek Text of Genesis* (1993). In Gen 6:6–7, where G reads ο θεος twice in contrast to twice יהוה in M, Wevers comments that G has "avoided κυριος in favor of ὁ θεός. It is God as creator, not as covenantal Lord, who confronts the creation he had brought into being" (1993: 79). Wevers now appears to believe that the variation of divine names in G is an exegetical revision expressing the translator's theology of divine names, as in Rösel's theory.

In contrast to the conclusions of Skinner, Harl, and early Wevers, I submit that some sense can be made of the general pattern of divine names in G of Genesis. In contrast to Rösel and recent Wevers, I think it more likely that the variations in names in G stem from the Hebrew *Vorlage*, not from the freewheeling pen of the G translator. Harmonizing tendencies in the proto-G scribal tradition are the solution to the problem.

First, let us consider the relevant Qumran evidence. There are no fragments of Genesis that are germane to this issue but some nice instances in Numbers, Deuteronomy, and Samuel:

Num 23:3   יהוה M
        אלהים 4QNum[b] S G (ο θεος) (DJD 12: 235)

Deut 3:20   יהוה 4QDeut[d] M S
        יהוה אלהיכם 4QDeut[m] (יהוה אלוהיכמה) G (κυριος ο θεος υμων)
        (DJD 14: 115)

Deut 31:17   אלהי M S
        יהוה אלהי 4QDeut[c] (יהוה א[להי]) G (κυριος ο θεος μου) (DJD
        14: 33)

1 Sam 2:25   אלהים M
        יהוה 4QSam[a] G (κυριος) (Cross 1953: 23)

1 Sam 23:14   אלהים M
        יהוה 4QSam[b] G (κυριος) (Cross 1955: 171)

These examples, which could be multiplied, support our current understanding of the text-critical value of G (see §2.1). Where the G reading of the divine name diverges from M, it is unwarranted to assume posthaste that the G translator has revised the reading of M. The character of G as conservation of its *Vorlage*, which was not identical to (proto-)M, is well established for these books.

The data on the variations of divine names in M and G for all of Genesis can be charted roughly as follows (revised from Wevers 1985: 32–33; and Rösel 1991: 363–71):

יהוה M ca. 141 times
   = G (κυριος) ca. 104 times
   ] אלהים G (ο θεος) 22 times
   ] יהוה אלהים G (κυριος ο θεος) 14 times
   ] om G once (14:22; a secondary plus in M)

אלהים M ca. 167 times
   = G (ο θεος) ca. 157 times
   ] יהוה G (κυριος) 3 times (19:29; 21:2,6)
   ] יהוה אלהים G (κυριος ο θεος) 4 times (6:12,22; 8:15; 9:12)
   ] om G 3 times (1:28; 31:50,53 [see Seebass 1986])

האלהים M 19 times
   = G (ο θεος) 19 times

יהוה אלהים M 23 times
   = G (κυριος ο θεος) 15 times
   ] אלהים G (ο θεος) 8 times

The raw data show no obvious pattern. Although G more often varies from M יהוה than from M אלהים, there are exceptions. G varies from M יהוה אלהים only in the direction of אלהים, never יהוה. The reasons for the variations are obscure.

If we narrow our scope to Genesis 1–11, however, the motives for variation may be discernible. I have suggested before that the use of אלהים in G of Gen 2:4–7, where M and S read יהוה אלהים, is explicable as a leveling through or harmonization of the name אלהים that is used exclusively up to that point (see §2.2 at Gen 2:4). The subsequent use of divine names in G of Genesis 1–11 can easily be explained as a continuation of this tendency to harmonize the variation of divine names. The motives for variation are best seen in the transitions between the following sections in Genesis 1–11:

1. Genesis 1:1–2:3. There is no variation between M and G in the use of divine names (exclusively אלהים). The textual differences in Gen 1:7, 8, 28 affect the total number of repetitions of this name in each version (see §2.2 ad loc.). The divine name אלהים occurs 35 times in M and 34 times in G.

2. Genesis 2:4–3:24. Genesis 2:4 introduces the shift in divine names from אלהים to יהוה אלהים in M (with the exception of אלהים in direct discourse), corresponding to a literary shift from the P source to J. The use of אלהים is continued by G in 2:4–7, arguably a harmonization with previous usage. Beginning in Gen 2:8, G uses the name יהוה אלהים in variation with אלהים. The use of both divine names is explicable as a compromise between harmonization with אלהים of Gen 1:1–2:3 and fidelity to יהוה אלהים of the parent text. The changes in this section are attributable to a harmonizing scribe (or scribes) in the proto-G tradition.

3. Genesis 4–11. The pattern of variation between יהוה אלהים and אלהים in
   G of Gen 2:8–3:24 continues. The only exceptions to this pattern are four
   instances (4:3, 13; 9:26; 10:9) in which G reads the name יהוה (= M). In
   all other instances, G reads either יהוה אלהים (19 times) or אלהים (29
   times). The variations between M and G in this section can be charted as
   follows:

   יהוה M 26 times
     = G (κυριος) 4 times
     ] אלהים G (ο θεος) 8 times
     ] יהוה אלהים G (κυριος ο θεος) 14 times

   אלהים M 26 times
     = G (ο θεος) 21 times
     ] יהוה אלהים G (κυριος ο θεος) 5 times

   To conform with the pattern established in Gen 2:8–3:24, יהוה was
   expanded to יהוה אלהים or changed to אלהים (with four exceptions =
   יהוה), and אלהים was either unchanged (predominantly) or expanded to
   יהוה אלהים.

After Genesis 11, the double name יהוה אלהים is no longer used in G, and the
names in the parent text are more consistently followed. Significant variation
occurs only in the case of אלהים ← יהוה (14 times in Genesis 12–50).

Harmonization was a common tendency in biblical scribal traditions; it is
characteristic of the proto-G tradition in Genesis 1–11 and the proto-S tradition
generally (see chapter 5). I have argued that the motive for harmonization in the
variation of divine names in Genesis is the abrupt transition from one pattern of
use to another: God's name changes from אלהים in Gen 1:1–2:3 to יהוה אלהים
(predominantly) in 2:4–3:24, and then varies between יהוה and אלהים in the rest
of the text. Many interpreters, including Philo, the classical rabbis, and modern
critical scholars, have tried to make sense of these changes in divine name, with
differing degrees of success. A scribe or scribes in the proto-G textual tradition
may have been the first to try to solve this problem or at least to ameliorate its
effect. The pattern of divine names in G of Genesis is explicable as a product of
such scribal harmonization.

In sum, it is most plausible to regard the vast majority of G variants in the
divine names in Genesis as secondary. These variants were, however, produced
by a coherent method. The opposite argument—that a scribe in the proto-M
tradition created the consistent source-critical pattern of divine names in M from
the pattern preserved in G—is implausible. Such an event, like the hypothetical
monkeys typing *Hamlet*, is an astronomical improbability. We may conclude

that the variants in divine names stemming from the proto-G text of Genesis are, for the most part, of negligible text-critical value. But they are of interest in revealing something of the conceptual world of ancient biblical scribes.

CHAPTER THREE

Textual Problems in M of Genesis 1–11

3.1 THE LAW OF SCRIBES: TEXTUAL CHANGE

It is nothing new to suggest that M of Genesis is an imperfect text. The *Kĕtîb-Qĕrê* system implemented by the Masoretes is a text-critical apparatus designed to improve the base text, probably reflecting some kind of collation of variant readings (see Tov 1992a: 58–63; Yeivin 1980: 52–61). The Talmud records a warning to scribes to beware graphic and auditory errors when copying biblical texts:

> In order that the text be perfect one must write no א for ע and no ע for א; no ב for כ; no ג for צ and no צ for ג; no ד for ר and no ר for ד; no ה for ח and no ח for ה; no ו for י and no י for ו; no ז for נ and no נ for ז; no ט for פ and no פ for ט; no curved letters for straight [i.e., final letters]; no מ for ס and no ס for מ. (*B. Šabbat* 103b)

A story about Rabbi Ishmael (ca. early second century C.E.) makes this case in more dramatic terms: "When I came to Rabbi Ishmael he said to me, 'My son, what is your occupation?' I said to him, 'I am a copyist.' He said to me, 'My son, be careful in your work, for your work is heaven's work; for should you omit one letter or add one letter, you will destroy the entire universe'" (*B. ʿErubin* 13a). One can see that great care was taken in the transmission of the rabbinic-M text, but there remained a certain anxiety about the commission of scribal errors.

To the traditional הלכות ספר תורה, "laws of (writing) Torah scrolls" (Yeivin 1980: 36–38), Goshen-Gottstein has added a text-critical supplement: the "law of scribes" (1957: 198 n. 3; 1965: 17; 1967: 275). By this law, he means that all scribes at all times and places make certain predictable kinds of errors, most of them accidental, including such commonplaces as graphic confusion, dittography, and haplography. It is to the effects of this law in M of Genesis 1–11 that we now turn.

The significant types of scribal error or change in M of Genesis 1–11 can be classified as follows:

graphic confusion: Gen 1:9; 2:12; 4:18; 10:3; 10:4; 11:30
simple haplography or dittography: Gen 2:11; 4:7; 5:23; 5:31; 8:10
haplography by homoioteleuton or homoioarkton: Gen 1:9; 1:26; 2:20; 5:3
word misdivision: Gen 8:14 (with other consequent errors)
assimilation by reminiscence or anticipation: Gen 1:29; 2:2; 7:20; 9:7
parablepsis: Gen 1:14; 4:8; 4:22; 4:26 (twice); 8:19; 10:5; 11:31
orthographic modernization: Gen 2:15; 4:7; 9:21
harmonization: Gen 1:11; 4:26; 7:3; 7:6; 7:22; 8:17
explication: Gen 2:23; 3:6; 3:22; 4:25; 6:16; 7:2; 7:14 (twice); 8:22; 9:10
    (twice)
editorial revision: Gen 5:18, 19, 25, 26, 28, 30, 31; 11:17

By "simple" haplography or dittography, I refer to the accidental change of a single letter (either two letters written singly or one letter written doubly). By parablepsis ("wrongly seen"), I refer to an apparently unmotivated error. Otherwise, my terminology is essentially equivalent to that of McCarter (1986: 26–61) and Tov (1992a: 236–85) in their exemplary treatments of the kinds of textual change in biblical texts.

3.2 TEXTUAL CHANGE IN M

Gen 1:9   מִקְוֵה 4QGen^h G (συναγωγην)] מָקוֹם M 4QGen^b S Jub 2:5 LAB 15:6
    Perhaps a graphic confusion (ה/ם); see §2.2.

Gen 1:9   ותרא) 4QGen^k# ויקוו המים מתחת השמים אל מקויהם ותרא היבשה
    (היבֹ[שה]) G (και συνηχθη το υδωρ το υποκατω του ουρανου εις τας
    συναγωγας αυτων και ωφθη η ξηρα) sim Jub 2:6] om M 4QGen^bg S

    A haplography by homoioarkton (ויק- ∩ ויק-) or possibly by homoioteleuton
    (היבשה ∩ היבשה); see §2.2.

Gen 1:11   פרי 2° M 4QGen^b S G (καρπον)] + למינו M 4QGen^b S
    Perhaps a harmonizing plus with למינהו 2° v 12; see §2.2.

Gen 1:14   ולש[נים] 4QGen^k G (και εις ενιαυτους) Syr] ושנים M S
    A parablepsis. This minor variant is of interest because of the testimony of a
4Q fragment. In the coordinated series of four nouns in the construction . . . והיו
ל, "they shall be(come)," M and S lack the preposition ל before the last noun in

the series, ושנים. Grammatically, one would expect the preposition before all four nouns, which one finds in G, Syr, and now 4QGen[k]. The grammatically correct and now clearly attested reading is to be preferred (so Davila 1990: 11; but correct his S reading there and in DJD 12: 77 to ושנים).

Gen 1:26 ובבהמה M S G (καὶ τῶν κτηνῶν)] + ובכל הארץ M S G (καὶ πάσης τῆς γῆς); + ובכל חית הארץ Syr

Perhaps a haplography (-ל ה- ∩ -ל ה-). The lists of animals in vv 24, 25, 26, 28, and 30 vary significantly in diction, yet they are semantically equivalent in referring to all animals. These variations were at times subject to scribal harmonizations (see §2.2 at Gen 1:28, 30). In v 26, the phrase ובכל הארץ occurs between ובבהמה and ובכל הרמש as an object of human rule. While humans are told to subdue the earth (וכבשה) in v 28, the reference to "all the earth" seems odd in the zoological context of v 26. For this reason, most commentators prefer the reading of Syr in v 26, ובכל חית הארץ, thereby seeing a reference to land animals, as suggested by the context (so Dillmann 1897: 81; Gunkel 1910: 112; Skinner 1930: 30; Speiser 1964: 7; Schmidt 1973: 127; Westermann 1984: 79; *BHS* ad loc.).

A problem with preferring the Syr reading is the possibility that Syr has a harmonistic text in this section of the list in vv 26 and 28. Whereas M and S list ובבהמה in v 26 and ובכל חיה in v 28, Syr lists both terms in both verses (for the different harmonistic reading of G in v 28, see §2.2):

v 26 (M S)	ובבהמה ובכל הארץ
v 26 (Syr)	ובבהמה ובכל חית הארץ
v 28 (M S)	ובכל חיה . . . הארץ
v 28 (Syr)	ובבהמה ובכל חיה . . . הארץ

It may be that the Syr readings in both verses have been expanded to harmonize with each other and with the comparable lists in vv 24 and 25, which include both terms (v 25: חית הארץ and הבהמה; v 24: היתו ארץ and בהמה). As a general rule, it is precarious to rely on a reading attested solely in one of the minor versions (see §1.3). In this case, the precariousness is magnified by the possibility that Syr has a harmonistic reading.

A more prudent solution is to posit that the anomalous phrase ובכל הארץ, shared by all the major versions, is an early scribal error. It may be a harmonizing or explicating plus, intended to include the earth under human rule in v 26 as it is in v 28 (note that וכבשה, "and subdue it [the earth]," precedes the blessing to rule over the animals). Perhaps more likely (since accidental), it may be the result of a haplography of an original phrase, ובכל הרמש הרמש על הארץ, in which the scribe's eye jumped from ובכל ה- to הארץ, triggered by the identical sequence -ל ה-. To complete this explanation, the corrupt phrase may then have been corrected by the insertion of the correct (original) phrase, yielding a final text: ובכל הארץ ובכל הרמש הרמש על הארץ. This solution, while conjectural, is perhaps more satisfactory than the alternatives: either staying with the the dubious reading of the major versions or preferring the probably harmonistic reading of Syr.

Gen 1:29   פרי M S G (καρπον)] + עץ M S (om G)

    Perhaps an anticipation of פרי עץ (3:2 and 3:3); see §2.2.

Gen 2:2   השׁשׁי S G (τη εκτη) Syr Jub 2:16] השׁביעי M

    An anticipation of השׁביעי v 2 (note the similar phraseology in both halves of v 2: ביום . . . מלאכתו אשׁר עשׂה); see §2.2.

Gen 2:11   חוילה S^mss] החוילה M S

    A simple dittography with graphic confusion of ח/ה. Elsewhere, the land of Havilah is written without the definite article, which is expected for a proper noun (Gen 25:18; 1 Sam 15:7; cf. Gen 10:7, 29). The presence of the definite article in 2:11 is easily accounted for by a simple dittography, aided by ה/ח confusion.

Gen 2:12   ההיא M^Q S Tg^P Syr] ההוא M^K T^O (mult)

    A graphic confusion of י/ו, a *qĕrê perpetuum* in the Pentateuch. This frequent error occurs seven times in M^K of Genesis 1–11 (2:12; 3:12, 20; 4:22; 7:2; 10:11, 12). The correct form, היא, occurs three times in M^K of Genesis, at Gen 14:2; 20:5; and 38:25. According to the Masoretic note at these vv, the correct form occurs 11 times in M^K of the Pentateuch. This is a systematic error limited to this form, in which graphic confusion triggered the assimilation of היא to הוא. Cross has proposed a plausible paleographic context for this scribal error: "In one style of [early Herodian] script *waw* and *yod* were not distinguished . . . the error must have been introduced when such a manuscript in later Herodian times was copied when *yod* had shortened, and to the scribe the older form of *yod* looked like *waw*" (personal correspondence, 10/12/92). In one instance in Genesis, a Qumran fragment preserves the correct form where M has the *qĕrê perpetuum* (4QGen^f at Gen 48:7; see Davila 1992: 174 n. 21).

Gen 2:15 הֹ- (2×: לעבדה ולשמרה)] הָ- (2×: לעבדה ולשמרה) M

The problem in this verse concerns the proper interpretation of the ה *mater* and is therefore a problem of vocalization and not of text as such. Nonetheless, it illustrates a problem of orthographic modernization, in which an unmodernized text was misunderstood. Numerous commentators have noted that גֹן, the referent of the pronominal suffixes on the infinitives לעבדה ולשמרה, is a masculine noun and requires the suffix to be -ô (Kuenen 1884: 138 n. 1; Gunkel 1910: 10; Skinner 1930: 66; GKC §122.l). The easiest explanation of the M vocalization is that the final ה was read as a *mater* for -â in the reading tradition fixed by the Masoretes, according to the standard orthography in postexilic texts. Grammatically, it is preferable to read the final ה as a *mater* for -ô, following the earlier, preexilic orthography (on this orthographic change, see Freedman 1962: 93; Andersen and Forbes 1986: 183–85; Barr 1989a: 208).

Gen 2:20 ולכל עוף G (και πασιν τοις πετεινοις) Tg^J Syr Vg] ולעוף M S

A haplography by homoioteleuton (ל- ∩ ל-). Although the reading of M and S is certainly possible, the context seems to require כל before עוף השמים, as is the case for the other animals listed, הבהמה and חית השדה. The loss of כל would be an easy haplography in an original reading ולכל because the scribe's eye need only skip from ל to ל (see Gunkel 1910: 11; Skinner 1930: 68; Speiser 1964: 15; *BHS* ad loc.).

Gen 2:23 לקחה M S G (ελημφθη)] + זאת M S (om G Syr)

An explicating plus. In the man's parallelistic discourse about the newly created woman, the demonstrative pronoun זאת occurs three times in M but only twice in G (and Syr). The third זאת is plausibly an explicating plus, specifying the subject of the passive verb לקחה. The subject is implicit; hence, this small plus may illustrate the scribal tendency to make the implicit explicit. With respect to parallelistic style, the rhythm and end rhyme of the line may lend support to this text-critical decision: לזאת יקרא אשה // כי מאיש לקחה.

Gen 3:6 ונחמד M S G (και ωραιον)] + העץ M S (om G Vg)

An explicating or harmonizing plus (cf. העץ 1° v 6). The three subordinate clauses expressing the woman's changed perceptions of the tree are stylistically parallel in M of v 6:

כי טוב העץ למאכל
וכי תאוה הוא לעינים
ונחמד העץ להשכיל

The common object of perception is specified in the three clauses as הוא, העץ, and העץ, respectively. Though G preserves a unit-by-unit correspondence in other respects, it lacks the last העץ, raising the suspicion that this word is secondary in M. An interesting stylistic progression in the three clauses heightens this suspicion: the first two clauses are marked with כי, but in the third clause כי is only implied. It would be stylistically apt, in view of this ellipsis in the third clause, for the subject of the clause also to be implied. The brevity of the third clause as ונחמד להשכיל may stylistically accentuate the end point of the woman's perception. In a clause with an implied subject, it is plausible that a scribe might secondarily supply the subject. The evidence of G suggests that this was the case in proto-M. Because there is no motive for a haplography in G, it is reasonable to conclude that the M reading has been expanded by the explication of the subject in the third clause.

Gen 3:22 ולקח M S G (καυ λαβη)] + גם M S (om G Syr^mss)

An explicating plus (cf. 3:6). Yahweh's fear that the man "will reach out his hand and take (ולקח) from the tree" has been realized once before, when the woman "took (ותקח) from its fruit and ate" (3:6). A scribe apparently added גם to ולקח in v 22 to create an explicit link with the previous taking of forbidden fruit in v 6. A simple "also" binds the story together more clearly and perhaps softens the problem of the absence of the tree of life in the earlier events of Genesis 3 (see the commentaries).

Gen 4:7   *תרבץ] רבץ M 4QGen^b# S G (ησυχασον)

A simple haplography of תת. Skinner notes of this difficult verse that "it is nearly certain that the obscurity is due to deep-seated textual corruption" (1930: 107). The problem with the clause לפתח חטאת רבץ, "sin crouches at the door," is the lack of agreement between the feminine noun חטאת and the masculine participle רבץ. This problem of lack of concord recurs for the masculine pronominal suffixes of תשקתו and תמשל בו in the following clause (see next entry).

One possible solution is to read רבץ as a noun, "croucher-demon" (or the like), functioning as a predicate nominative: "sin is/shall be a croucher-demon at the door" (so Cassuto 1961: 210–11; Speiser 1964: 32–33; and, with reservations, Westermann 1984: 299–301; Wenham 1987: 105–6). The metaphor of sin as a croucher-demon would be plausible in Mesopotamia, where the *rābiṣu lemnu*, the "evil Rābiṣu-demon" (or "evil croucher-demon"), is a malevolent spirit who ambushes his victims in everyday places (see Barré 1995). But there

are at least two serious problems with reading רבץ as a noun here: (1) to take
רבץ, understood as a predicate nominative, as the antecedent of תשקתו and
תמשל בו is grammatically difficult in that one would expect the pronominal suffixes to refer to the subject of the clause (Barré 1995: 1289); (2) no "croucher-
demon" (Rābiṣu/Rōbēṣ) is attested in any West Semitic religion, including the
Bible. With the variety of West Semitic malevolent spirits and demons available,
it is difficult to think that in this verse Yahweh casually alludes to a minor
Mesopotamian demon.

A far simpler analysis follows Skinner's insight that the problem is a text-
critical one. The most plausible text-critical solution is that tentatively advanced
by Dillmann (1897: 189; Driver 1946: 158), that an original sequence, חטאת
תרבץ, became חטאת רבץ by a simple haplography of תת. This simple and
elegant solution requires no grammatical or mythological inconcinnities and
yields the apt and memorable admonition, לפתח חטאת תרבץ, "sin crouches at
the door."

Gen 4:7   *הָ־ (2×: בה, תשוקתה) וֹ־ (2×: בו, תשוקתו) 4QGen^b (בו only) M S

An orthographic modernization. The problem in 4:7 is analogous to that in
2:15. The referent of the pronominal suffixes is חטאת, a feminine noun. In M,
both suffixes have a final ו *mater*, indicating the masculine suffix -ô. Dillmann
aptly suggests the restoration of תשוקתה and בה for the M readings תשוקתו and
בו (1897: 189). While few have adopted this suggestion (only Driver 1946:
158), it is an economical and elegant solution. In this case, we can suppose that
a text with the older orthography of final ה (for -â) has been wrongly modernized to final ו (for -ô). An incorrect orthographic modernization is the easiest
solution to this problem, yielding a reconstructed reading of two ה *matres*.

Gen 4:8   נלכה השדה S G (Διελθωμεν εις το πεδιον) T^P Syr Vg] om M 4QGen^b

A parablepsis. The mystery of what Cain said to Abel has long exercised biblical interpreters (see most elaborately Tg^P). Something is missing in the text, a
point noted in some M manuscripts by a *pisqâ bĕʾemṣāʿ pāsûq*, a section division in the middle of a verse (see Tov 1992a: 53). Some have tried to make
sense of the M phrase ויאמר קין אל הבל אחיו, "Cain said to his brother Abel," by
construing ויאמר as something other than "(he) said" (e.g., Cassuto 1961: 213–
15; but see the apt cautions of Dillmann 1897: 189–90). But ויאמר occurs six
times in the Cain and Abel story, each time in the same syntactic position
(clause-initial), and clearly each time it means "(he) said." To posit a different
meaning for one of these six occasions is unwarranted in view of the consistent

grammar of the text. Most commentators have concluded that the absence of a quote following ויאמר indicates a corrupt text. As Dillmann observes, "It is yet as good as certain that the author cannot have so written" (1897: 189–90).

In contrast to M, 4QGen[b], and Tg[O], all the other major and minor versions share the reading נלכה השדה (Hebrew in S), "Let us go to the field" (on the Syr rendition, פקעתא, "valley," see Brock 1979: 216-17.) This reading is either the archetype (or original) or a popular secondary correction. Skinner (1930: 107), Driver (1905: 65), and others (Speiser 1964: 29; *BHS* ad loc.) prefer the longer text as the original reading, while the majority of commentators are noncommittal.

The first step in adjudicating among the variants is to determine whether there is a scribal mechanism by which one reading gave rise to the other. One can imagine that a text with an obvious gap might be supplied with a filler such as נלכה השדה. It seems curious, however, that so many texts would have supplied the same filler, particularly one so nondescript. If, conversely, a text originally read נלכה השדה, how might this phrase have been lost? A plausible solution, suggested by Robert Cole (oral communication), is that a scribe lost this phrase by accidental assimilation to a similar sequence in the second half of the verse. Note the following correspondence of sequences:

v 8a   קין אל הבל אחיו נלכה השדה ויהי

v 8b   קין אל הבל אחיו ויהרגהו

It is plausible that a scribe may have accidentally anticipated the second sequence, -קין אל הבל אחיו וי, before resuming with ויהי of the first sequence. Such an explanation would account for the loss of נלכה השדה in M by ordinary scribal error.

Our new respect for the non-M versions in the post-Qumran era—plus a plausible explanation for scribal error in M—yields the most likely conclusion that the short text of M is secondary and that the archetypal or original reading is נלכה השדה, preserved in S, G, and most of the minor versions.

Gen 4:18 מחייאל 1–2° M (2° only); sim S (מחיאל 1–2°) G (Μαιηλ 1–2°); cf vocalic pattern of Vg (Maviahel 1–2°)] מחויאל 1–2° M (1° only) Tg[P] (1–2°); מחואל 1–2° Syr

A graphic confusion of ׳/ו. Two variant readings of the name of Irad's son are preserved by M in successive clauses: מחויאל ומחייאל. The M vocalization appears to read both variants as "destroyed (one) of God," from √מחה, using the passive adjectival patterns *qatûl* and *qatîl*. As Skinner notes, the most likely analysis of the name according to ordinary Hebrew onomastics is from the root

√חיה, probably מְחִיָּאֵל (Piel) or מַחְיִאֵל (Hiphil), either form meaning "God preserves my life" (or "enlivens me") or "God is my preserver/enlivener" (1910: 117; similarly Hess 1993: 41–43). The alternate reading in M, מחויאל, is easily attributable to a י/ו confusion, perhaps motivated by anticipation of the vocalic pattern of מתושאל, the following name in v 18.

Conversely, it is possible to argue that מחויאל preserves the older allomorph √חוה, like the name חוה, Eve (so Layton 1997: 25-26). In this explanation, the variant form מחייאל could be the product of linguistic modernization. Adjudicating between these two arguments is not simple because both phenomena—י/ו confusion and archaic traits in personal names—are attested in Genesis 1–11. It may be easier to prefer the solution with the simpler change of graphic confusion.

Gen 4:22 <אבי כל>] om M S G

A parablepsis. Most commentators recognize that the text is awry in v 22. The phrase תובל קין לטש כל חרש נחשת וברזל is disturbed, presumably missing אבי כל or הוא היה אבי כל, judging from the parallel descriptions of Tubal Cain's two older brothers (vv 20–21; cf. the renderings of Tg[O]: הוא הוה רבהון דכל; and Tg[J]: רב לכל). As a diagnostic conjecture in the absence of textual variants or a plausible reconstruction of textual change (see §1.2), it is feasible to read אבי כל after תובל קין, yielding the phrase תובל קין אבי כל לטש כל חרש נחשת וברזל. If this or something like it was the original text, then one might see how the phrase כל חרש could have been inserted as an explicating gloss for the rare כל לטש (similarly Freedman 1952: 192). This solution to the problem is possible, though it bears little weight in the absence of supporting textual data.

Gen 4:25 אדם M S G (Αδαμ)] + עוד M S (om G)

An explicating plus (cf. 4:1). Adam and Eve's second reported sexual congress is linked to the first report in M (= S) and G, but by different means: M reads "Adam knew his wife again," with a simple עוד providing an explicating link between the two events; G provides continuity by a harmonizing expansion of the archetype את אשתו, "his wife," to את חוה אשתו, "Eve, his wife," after the sequence in 4:1. Notably, the G text of 4:25 is not precisely harmonized to 4:1, as it preserves the different word order (verb-initial). Thus, even though G has been expanded by חוה (and elsewhere in the verse by ותהר) to harmonize with 4:1, it preserves the rest of the text of 4:22, in which עוד (M) is conspicuously lacking. Because there is no motive for the loss of this word in G, it is reasonable to regard it as an explicating plus in the proto-M tradition.

Gen 4:26 ולשת M S G (καὶ τῳ Σηθ)] + גם הוא M S (om G)

A harmonizing plus with וצלה גם הוא ילדה (4:22) and ולשם ילד גם הוא (10:21). The notice of Seth's fatherhood has attracted a גם הוא, "him too," from the parallel phrases in which Zillah and Shem have children. Each of these phrases occurs after a previous notice of birth; in each phrase, the parent's name (Seth, Zillah, Shem) occurs in clause-initial position as a nominative absolute (*casus pendens*), and in the cases of Seth and Shem the verb ילד is a Qal passive (though vocalized as a Pual). In view of these similarities, it is easy to see how a scribe might have filled out the phrase for Seth with גם הוא. The absence of this remark in G of 4:26 indicates that it is a secondary expansion shared by M and S.

Gen 4:26 זה G (ουτος) T^P Syr Vg 11QJub^M 3.2 (= Jub 4:12)] אז M S

A parablepsis, perhaps with a simple haplography (-ה ה-). The variation of זה versus אז is not great. If זה was the original, then one may account for the lost ה by simple haplography in the sequence זה החל- and for the addition of א as a secondary correction. Conversely, one might imagine that אז became זה by a random loss of א and a dittography of ה. One can only construct a sound argument for the preferred reading on the basis of the grammatical and semantic context (see next entry).

Gen 4:26 החל S Syr cf 11QJub^M 3.2 (ריא[ש]ו[ן]) (= Jub 4:12)] הוחל M G (ηλπισεν, from √יחל)

A parablepsis. The sequence in M, אז הוחל לקרא, "then was begun to call on (the name of Yahweh)," seems ungrammatical and semantically obscure in its context. The phrase זה החל has textual warrant and is a plausible archetypal reading (so Dillmann 1897: 210; Gunkel 1910: 54; Skinner 1930: 126). The grammatical construction of החל + ל + infinitive is found in two other J texts in Genesis 1–11: הוא החל להיות (Gen 10:8) and ויהי כי החל האדם לרב (Gen 6:1). This consistent usage supports reading החל (with S and G) as Hiphil, not Hophal (note, however, that G reads the verb as a Hiphil of √יחל, "to hope for"), and reading זה as the governing pronoun, referring to Enosh as the one who "began to call on the name of Yahweh."

Gen 5:3 *בן] om M S G

A haplography by homoioarkton (-ב ∩ -ב). The verb ויולד, "he begot," requires an object, as it has in the other 35 occurrences of the form in the Book of Generations (ספר תולדת) of Genesis 5 and 11. It is possible that the object, בן, is implied by the verb and its context (so Dillmann 1897: 223; Speiser 1964:

40). It is also possible that the original text read ויולד בן (cf. 5:28) and that בן has been lost (so Skinner 1930: 130). The latter possibility is explicable by a simple scribal error. In an original sequence of ויולד בן בדמותו, it would be easy for a scribe's eye to skip from ב to ב, thereby losing בן. The symmetrical cluster of letters in this reading, -דבנבד-, makes this haplography quite plausible. Although this would be an early scribal error, inherited by all the major versions, it seems to be an easier solution than a unique instance of an implied object for ויולד.

Gen 5:18 62 S] 162 M G

An editorial revision; see §4.2.

Gen 5:19 *900] 800 M G; 785 S

An editorial revision; see §4.2.

Gen 5:23 ויהיו S G (και εγενοντο)] ויהי M

A simple haplography with a graphic confusion of י/ו. The formula ויהיו כל ימי PN, "all the days of PN were . . . ," occurs seven times in M of Genesis 5 (vv 5, 8, 11, 14, 17, 20, 27). In two other instances, the initial word of the formula in M is ויהי (vv 23 and 31). Because the plural noun ימים requires the plural verb ויהיו (so S and G), it is clear that M's ויהי in these two instances is an error, most likely the result of a simple haplography of יו aided by י/ו confusion.

Gen 5:25 67 S] 187 M; 167 G

An editorial revision; see §4.2.

Gen 5:26 *902] 782 M; 653 S; 802 G

An editorial revision; see §4.2.

Gen 5:28 *88] 182 M; 53 S; 188 G

An editorial revision; see §4.2.

Gen 5:30 *665] 595 M; 600 S; 565 G

An editorial revision; see §4.2.

Gen 5:31 ויהיו S G (εγενοντο)] ויהי M

A simple haplography with a graphic confusion of י/ו; see the previous discussion at 5:23.

Gen 5:31 753 G] 777 M; 653 S

An editorial revision; see §4.2.

Gen 6:16 ‏ופתח‎ M S G (την δε θυραν)] + ‏התבה‎ M S (om G)

An explicating plus. God's instructions to Noah on the construction of the ark include building an entry or doorway. Where M reads ‏ופתח התבה בצידה‎ ‏תשים‎, "make the entrance of the ark in its side," the literalistic G text lacks the equivalent of ‏התבה‎, "the ark." That the ark is the object of construction has already been specified earlier in the verse, and it is clear that the instruction to make a ‏פתח בצדה‎, "entrance in its side," refers to the ark. The pronominal suffix "its" makes this identification unambiguous. Nonetheless, an explicating scribe appears to have inserted ‏התבה‎ to make this identification crystal clear.

Gen 7:2 ‏לא טהרה‎ M S G (μη καθαρων)] + ‏היא‎ M (‏הוא‎) S (om G)

An explicating plus. In the instruction to take a pair of each unclean animal into the ark, the governing verbal phrase, ‏תקח לך‎, "take," is implicit from the previous clause in v 2a. To clarify the stylistic ellipsis in this command, an explicating scribe apparently added ‏היא‎ after the prepositional phrase, ‏ומן הבהמה‎ ‏אשר לא טהרה‎, to clarify that it is this group to which the implicit command pertains. As in previous instances, this explicating plus is unnecessary for all but the most punctillious reader.

Gen 7:3 ‏על‎ M S G (επι)] + ‏פני‎ M S (om G, sim Tg[J])

A harmonizing plus with ‏על פני כל הארץ‎ (8:9, 1:29). The absence of ‏פני‎ in this phrase in G indicates that M has an expanded reading. This is the sole instance in Genesis of the phrase ‏על כל הארץ‎, "on the whole earth"; the longer phrase ‏על פני כל הארץ‎, "on the face of the whole earth," occurs several times. In the flood story, the longer phrase occurs in 8:9 in connection with the dove (note the birds in 7:3). In the creation story, the longer phrase occurs in connection with ‏זרע‎, "seed," as in 7:3. These similarities in diction make it plausible that a scribe in the proto-M tradition has harmonized the phrase in 7:3, whether wittingly or accidentally, to the familiar longer phrase in the other verses.

Gen 7:6 ‏היה‎ M S G (εγενετο; ην G[A])] + ‏מים‎ M S G (υδατος) (om G[A])

A harmonizing plus with ‏המבול מים על הארץ‎ (6:17). The word ‏מים‎, "water," in 6:17 and 7:6 is often taken to be an explicating gloss for the infrequent term ‏מבול‎, "flood." Alternately, it may be, as Skinner puts it, "a peculiar case of nominal apposition" (1930: 162). The case is difficult to decide on a textual or grammatical basis, as Skinner observes.

In 6:17, the sequence המול מים is attested in all versions and hence is either an original apposition or an early gloss. In the absence of textual variants, it is prudent to accept this reading as the archetype or original (so Tov 1985: 281 n. 71). In 7:6, the use of מים is much more awkward, as the verb היה intervenes between the two nouns, yielding a fractured syntax: והמבול היה מים על הארץ, "and the flood was water on the earth." The word מים seems clearly intrusive in this sentence. Because a major codex of G, G^A (Alexandrinus), lacks a corresponding term for מים in this verse, there is some textual warrant for regarding the word as secondary in M. With most commentators (Gunkel 1910: 142; Westermann 1984: 391; McCarter 1986: 32–33; *BHS* ad loc.), it is feasible to regard מים in 7:6 as a secondary expansion. This plus may be regarded as a harmonizing link with המבול מים in 6:17, creating a verbal continuity between God's stated intention (6:17) and the realization of that intention (7:6). In this respect, the attempt to harmonize the two verses is comparable to the harmonizations of *Wortbericht* and *Tatbericht* in Genesis 1 (see §2.2).

In this explanation, I have cited the reading of G^A, which lacks υδατος = מים. However, both the critical editions of Wevers and Rahlfs prefer the reading of G^911 (Berlin Papyrus) to that of G^A in 7:6b. The two texts read as follows:

G^911 και ο κατακλυσμος εγενετο υδατος επι της γης
G^A   και ο κατακλυσμος ην επι της γης

The variation is εγενετο υδατος = היה מים (G^911) versus ην = היה (G^A). According to Wevers's apparatus, most of the other Greek manuscripts have readings related to that in G^911, and only one (54) other than G^A lacks υδατος. Although the preference for the reading of G^911 is certainly defensible, it is also arguable that in this case the reading in G^911 (and the related readings) reflects a correction of a G^A-type reading toward M. In text-critical terms, it is easier to account for the textual change from ην (G^A) to υδατος (G^911) than vice versa in this case. Wevers has shown that G^911 shares a number of readings with M against G, thus suggesting "the possibility of a prehexaplaric revision towards the Hebrew" (1974: 220–22). In light of this situation, I would suggest that υδατος in 7:6 is another instance of a secondary revision of G toward M and that the reading in G^A is plausibly the preferred G reading.

Gen 7:14 init] + המה M S (הם) (om G)

An explicating plus. The pronoun המה, lacking in G, in the entry procession of v 14 can be identified compellingly as an explicating gloss. This pronoun refers back to the entrants listed in v 13 (Noah and his family), joining them to the list of animals in v 14. But in v 15 we are told, ויבאו אל נח אל התבה, "they came to Noah into the ark." Clearly, the subject of this verb is the list of animals in v 14. The המה that is prefixed to this list implies that Noah and his family also "came to Noah into the ark." Not only is it impossible for Noah to come to Noah, but Noah and family have already entered the ark in v 13 (בא נח אל התבה . . .). The attempt to complete the list of ark entrants in v 14 with המה only serves to disrupt the logical continuity of the narrative. The textual evidence and the sense of the narrative mutually support the judgment that the pronoun is a scribal explicating plus.

Gen 7:14 fin] + כל צפור כל כנף M S (om G)

An explicating plus (cf. כל צפור כל כנף Ezek 17:23). This curious phrase, lacking in G, is in apposition to the previous phrase, וכל העוף למינהו, "every flying creature (or bird) according to its kind." Cassuto observes nicely that "the significance of this apposition is not at first glance quite clear" (1964: 90). Dillmann plausibly suggests that the second phrase "singles out the bird species proper from the mass of the עוף" (1897: 279), that is, clarifies that not all "flying things" entered the ark, only winged birds. Presumably, this specification has been added to exclude other flying things, such as insects. The wording of this explicating phrase may be borrowed from Ezek 17:23. Again in this case, the textual evidence coheres with the semantic and grammatical superfluity of the phrase to identify this reading as an explicating plus. It is worth noting that this scribal explication of the kinds of flying creatures on the ark anticipates the considerable exegetical interest in such details in later periods (see Lewis 1968).

Gen 7:20 גבהו G (υψωθη)] גברו M S

A reminiscence of המים גברו v 19. The root √גבר is used four times in the flood story in M (7:18, 19, 20, 24). On only one of those occasions, 7:20, G reads a form of √גבה rather than a form of √גבר. In the three verses where M and G agree (7:18, 19, 24), the meaning of the verb is "be strong" or "prevail." In 7:20, the meaning of the verb refers to the height of the waters. Although "be strong" is possible in v 20, it is more likely that the reading in M, גברו המים, was caused by an accidental reminiscence of the phrase המים גברו in v 19. The difference of only a single letter between גברו and גבהו makes such reminiscence an easy error. A graphic confusion of ה/ר may have contributed to this change. Skinner (1930: 165) rightly prefers גבהו here.

Gen 7:22 נשמת M S G (πνοην)] + רוח M S (om G Vg)

A harmonizing plus with רוח חיים (6:17, 7:15). Most commentators have recognized that the phrase נשמת רוח חיים in 7:22 is a conflation of two synonymous phrases, נשמת חיים and רוח חיים, meaning "breath of life." Because the phrase with נשמת occurs in J (Gen 2:7) and the phrase with רוח occurs in P (Gen 6:17; 7:15), it is usually concluded that נשמת חיים is the original reading of 7:22, a J text (Dillmann 1897: 280; Gunkel 1910: 63; Skinner 1930: 154; Westermann 1984: 392). It seems to have escaped notice that this argument is more forceful than it seems in that the G reading provides direct textual warrant.

Where M has נשמת רוח חיים in 7:22, G reads πνοην ζωης. This is the same wording as in G of 2:7, where M has נשמת חיים. In contrast, in the verses where M has רוח חיים (6:17; 7:15), G reads πνευμα ζωης. The lexical choices in G are consistent here and elsewhere in Genesis: πνοη corresponds to נשמה; πνευμα corresponds to רוח. Given the lexical regularity of G, the absence of πνευμα = רוח in 7:22 indicates that the *Vorlage* lacked this word. The textual data of G support the frequent analysis that רוח in 7:22 is a secondary expansion, harmonizing the phrase נשמת חיים with the two occasions in the flood story where רוח חיים is used. This is yet another case of the harmonization of God's word (6:17; P) and its fulfillment (7:22; J). We may conclude that this harmonizing plus was not the work of the redactor of the flood story, R[JEP] (pace Westermann 1984: 392) but was added by a harmonizing scribe in the proto-M (or proto-S) textual tradition.

Gen 8:10 וייחל G (και επισχων)] ויחל M S (also v 12) 4QCommGen[a]

A simple haplography of יי (cf. וייחל v 12). The verb יחל, "to wait," occurs clearly only in the Piel and Hiphil (*BDB* 403–4). In 8:12, the form וייחל is probably to be read as a Piel (though oddly it is vocalized in M as a Niphal). In v 10, the form ויחל is vocalized as a Hiphil, but if it were Hiphil the form should be ויוחל. With Dillmann (1897: 286), Skinner (1930: 156), and others (e.g., *BHS* ad loc.), it is probable that an original וייחל in v 10 became ויחל by a simple haplography of יי.

Gen 8:14 עשר יום 4QCommGen[a] Jub 5:31] ועשרים יום M S; ועשרים G (εικαδι)

A word misdivision with a graphic confusion and simple haplography of י, with secondary corrections. The differences between M, G, and other texts in the flood chronology of Genesis 7–8 have long been noted, but it has not been observed that the differences are explicable by text-critical means (see Hendel 1995b). The chief difference is the variation between the 17th day (שבעה עשר יום) of the month and the 27th day (שבעה ועשרים יום) for three key dates of the flood: Gen 7:11, 8:4, and 8:14. The textual variations are as follows:

7:11 שבעה עשר יום M S 4QCommGen[a] (שבעה עשר בו) Jub 5:23
שבעה ועשרים G (εβδομη και εικαδι)

8:4 שבעה עשר יום M S 4QCommGen[a] (שבעה עשר בחודש)
שבעה ועשרים G (εβδομη και εικαδι)

8:14 שבעה ועשרים יום M S
שבעה עשר יום 4QCommGen[a] Jub 5:31 G[mss] (επτακαιδεκατη ημερα)
שבעה ועשרים G (εβδομη και εικαδι)

The variations in 7:11 and 8:4 are identical, with the G reading differing from that shared by all the other versions and ancillary sources (Jub and 4QCommGen[a]). There are two differences between the two readings: (1) the numerical difference of 17 versus 27 and (2) the presence or absence of the word יום. To the textual critic, the two differences are mutually intelligible. In all three verses, G lacks יום (ημερα), the only three cases of 150 in Genesis where G lacks a corresponding term for יום (Hendel 1995b: 76–77). In these three cases, the G reading is easily explained as the result of simple scribal error in which the two words עשר יום were misread as עשרים (with a secondary correction of -ו). A scribe (or scribes) committed a simple haplography of יו, two letters barely distinguishable in the square scripts of the Hellenistic period, and a word misdivision. The archetype of the G reading is clearly שבעה עשר יום, as it is in M and the other versions for 7:11 and 8:4.

The third verse, 8:14, is somewhat more complicated. The situation for G is the same, presupposing an archetypal reading שבעה עשר יום. This archetypal reading may be preserved in two ancillary sources, 4QCommGen[a] and Jub 5:31, though it appears also in some G manuscripts (see apparatus in Wevers's edition; note the consistent representation of יום as ημερα). Where G reads עשרים, presupposing an archetype of עשר יום, M and S read עשרים יום. The most viable solution of this variation is that an archetypal עשר יום was misread as עשרים (so G) and then secondarily corrected to עשרים יום (M S). Alternatively, it is also possible that the final יום was the result of a dittography of the original יום. In this explanation, we can trace the textual history from an archetypal reading שבעה עשר יום to the variant readings preserved in the versions. Hence, it is reasonable to prefer in 8:14 the reading שבעה עשר יום, indirectly attested in G and possibly preserved in 4QCommGen[a] and Jub, over the variant in M.

In this text-critical analysis, we not only arrive at a plausible solution for all the variants in 8:14 but also solve the problem of the flood chronology in P: the flood begins on 2/14 (Gen 7:11) and ends on 2/14 (Gen 8:14), a complete year. For other implications concerning the calendar of P (probably lunisolar) and the later solar calendar of 1 Enoch, Jub, 11QTemple, and Qumran sectarian literature, see Hendel 1995b.

Gen 8:17 אתך 2° M S G (μετα σεαυτου)] + ושרצו בארץ M S (om G)

A harmonizing plus with שרצו בארץ (9:7). In M of 8:17, God says of the animals after the flood, ושרצו בארץ ופרו ורבו על הארץ, "Let them swarm on the earth, and let them be fruitful and multiply on the earth." Here G lacks the first clause, ושרצו הארץ. As Skinner notes (1930: 167), G probably has the better text; M appears to have been expanded by a harmonization with the comparable blessing to humans in 9:7, פרו ורבו שרצו בארץ. Because there is no motive for haplography in G, its reading is to be preferred. Hence, we may take as the archetype or original in 8:17 ופרו ורבו על הארץ. This blessing has been expanded in proto-M or proto-S to harmonize God's parallel blessings to animals and humans in the postdiluvian era.

Gen 8:19 וכל העוף וכל הרמש ה- S G (και παν πετεινον και παν ερπετον) Syr] כל הרמש וכל העוף M; om וכל העוף Vg

A parablepsis. The chief variation here consists of the order of כל העוף, "all the birds," and כל הרמש, "all the creeping things." Because the verse continues with the phrase רומש על הארץ, it is natural to think that the reading of S and G, כל הרמש הרומש על הארץ, "all the creeping things that creep on the earth" (cf. 7:14; 1:26), is the archetype or original (so Gunkel 1910: 147; Skinner 1930: 167; Speiser 1964: 53; *BHS* ad loc.). For some unknown reason, M appears to have suffered a metathesis of כל הרמש and כל העוף, and someone has secondarily adjusted the text by adding כל before רומש על הארץ (probably influenced by 1:30 כל רומש על הארץ). The separation of the noun רמש from the participle רומש in the M enumeration of animals makes little sense and is most plausibly a corruption of the reading shared in S, G, and Syr. Note also that Vg has suffered a haplography in this sequence (וכל ∩ וכל).

Gen 8:22 init] + עד M S (om G Vg)

An explicating plus. The עד in God's promise that the cycles of nature will never cease appears to be connected to the verbal negation, לא ישבתו, "will not cease." The עד emphasizes that these will "never again" cease, with the construction, עד . . . לא (BDB, 729). Twice in v 21, one finds the more usual construction, לא . . . עוד. In view of the absence of this clarifying adverb in G, it may be identified as a probable explicating plus, influenced by the grammatical construction of the previous verse.

Gen 9:7 *ורדו cf G^mss (και κατακυριευσατε)] ורבו M S G (και πληθυνεσθε)

A reminiscence of ורבו v 7 (cf. ורדו 1:28). The imperative ורבו, "multiply," occurs twice in the divine command in the major versions of 9:7. Many commentators, possibly going back to Greek scribes in the inner-G tradition, have corrected the second of these to ורדו, "rule," based on the obvious allusion to the blessing in 1:28, where one finds the phrases פרו ורבו and ורדו in close proximity (Gunkel 1910: 150; Skinner 1930: 171; Speiser 1964: 57; *BHS* ad loc.; Westermann 1984: 460). It is possible that the inner-Greek variant κατακυριευσατε (= רדו) is the original G reading, as the families *b* and *d* elsewhere have affinities with the pre-Hexaplaric papyri 911 and 962, and *d* may reflect in part the old Lucianic G text (Wevers 1974: 228). In this possibility, the G reading (= רדו) is the original, superior reading. In any case, the difference between ורדו and ורבו is a single letter, making assimilation by reminiscence an easy error. It is not likely that a graphic confusion of ב/ד aided this change, though such a confusion is possible in some periods.

Gen 9:10 הארץ M S G (της γης)] + אתכם M S (om G Vg)

An explicating plus. After the phrase כל נפש החיה אשר אתכם, "every living thing that is with you," a scribe appears to have added another אתכם to the similar phrase ובכל חית הארץ, "and all (wild) creatures of the earth." This word is lacking in G. It is plausibly an explicating plus, an attempt to clarify what is implicit in the text.

Gen 9:10 fin] + לכל חית הארץ M S (om G)

An explicating plus (cf. ובכל חית הארץ v 10). This final phrase of 9:10, lacking in G, appears to be an explication of the previous phrase, מכל יצא התבה, "of all that exited the ark." The meaning of this clarifying gloss is obscure (similar to the gloss in 7:14, discussed earlier). Dillmann's attempt to make sense of it is instructive: "*any which* went out of the ark, *in respect of*, i.e., *namely, all* the animals of the earth" (1897: 296) The secondary nature of this gloss is evident by comparison with the virtually identical phrase earlier in the verse, ובכל חית הארץ, which appears to refer to wild animals, while the final phrase must refer to all the animals. Dillmann's decipherment shows also the oddity of the series of prepositions in this sequence (מכל . . . לכל). Again, the grammar and the textual evidence correspond in the judgment that this is an explicating plus. Ironically in this case, as in several others, the explicating plus tends to add less clarity rather than more. This is not uncommon for scholarly annotations (Merton 1965).

Gen 9:21 אהלה M^K] אהלו M^Q S

An orthographic modernization. The M text of 9:21 illustrates the process of orthographic modernization of the final *mater* ה- to ו-. The compilers of the

Kĕtîb-Qĕrê apparently consulted texts with modernized and unmodernized readings of this word. For some unknown reason, the form with the older orthography was retained in the *Kĕtîb* (perhaps this was the majority reading or that of the base text), and the modernized reading was taken as the *Qĕrê*. This purely orthographic variant shows the type of modernization that caused problems in 2:15 and 4:7 (discussed previously).

Gen 10:3 דיפת 1 Chr 1:6 (M) cf Syr (דיפר)] ריפת M S G (Ριφαθ) 1 Chr 1:6 (G)

A graphic confusion of ד/ר. Lipínski has argued plausibly that this word corresponds to *dahyu-pati*, a Persian title meaning "chief of the people/region" (1990: 49–50). In Elamite texts at Persepolis, this term is written as *da-a-ú-bat* (plus an affix, *ti-iš*) and *da-i-bat* (plus *ti-iš*). The term may also be found in an Assyrian inscription of Esarhaddon with reference to a local Medean chief (under the logogram EN.URU). The association of דיפת with the Scythians (אשכנז) in v 3 may be explained by the joint presence of Medes and Scythians in Anatolia during 590–585 B.C.E. (Lipínski 1990: 50).

Lipínski has also argued that the following name in M, תגרמה, ought to be read תגדמה, after a Cimmerian ruler referred to in Assyrian as *Tug-dam-me-i* and in Greek as Lygdamis (1990: 50). The forces of Tugdamme were active in Anatolia from 652 to 636 B.C.E. If this analysis is correct, then תגרמה has also suffered a ד/ר confusion. The absence of textual variants, however, warrants a cautious preference for the existing reading, though it may be historically incorrect.

Gen 10:4 רדנים S (רודנים) G (Ροδιοι) 1 Chr 1:7 (רודנים)] דדנים M; דורנים Syr

A graphic confusion of ד/ר; see §1.2.

Gen 10:5 <אלה בני יפת>] om M S G

A parablepsis. Dillmann notes, "Since the author in vv 20 and 31 concludes each of the other peoples with a subscription, and always shows himself very uniform in the use of his formulae, we expect here also an "אלה בני יפת (1897: 337–38; also Gunkel 1910: 153; Skinner 1930: 200; *BHS* ad loc.; and most others). The subscription formula has some variation to it, but Dillmann's point is apposite. Compare the slight variations in order and phrasing:

v 5   <אלה בני יפת> בארצתם איש ללשנו למשפחתם בגויהם

v 20   אלה בני חם למשפחתם ללשנתם בארצתם בגויהם

v 31   אלה בני שם למשפחתם ללשנתם בארצתם לגויהם

As Dillmann and others observe, the first part of v 5, מאלה נפרדו איי הגוים, can only refer to the Mediterranean peoples of v 4 (the sons of Javan), and the second half of v 5 includes all the sons of Japheth. The alternative explanation, that the descent of the איי הגוים, "islands of the nations," refers to all the sons of Japheth is implausible (pace Horowitz 1990). So, the missing part of the subscription can be placed with some confidence. This solution, although it lacks direct textual support from the versions, is compelling. However, in the absence of textual evidence or a cogent explanation of scribal error, this reading must be labeled a diagnostic conjecture.

Gen 11:17   370 G] 430 M; 270 S
   An editorial revision; see §4.3.

Gen 11:30   ילד S] ולד M cf להולד G ($\varepsilon\tau\varepsilon\kappa\nu o\pi o\iota\varepsilon\iota$)

A graphic confusion of י/ו. The noun ילד, "child," occurs more than 100 times in the Hebrew Bible, including 20 times in Genesis, and only here is it written with initial ו instead of י. Although *wald-* is the ancestral proto-Semitic form (preserved in Arabic and Ethiopic), the shift of word-initial *waw* → *yod* is one of the characteristic phonological features of the Northwest Semitic language group. This shift occurred by the early second millennium B.C.E., as evidenced by Northwest Semitic names attested in Egyptian and Akkadian texts (see Huehnergard 1992: 159). It is hardly conceivable that in one instance of more than 100 in the Hebrew Bible we find the proto-Semitic or proto-Northwest Semitic form intact. It is far more likely that M has suffered a simple graphic confusion of י/ו (so tentatively Skinner 1930: 237).

This reading, אין לה ולד, has an interesting *Nachgeschichte*. In (proto-)G, this reading is reflected with an additional error of word misdivision, such that אין לה ולד was misread as אין להולד, "unable to give birth," an understandable error given the hapex ולד. In Qumran and Rabbinic Hebrew, the word ולד takes on a special meaning, "embryo" (Qimron 1986: 99). At a later time, this textual and semantic development apparently influenced some eastern M manuscripts at 2 Sam 6:23, where Kennicott records the variant, לא היה לה ולד (*BHS* ad loc.).

Gen 11:31   ויצא אתם S (ויציא) G ($\varepsilon\xi\eta\gamma\alpha\gamma\varepsilon\nu$ $\alpha\upsilon\tau o\upsilon\varsigma$) Vg] ויצאו אתם M

A parablepsis. The statement in M, ויצאו אתם, "they went with them," makes no sense (see Dillmann 1897: 412; Skinner 1930: 166; Emerton 1994: 177–79). The reading in S and G, ויצא אתם, "he sent them," makes grammatical sense, though we are surprised at the end of v 32 to find that Terah, who "sent them," is also in Haran. The Syr text printed in the London Polyglot of 1654 (ed. Walton) reflects a reading ויצא אתם, "he went with them," which makes best sense of all, but this is from a minor Syr manuscript. On text-critical grounds, the reading of S and G, which is grammatically and semantically possible, is preferable to the reading of M. The difference between these two variants is simply the placement of a ו *mater*. It is possible that ויצא suffered a simple haplography of י(ו), with the requisite י/ו confusion, and a scribe in the proto-M tradition wrongly corrected the form to plural, ויצאו, perhaps anticipating the plural forms ויבאו and וישבו that follow in v 31. This is the easiest and best supported solution (and followed by most commentators). Note that S has modernized the form of ויצא from jussive (or old preterite) to imperfect, a frequent type of linguistic revision in S.

CHAPTER FOUR

The Chronologies of Genesis 5 and 11

4.1 THE PROBLEM

The problem of the ages of the ancestors in Genesis 5 and 11 is hinted at by Josephus in an intriguing aside: "The reader should not examine the ages of the individuals at death, for their lifetimes extended into those of their sons and of their sons' descendants, but should confine his attention to their dates of birth" (Ant 1.88; trans. Thackeray). If one examines the ages of these individuals at death, one discovers the scandal that in G (and its congeners) Methuselah survives the flood by 14 years (see §4.2 on Josephus's biblical *Vorlage*). Further, as Eusebius of Caesarea first observed in his *Chronicle*, the chronlogies of Genesis 5 and 11 diverge significantly among M, S, and G. Jerome notes in his *Hebrew Questions on Genesis*: "this is a celebrated question, and one which has been publicly aired in argument by all the churches" (Hayward 1995: 35). For Jerome, this problem provided a prime opportunity to argue for the *hebraica veritas*, against the sins of G. Augustine defended G as inspired Holy Writ, though even he felt compelled to admit: "One thing remains certain: Methuselah did not live on after the Flood" (*City of God* 15.11; trans. Bettenson [Penguin]), reluctantly following M in this instance.

The problem of the death of Methuselah in G is emblematic of the problem of the different chronologies in M, S, and G of Genesis 5 and 11. In what follows, I will examine and refine the solution advanced by Klein (1974a), that the variant chronologies of M, S, and G are the result of conscious and systematic revisions of Genesis 5 and 11, motivated by problems implicit in the ages of the individuals at death, as Josephus cautioned. Most remarkably, these problems were solved independently in the textual traditions ancestral to M, S, and G. The nature of these chronological problems can be sketched as follows.

In the antediluvian chronology from Adam to Noah in Gen 5:3–32, three patriarchs—Jared, Methuselah, and Lamech—die in or near the year of the flood

61

in all the major versions. In S, all three die in the year of the flood. In M, Methuselah dies in the year of the flood, and Jared and Lamech die earlier. In G, Jared and Lamech die before the flood, and Methuselah survives the flood by 14 years. It is notable that only for these three patriarchs do the numbers of M and S diverge. When one considers these variations among the versions, the suspicion arises that the death of these three patriarchs and the date of the onset of the flood may once have clashed, as they still do for Methuselah in G. If in the archetypal chronology of Genesis 5 Jared, Methuselah, and Lamech survived the flood, this problem would provide sufficient warrant for scribes to correct the text by adjusting the chronology. This is the solution proposed by Klein: "the original chronology implied that three patriarchs lived through the flood, and this was resolved in quite different ways" (1974a: 263).

The narrative of the flood story precludes the possibility that these men survived the flood. The only humans saved from the flood are Noah, his wife, his sons, and his sons' wives (Gen 6:18; 7:7, 13; 8:18); after the flood, "there remained only Noah and those with him on the ark" (Gen 7:23). There is no room in the narrative for other human survivors. Recent studies of this issue by Hughes and Etz agree with Klein on this point: "The coincidence between the year of Methuselah's death and the year of the flood in MT's chronology, and similar coincidences in the case of Jared, Methuselah, and Lamech in SP's chronology, seem to have resulted from application of the minimum adjustment that would ensure that these ancestors died before the start of the flood" (Hughes 1990: 14; similarly Etz 1993: 172–75). This is a plausible explanation for the chronological variants in Genesis 5 that is far more appealing than the complicated algebra of most treatments (see the reviews of scholarship in Dillmann 1897: 217–22; Skinner 1930: 134–36; Wenham 1987: 130–34, 250–51; Hughes 1990: 6 n. 1; Etz 1993: 177 n. 13).

As for the postdiluvian chronology from Shem to Abraham in Gen 11:10–32, an examination of the ages of these individuals at death uncovers another potentially disturbing result. In the M chronology, Noah, Shem, and *all* the postdiluvian patriarchs are still alive during Abraham's lifetime, and several survive him. This circumstance explains why in rabbinic traditions it is possible for Isaac to study Torah with Shem and for Jacob to study with Eber (e.g., *Gen. Rab.* 56.11; 63.10; 68.5). This problem was noted by Dillmann: "One can scarcely imagine it to have been part of our author's conception that Noah did not die till Abraham was fifty-eight years old, or that Shem lived on till after Jacob's birth, and that Eber was still alive after the death of Abraham" (1897: 399). Klein proposes that in the scribal traditions ancestral to S and G this overlap of generations was perceived as a problem. He posits that the "numbers were given originally without their implications for absolute chronology being fully noted. When the difficulties with this absolute chronology were noted, corrections were made in the archetype behind LXX and SP" (1974a: 259; similarly Etz 1993: 184).

In contrast, Hughes argues that the adjustments in S and G for the post-diluvians of Genesis 11 reflect larger chronological concerns, either to emphasize the date of the founding of the Samaritan Temple at Mt. Gerizim (S) or to highlight the date of the exodus (G) (1990: 237–38, 240–41). If, as I will argue later, Klein's solution more easily accounts for the data, the theory of two or more complicated chronological systems secretly pointing toward historical events is unnecessary (especially since the numbers do not quite fit the scheme in each case; see Hughes 1990: 240, and later here).

This motive for the chronological variants of Genesis 5 and 11—that the ancestors' ages originally extended across narrative boundaries—is consistent with the widely held view that these genealogical texts derive from an originally independent document, the ספר תולדת אדם, "Book of the Generations of Adam" (Gen 5:1; see Cross 1973: 301–5; Wallace 1990; Carr 1996: 70–73). When the P writer or redactor integrated this work into the narrative context, he may not have perceived (or may have been unconcerned with) the implicit chronological conflicts. It remained for later scribes to detect the problems and to incorporate their textual solutions.

Most modern treatments of the textual and chronological problems of Genesis 5 and 11 begin with "the working hypothesis . . . that the original chronology is identical with that of the MT" (Larsson 1983: 401). As we have seen (§2.1 and passim), this hypothesis is no longer tenable. It is necessary to examine all of the textual data and explore the textual relationships among all the significant variants, with the ideal of arriving at the archetypal or original set of readings. As Skinner aptly notes in this regard, "A presumption in favour of MT would be established only if it could be shown that the numbers of S and G are either dependent on MT, or involve no chronological scheme at all" (1930: 136). This standard also applies to the occasional scholarly preference for the chronologies of G (Ewald 1869: 276 n. 1) or S (for Genesis 5: Budde 1883: 111; Dillmann 1897: 220).

Among modern studies of Genesis 5 and 11, only those of Klein, Hughes, and Etz come reasonably close to the goal of accounting for most or all of the textual data. Hence, it is notable that their reconstructions of the archetypal numbers are nearly identical, with the primary exception of the dates for Lamech (see §4.2; Hughes also makes an adjustment for Methuselah; see §4.3). If by careful method it is possible to reconstruct a parent text that can by normal scribal events give rise to the extant readings in the chronologies of Genesis 5 and 11, then we can claim that the textual problem has been solved and can draw appropriate inferences.

4.2 GENESIS 5:3–32

The textual data and the proposed archetype are charted in table 4-1. With the exception of the numbers for Jared, Methuselah, and Lamech, there is a clear pattern among the textual variants: M and S are identical, and G differs by $b + 100$ and $r - 100$. Because these variations in G cancel out in their sum, the number for t is identical in M, S, and G.

The increase in the figure for b in proto-G ($b + 100$) serves to delay the onset of the flood (A.M. 2242 in G), and the corresponding decrease in r preserves the original set of lifespans. By this simple systematic adjustment, the G chronology manages to have all of Noah's ancestors die before the flood, with the curious exception of Methuselah. This mishap may be an unintended consequence of a systematic application of the revision. For Methuselah to have died at or before the flood, a scribe would have had to alter the system, and this may have seemed too radical for a systematizing scribe. As the Church Fathers noted, the death of Methuselah remains a problem in G.

In light of the probability that the G variants for b and r are the result of systematic revision, we may posit that the archetypal numbers in all cases except Jared, Methuselah, and Lamech are preserved as follows:

$$b = \text{M S} \ (\text{G} - 100)$$
$$r = \text{M S} \ (\text{G} + 100)$$
$$t = \text{M S G}$$

Because this consistent pattern of agreements and disagreements is lacking in the textual variants for Jared, Methuselah, and Lamech, their cases require individual analysis.

Jared

The variants for Jared's t (Gen 5:20) are 962 (M), 847 (S), and 962 (G). Because agreement between M and G preserves the archetype for t elsewhere, 962 is plausibly the archetype here. In S, the value of $t = 847$ ensures that Jared dies in the year of the flood (A.M. 1307 in S). This is likely a secondary revision of t.

Table 4-1. The Chronology of Gen 5:3–32: Major Versions and Archetype

		M	S	G	Archetype
Adam	b	130	130	230	130
	r	800	800	700	800
	t	930	930	930	930
	A.M.	(1–930)	(1–930)	(1–930)	(1–930)
Seth	b	105	105	205	105
	r	807	807	707	807
	t	912	912	912	912
	A.M.	(130–1042)	(130–1042)	(230–1142)	(130–1042)
Enosh	b	90	90	190	90
	r	815	815	715	815
	t	905	905	905	905
	A.M.	(235–1140)	(235–1140)	(435–1340)	(235–1140)
Kenan	b	70	70	170	70
	r	840	840	740	840
	t	910	910	910	910
	A.M.	(325–1235)	(325–1235)	(625–1535)	(325–1235)
Mehalel	b	65	65	165	65
	r	830	830	730	830
	t	895	895	895	895
	A.M.	(395–1290)	(395–1290)	(795–1690)	(395–1290)
Jared	b	162	62	162	62
	r	800	785	800	900
	t	962	847	962	962
	A.M.	(460–1422)	(460–1307)	(960–1922)	(460–1422)
Enoch	b	65	65	165	65
	r	300	300	200	300
	t	365	365	365	365
	A.M.	(622–987)	(522–887)	(1122–1487)	(522–887)
Methuselah	b	187	67	167	67
	r	782	653	802	902
	t	969	720	969	969
	A.M.	(687–1656)	(587–1307)	(1287–2256)	(587–1556)
Lamech	b	182	53	188	*88
	r	595	600	565	*665
	t	777	653	753	753
	A.M.	(874–1651)	(654–1307)	(1454–2207)	(654–1407)
Flood	A.M.	(1656)	(1307)	(2242)	(1342)

b = age at begetting
r = remainder
t = total lifespan
A.M. = year after creation (*anno mundi*)

The variants for Jared's *b* (Gen 5:18) are 162 (M), 62 (S), and 162 (G). Because S and G preserve the expected relationship for *b* (where G = S + 100), the archetype is plausibly 62. In M, the value of *b* = 162 delays the onset of the flood by 100 years, ensuring that Jared dies before the flood. This value is likely a secondary revision of *b*.

These revisions in M, S, and G account for all the textual variation for Jared, yielding the archetypes: *b* = 62, *r* = 900, and *t* = 962.

Methuselah

The case of Methuselah has the same pattern of agreements and disagreements as Jared. The variants for Methuselah's *t* (Gen 5:27) are 969 (M), 720 (S), and 969 (G). The number shared by M and G is plausibly the archetype, as is the pattern elsewhere. In S, the value of *t* = 720 places the death of Methuselah in the year of the flood. This is likely a secondary revision.

The variants for Methuselah's *b* (Gen 5:25) are 187 (M), 67 (S), and 167 (G). In S and G, there is the expected relationship for *b*, yielding an archetype of *b* = 67. In M, the value of *b* = 187 delays the onset of the flood so that Methuselah dies in the year of the flood (A.M. 1656 in M). This is likely a secondary revision.

These revisions in M, S, and G account for all the textual variation for Methuselah, yielding the archetypes: *b* = 67, *r* = 902, and *t* = 969.

In the similar strategies of revision for Jared and Methuselah, the G readings conform to its consistent system of revising *b* + 100 and *r* − 100, M has raised *b* by 100 and 120, and S has lowered *t* by 115 and 249. The revisions in M and S ensure that Jared and Methuselah do not survive the flood, and the systematic revision in G achieves this result for Jared but, famously, not for Methuselah.

Lamech

In the case of Lamech, a discernible pattern of agreements and disagreements is lacking. Therefore, a solution is more difficult to ascertain.

The variants for Lamech's *t* (Gen 5:31) are 777 (M), 653 (S), and 753 (G). Because the number in S has Lamech die in the year of the flood, the S figure is likely a revision, as in the previous two cases. It is not clear whether the variation between S and G (100 years) is significant. In M, *t* = 777, which is likely a secondary figure influenced by the fate of the other Lamech in Gen 4:24, whose vengeance is 77 compared to Cain's sevenfold (so Dillmann 1897: 221; Klein 1974a: 261; and others). The reading in M for Lamech's *t* may be an intentional revision (so Hughes 1990: 15) or an accidental assimilation by reminiscence of 4:24:

למך שבעים ושבעה (M) 4:24
למך שבע ושבעים שנה ושבע (M) 5:31

Because the values for Lamech's t are arguably secondary in M and S, the archetypal reading is most plausibly that of G, as is the case in every other instance in Genesis 5. Hence, we may prefer the G evidence for the archetype of Lamech's $t = 753$, though because of the absence of agreement with S or M there is more uncertainty than in the other cases.

The archetype for Lamech's b (Gen 5:28) is also difficult to isolate because of the absence of pattern among the variants: 182 (M), 53 (S), and 188 (G). In this instance, the reconstructions of Klein, Hughes, and Etz diverge because of the unclarity of the data. Klein relies on the consistency of the G revision formula ($b + 100$) to suggest an archetype of $b = 88$. He proposes that the divergent numbers for b in M and S are the result of scribal errors. For M's figure, he posits a revision of $b + 100$ (as in the case of Jared in M), yielding 188, with a subsequent change to 182 by an accidental assimilation by reminiscence of Gen 5:26 (Methuselah's r):

למך שתים ושמונים שנה (M) 5:26
למך שתים ושמנים שנה (M) 5:28

This scenario of assimilation by reminiscence is plausible and would easily yield the text in 5:28 (M). The proposal that the revised figure in proto-M was 188 ($b + 100$) is only a guess, though it would provide an easy textual basis for this scribal error.

Klein suggests that the scribal error behind the S figure, $b = 53$, is an assimilation by anticipation of Lamech's archetypal t in 5:31 (preserved in G as noted previously):

למך שלש וחמשים שנה (S) 5:28
למך שלש וחמשים שנה (G) 5:31

This, too, is an easy scribal error and accounts well for the S reading. Hence, from an archetype of Lamech's $b = 88$, one can account for the extant readings by the expected systematic revision in G and by simple scribal errors in M and S. This result is far from certain, but it is plausible.

In contrast to this solution, Hughes relies on the consistency of S in preserving the archetype for b elsewhere in Genesis 5 to yield an archetype of $b = 53$. However, if the S figure is the archetype, G should read 153, whereas it reads 188. Hughes is puzzled by the unexpected extra 35 years in G, noting that "this adjustment was not required for purposes of chronological harmonization" (1990: 15) and finds no motive for it. Hughes then suggests that proto-M had the same number as proto-G for Lamech's b, but reduced it by 6 years to make it a multiple of 7. He admits that this too is a "somewhat complex adjustment" (1990: 15). Hughes later indicates that his chief motive for preferring S rather than G ($-$ 100) in his reconstruction of Lamech's *b* is that the S reading yields a round number for the archetype of Abraham's birthdate (if coupled with a 2-year adjustment to Methuselah's chronology; see later). According to Hughes's reconstruction of the original Priestly chronology, Abraham is born in A.M. 1599. By appeal to the custom of postdating, Hughes concludes that "Abraham's first year was 1600 from creation" (1990: 21). For this reason, he argues against Klein's reconstruction of Lamech's *b* = 88 (from G $-$ 100), because in that case "1600 A.M. loses its significance, and Abraham is born insignificantly in either 1632 or 1634 A.M." (1990: 21). Because it is not clear why 1600 A.M. should be an appropriate date for Abrahamn's birth, and Hughes relies on questionable maneuvering to get to this date, his argument carries little weight. Text-critically, his argument is additionally flawed by having no plausible explanation for the readings in M and G.

In contrast to the solutions of Klein and Hughes, Etz tentatively prefers M for the reconstruction of Lamech's *b*, though (like Klein) he suggests that it has been revised upward by 100, as in the case of Jared. He posits an archetype of *b* = 82 (M $-$ 100) because it "fits the pattern of nearly all the other numbers, in all forms of the text. 74 of the 81 numbers are values divisible by 5, or divisible by 5 with 2 added" (1993: 175). This argument, too, has little text-critical significance; like Hughes's proposal, it fails to account for two of the three readings.

The archetype of Lamech's *b* is ambiguous and contested, and a clear determination may not be possible. In view of the alternative arguments, one should prefer the explanation that most easily accounts for all the data. Because Klein's proposal meets this standard and Hughes's and Etz's do not, one should tentatively prefer the reconstruction that Lamech's *b* = 88, derived from the G reading. The readings of S and M are plausibly the result of ordinary scribal errors. In this case, it is reasonable to prefer G as a basis for establishing the archetype of Lamech's *b*, though in the absence of a clear relationship with the readings in M or S, there remains a considerable degree of uncertainty.

Aside from the residue of uncertainty in the numbers for Lamech, the archetypal numbers for the chronology of Genesis 5 are easily ascertainable by this analysis, predicated on the desire of ancient scribes to have the antediluvian ancestors of Noah die at or before the year of the flood. In proto-G, the solution adopted was to revise upward by 100 years each year of begetting, thereby delaying by 900 years (100 $\times$ 9) the date of the onset of the flood. In proto-M and proto-S, the textual revisions were confined to the ages of the three problematic patriarchs, Jared, Methuselah, and Lamech. Proto-M revised upward the year of begetting for each of the three, and proto-S revised downward the year of death for each of the three. By these three different strategies of revision, the problem was solved, with the notorious exception of Methuselah in G. By identifying the problem and the strategies adopted to solve it, it is possible to reconstruct with some confidence the archetypal chronology of the text ancestral to M, S, and G.

Minor Versions and Ancillary Sources

The testimony of the minor versions (Tgs, Syr, Vg) adds little to the picture, as they consistently agree with M. The testimony of the ancillary sources (Jub, Ant, LAB) is more interesting, as these texts show some mixing among the chronologies of the major versions. The affinities of the ancillary sources are most easily shown by comparing the values for b and the year of the flood (the year of the flood = the sum of the b's), charted in table 4-2.

The chronology of *Jubilees* (Jub) has close affinities with S, as one can see particularly by the near agreements in the numbers for Jared, Methuselah, and Lamech and by the same year for the flood. Jub generally indicates the ages of begetting by listing the year according to its system of jubilees, but for Methuselah and Lamech it lists only the date of marriage, so the ages at begetting for these two are only approximate. The agreement of Jub with S is complicated by the fact that in the postdiluvian chronology it agrees with G in the inclusion of Kenan II (see §4.3). Hence, the biblical chronology used in Jub has close affinities with S, but in a significant expansion in the postdiluvian sequence it agrees with G.

Josephus's *Jewish Antiquities* (Ant) 1.83–88 agrees in its dates of begetting for the most part with G, with the notable exception of the date for Methuselah, which agrees with M. Fraenkel argues that this deviation from G is explicable by the widely held view that Josephus's biblical *Vorlage* was a G text that had been partially revised toward M (1984: 181–85, 198–99). The revision of 167 (G) to 187 (M) is widespread in G manuscripts and is plausibly a prehexaplaric revision. The revision of Methuselah's b to 187 in these G mss enables Methuselah to die before the year of the flood, thereby solving the notorious problem in G. The hypothesis that Josephus used a revised G text in this chronology may find some support by other instances in Genesis where Ant agrees with Aquila or other revisions of G (e.g., at Gen 1:1 Ant εκτισεν = Aquila, against G εποιησεν; see Brock 1992a: 328, 335 n. 13).

Table 4-2. The Chronology of Gen 5:3–32: Ancillary Sources

	Jub 4:7–28	Ant 1.83–88	LAB 1:2–22
Adam	130	230	—
Seth	98	205	105
Enosh	97	190	180
Kenan	70	170	170
Mehalel	66	165	165
Jared	61	162	162
Enoch	65	165	165
Methuselah	ca. 67	187	187
Lamech	ca. 53	188	182

	Jub 5:22–23	Ant 8.61	LAB 3:6
Flood, A.M.	1307/8	1662	1652

	S	G	M
Adam	130	230	130
Seth	105	205	105
Enosh	90	190	90
Kenan	70	170	70
Mehalel	65	165	65
Jared	62	162	162
Enoch	65	165	65
Methuselah	67	167	187
Lamech	53	188	182
Flood, A.M.	1307	2242	1656

In Ant 8.61, a chronological notice attached to the construction of the Solomonic Temple, Josephus is clearly using an M-type chronology. The date of the flood according to Ant 8.61 is A.M. 1662 and, with some textual reconstruction, the related chronology at Ant 10.147 might read a date of A.M. 1656 (Fraenkel 1984: 177–80). These readings indicate either the use of a revised G text or the use of M.

The chronology of Pseudo-Philo's *Biblical Antiquities* (LAB) agrees for the most part with G but also has a number of M readings. LAB agrees with M in the dates of *b* for Seth, Methuselah, and Lamech but agrees with G for all the others (with a 10-year difference for Enosh, likely a scribal error). Because LAB was probably written in Hebrew before its translation into Greek (and thence Latin; see Harrington 1971), these numbers may reflect a Hebrew text with some affinities to the G *Vorlage* in this section (so Harrington 1971: 8, 16), or they may be due to the Greek translator of LAB, who may have consulted a revised G text (so Brock 1992a: 318, 337 n. 29). The mixed readings may be better explained by the latter hypothesis, which would provide a scenario similar to that in Ant 1, namely, the common use of revised G texts in the early centuries C.E.

The testimony of the ancillary sources allows us to detect the use of a Hebrew text of Genesis with affinities to proto-S in the mid-second-century B.C.E. (Jub) and possibly the use of revisions of G toward M in the first century C.E. and later (Ant and LAB).

4.3 GENESIS 11:10–32

The textual data and the proposed archetype are charted in table 4-3. The chronological variants in Genesis 11 occur primarily in the sequence from Arpachshad to Nahor, with one variant in the numbers for Terah.

The deviations between M and S and between M and G are regular during the span from Arpachshad to Nahor, with four exceptions that require further analysis. If we consider the relations to the numbers of M, the consistent pattern from Arpachshad to Nahor is as follows:

S: $b + 100$ (50 for Nahor)
$\quad r - 100$ (50 for Nahor)
G: $b + 100$ (50 for Nahor)

As we have seen in the revisions of Genesis 5, the effect of raising b is to delay a future event by the sum of the b's. It is plausible, therefore, that proto-S and proto-G have delayed the birth of Abraham by 650 (S) or 650 + 130 (G with Kenan II) years in order to solve the problem of the overlap of generations noted previously (§4.1). According to M (and the proposed archetype), all of the post-diluvian patriarchs plus Noah are alive at Abraham's birth, and three (Shem, Shelah, and Eber) survive him. If, following Dillmann and others, we identify this as a problem implicit in the archetypal chronology of Genesis 11, this circumstance provides ample motive for the revision of this chronology in proto-S and proto-G. Conversely, there is no identifiable motive for scribes in the proto-M tradition to reduce the numbers for b in this series, which would create the problem of contemporaneous generations at the time of Abraham.

By this reasoning, we may conclude that the archetypal numbers are preserved as follows:

$b = $ M
$r = $ M G

Table 4-3. The Chronology of Gen 11:10–32: Major Versions and Archetype

		M	S	G	Archetype
Shem	b	100	100	100	100
	r	500	500	500	500
	t	—	600	—	—
	A.M.	(1556–2156)	(1207–1807)	(2142–2742)	(1242–1842)
adjustment		+ 2	+ 2	+ 2	+ 2
Arpachshad	b	35	135	135	35
	r	403	303	430	403
	t	—	438	—	—
	A.M.	(1658–2061)	(1309–1612)	(2244–2674)	(1344–1747)
Kenan II	b	—	—	130	—
	r	—	—	330	—
	A.M.			(2379–2839)	
Shelah	b	30	130	130	30
	r	403	303	330	403
	t	—	433	—	—
	A.M.	(1693–2126)	(1444–1877)	(2509–2969)	(1379–1812)
Eber	b	34	134	134	34
	r	430	270	370	370
	t	—	404	—	—
	A.M.	(1723–2187)	(1574–1978)	(2639–3143)	(1409–1813)
Peleg	b	30	130	130	30
	r	209	109	209	209
	t	—	239	—	—
	A.M.	(1757–1996)	(1708–1947)	(2773–3112)	(1443–1682)
Reu	b	32	132	132	32
	r	207	107	207	207
	t	—	239	—	—
	A.M.	(1787–2026)	(1838–2077)	(2903–3242)	(1473–1712)
Serug	b	30	130	130	30
	r	200	100	200	200
	t	—	230	—	—
	A.M.	(1819–2049)	(1970–2200)	(3035–3365)	(1505–1735)
Nahor	b	29	79	79	29
	r	119	69	129	119
	t	—	148	—	—
	A.M.	(1849–1997)	(2100–2248)	(3165–3373)	(1535–1683)
Terah	b	70	70	70	70
	r	—	—	—	—
	t	205	145	205	205
	A.M.	(1878–2083)	(2179–2324)	(3244–3449)	(1564–1769)
Abraham	A.M.	(1948–2123)	(2249–2424)	(3314–3489)	(1634–1809)

b = age at begetting

r = remainder

t = total lifespan

A.M. = year after creation (*anno mundi*)

In the four cases where M and G differ on the value of *r* (Arpachshad, Shelah, Eber, Nahor), there is a possibility that scribal error has affected one or both versions. Klein has argued plausibly that the following scribal errors affected proto-G (three instances) and proto-M (one instance).

1. The variants for Arpachshad's *r* (Gen 11:13) are 403 (M), 303 (S), and 430 (G). The S value follows the expected formula (*r* − 100) for an archetype of 403 (= M). The G reading reflects a minor textual change from שלש → שלשים.

2. The variants for Shelah's *r* (Gen 11:15) are 403 (M), 303 (S), and 330 (G). The M and S values again indicate an archetype of 403. The G reading apparently reflects the same minor textual change from שלש → שלשים (perhaps assimilated to 11:13 or vice versa) and a change from ארבע → שלש in the hundreds position (perhaps a reminiscence of the שלשים/שלש two words previously).

3. The variants for Eber's *r* (Gen 11:17) are 430 (M), 270 (S), and 370 (G). In this case the G and S values indicate an archetype of 370, and it is the M reading that is anomalous. Klein suggests that the M reading has been affected by the number of Eber's *b* in v 16. I would suggest that the number of Shelah's *r* in v 15 adds to the possibility of confusion:

    11:15 עבר שלש שנים וארבע מאות שנה
    11:16 עבר ארבע ושלשים שנה
    11:17 עבר . . . שלשים שנה וארבע מאות שנה

    The occurrence of וארבע מאות שנה and שלשים שנה (plus another שלש and ארבע) in vv 15–16, all prefaced by the name עבר, make it plausible that the reading in v 17 has been assimilated to these phrases, yielding the secondary reading of 430 in M.

4. The variants for Nahor's *r* (Gen 11:25) are 119 (M), 69 (S), and 129 (G). For Nahor S and G follow the formula of *b* + 50, and S reduces *r* by this amount. The expected S formula of *r* − 50 yields an archetype of 119. The G reading reflects a minor textual change from עשרה → עשרים.

Allowing for the plausibility of these four scribal errors, the pattern noted previously accounts for all the textual variants in the chronology, with the exception of one variant for Terah and the curious inclusion of Kenan in G.

Terah's Death

The variants for Terah's *t* (Gen 11:32) are 205 (M), 145 (S), and 205 (G). As many commentators have noted, the lifespan of Terah in M creates a problem in the Genesis narrative (see recently Emerton 1994). Gen 11:32 relates that "Terah died in Haran." Immediately thereafter, Yahweh calls Abraham to the promised land (12:1-4). The narrative sequence implies that Terah died before Abraham's call and journey. But Gen 12:4 states that Abraham was 75 when he left Haran, in which case Terah was still alive according to the numbers in M and G, being only 145 at the time (Terah's $b + 75 = 145$). The apparent contradiction between the narrative sequence and the lifespan of Terah was felt in rabbinic and patristic traditions (e.g., *Gen. Rab.* 39.7; Jerome, *Questions*, at 12:4 [Hayward 1995: 43-44, 148-49]; Augustine, *City of God* 16.15; note that some medieval M mss had an inverted *nun* [antisigma] at 11:32 [so Rashi and the Masora parva of V], a scribal mark indicating a verse out of sequence [Tov 1992a: 54 n. 34]). The proto-S tradition solved the problem textually by revising Terah's *t* to 145. By this revision, Terah dies in the year of Abraham's departure, in concord with the sense of the narrative. (It is possible, though not necessary, that the S reading is reflected in Acts 7:4 and Philo, *Mig.* 177; see Emerton 1994: 171.) The alternative possibility, that proto-M and proto-G raised an archetype of 145 by 60 years, has no textual or exegetical motive and would have created an obvious narrative problem. The archetype is therefore most plausibly 205 (= M G).

The problem implicit in the year of Terah's death provides additional evidence for the proposal that the chronological problems of Genesis 5 and 11 are an accidental result of the combination of the ספר תולדת אדם with the preexisting Genesis narrative. In this instance, the implications of Terah's numbers conflict with a chronological notice in P (Gen 12:4b).

Kenan II

The inclusion of a second Kenan (Καιναν) in the G chronology at Gen 11:12-13 is a curious plus. As most commentators have observed, this is almost certainly secondary for several reasons: Kenan has already appeared in Gen 5:9-14 (son of Enosh); his numbers in Genesis 11 (G) duplicate those of his son, Shelah; and he is absent at this point in the genealogy of 1 Chron 1:18, 24 in both M and G (Dillmann 1897: 397; Gunkel 1910: 155; Klein 1974a: 258; Hughes 1990: 9). A plausible motive for the insertion of Kenan in this list (and in the corresponding point between Arpachshad and Shelah in 10:22-24) is the desire to harmonize the literary structure with that of Genesis 5, where the genealogy lists ten generations, ending with Noah (so most commentators). The addition of Kenan II in Genesis 11 yields a parallel list of ten generations, ending with Abraham. In this explanation, the inclusion of Kenan II in proto-G is another reflex of its harmonistic tendency regarding literary structure, as in Genesis 1 (see §2.2). The evidence of Jub (see later) corroborates the view that the insertion of Kenan II into this genealogical sequence occurred in the Hebrew textual tradition.

Other Harmonizations

A harmonistic tendency in G and S is also discernible in the filling out of the chronological formulae in Genesis 11 on the basis of the parallel formulae in Genesis 5. At the end of each entry, G consistently adds וימת, "and he died," as is the case in Genesis 5. S harmonizes the text more completely by including the formula and number for the total lifespan along with a statement of death (ויהיו שנה וימת . . . כל ימי), again parallel to Genesis 5.

It is possible that the formulaic structure of the original ספר תולדת אדם was consistent from Adam through Lamech or Abraham; if so, then the harmonizations of proto-G and proto-S in this regard may partially reconstruct the original document. There is no obvious reason, however, for the redactor to have truncated the original genealogical document. It is also possible that the genealogy from Shem to Abraham was a secondary supplement to the ספר תולדת אדם (so Carr 1996: 72 n. 47).

The Two-Year Gap

Another problem in the chronology of Genesis 11 concerns the statement, attested in all versions, that Shem fathered Arpachshad at the age of 100 "two years after the flood" (Gen 11:10). Because Noah fathered Shem at the age of 500 (Gen 5:32) and was 600 in the year of the flood (Gen 7:6), we expect Shem to have been 100 in the year of the flood, not two years later. Most commentators conclude from this contradiction that the phrase "two years after the flood" is a gloss, though its motive is obscure (Dillmann 1897: 401; Skinner 1930: 232; Hughes 1990: 18; cf. Budde 1883: 109).

Hughes speculates that the two-year gloss is "a chronological correction made after 2 years had fallen out of [the] antediluvian chronology through some process of textual corruption, when it was noticed that the remaining figures no longer added up to the correct totals required by Priestly tradition" (1990: 18, 22). He speculates further that the lost two years had originally belonged to Methuselah's *b*, and he therefore supplies these extra two years in his reconstruction of the archetype for Methuselah's *b*, yielding 69 rather than the expected 67 (see previously). Other unlikely solutions for the two-year gap have also been proposed (see the survey in Wenham 1987: 250).

In view of the other chronological problems attributable to the combination of the narrative and the ספר תולדת אדם, I suggest that this problem has a similar etiology. The flood story specifies that Noah, his wife, his sons, and his sons' wives enter the ark (Gen 7:7, 13) and that only they exit the ark (Gen 8:18; all P texts). As the glossator must have noticed, these statements (particularly 8:18) preclude the birth of a child during the year of the flood. Men and women exit the ark, but no infants. Yet, according to the chronology in Gen 5:32 and 11:10, this is Shem's 100th year, when Arpachshad is born. This implicit problem provides ample motive for a scribe to add an explicating gloss specifying that Arpachshad was born two years after the flood, not in the year of the flood. To make the text consistent, the glossator should have revised Shem's *b* two years upward (or revised upward Noah's *b* or age at the flood), but this was not done, leaving the problem of the two-year gap. (After formulating this solution I found that it had already been proposed by Budde [1883: 109] but not taken up since.)

This implicit clash between the flood narrative and Shem's *b* is sufficient motive for the gloss in Gen 11:10. This reading, while late in the compositional history of Genesis, is attested in all versions and hence is an archetypal reading. It is possible that this early gloss stems from the redactor who combined the ספר תולדת אדם with its narrative context. Whoever incorporated this explicating gloss, its presence is explicable by the same literary history that caused the other chronological problems in Genesis 5 and 11.

Minor Versions and Ancillary Sources

The testimony of the minor versions and ancillary sources is also of interest for the history of the chronology in Genesis 11. The minor versions consistently agree with M, with the sole exception of Vg at 11:13 (Arpachshad's *r*) where Vg reads 303 (= S) rather than the expected 403 (= M). This reading may reflect a simple haplography in the underlying Roman numerals, reading CCCIII rather than CCCCIII.

The affinities of the ancillary sources are less clear than in Genesis 5. The numbers for Jub, Ant, and LAB are charted in table 4-4. (Jub and Ant provide data for *b* only; LAB has six *b*'s and *r*'s.)

For Jub, the only chronological agreements with the major versions are the two-year adjustment and Terah's *b*, for which all texts agree. The numbers for Arpachshad through Nahor are unique, varying in the range between the values in M and S/G. No rationale has yet been proposed for these values in Jub. Jub agrees with G in the inclusion of Kenan II between Arpachshad and Shelah (but not on the date for Kenan's *b*). This striking agreement would seem to indicate that this plus existed in Hebrew manuscripts of the second century B.C.E., the time of the composition of Jub. Some have argued the insertion of Kenan II is secondary in Jub, added by its Greek translator under the influence of G, but the divergence in the chronologies of Jub and G make this a difficult supposition (see further VanderKam 1988: 75–80; 1995: 96). The evidence of Jub for the

Table 4-4. The Chronology of Gen 11:10–32: Ancillary Sources

	Jub 8–11	Ant 1.148–51	LAB 4:12–15
adjustment	+2	+12	—
Arpachshad	65	135	—
Kenan	57	—	—
Shelah	71	130	—
Eber	64	134	—
Peleg	32	130	—
Reu	108	130	$r = 119$
Serug	57	132	29; $r = 67$
Nahor	42	120	34; $r = 200$
Terah	70	70	70

chronology of Genesis 11, consisting for the most part of unique numbers and a significant plus shared with G, is curiously inconsistent with the evidence in Genesis 5, where Jub shows clear affinities with S.

Ant 1.148–51 for the most part reproduces the numbers of G with the following exceptions: 12 for the two-year gap (probably a scribal error), 120 for Nahor's b (probably a scribal error influenced by Nahor's $r = 129$), a switch in the numbers for Reu and Serug (should be 132 and 130), and the absence of Kenan II (see Fraenkel 1984: 186–90). The most significant variation from G is the absence of Kenan II, which may reflect a G text revised toward M. Because few G manuscripts lack Kenan II and those that do have hexaplaric affinities, Fraenkel argues for the possibility that Josephus himself made this correction toward M (1984: 189). Because the chronology in Ant 1.83–88 shows other signs of having been based on a revised G text (see §4.2), it is possible that Josephus's Greek *Vorlage* lacked Kenan II in Gen 11:12–13.

The numbers of LAB are as puzzling as those in Jub. With the exception of Terah, whose b agrees in all the texts, the numbers given are unique. Harrington (1971: 8) notes the likelihood of confusion in the manuscripts of LAB in which the numbers are represented by Roman numerals. This observation may account for the obscurity of the few numbers provided in this section of LAB.

The testimony of the ancillary sources is therefore mixed. Only Ant preserves a textual profile consistent with its version of the chronology in Genesis 5. The situations of Jub and LAB suggest the possibility of varying degrees of editorial revision, scribal error, or both. If editorial revisions have been made, no consistent pattern is discernible. It is conceivable that some of the unique numbers derive from unknown biblical texts, though this possibility seems unlikely in view of their textual affinities in Genesis 5.

4.4 RECENSIONS OF GENESIS

I have argued that the chronological problems of Genesis 5 and 11 are easily
accounted for by the theory that a redactor incorporated a document, the ספר
תולדת אדם, "Book of the Generations of Adam," into the preexisting text of
Genesis without harmonizing the chronological data of the two documents. From
this perspective, we can discern clearly the chronological clashes that motivated
the various scribal revisions. As first systematically worked out by Klein, the
initial problems were (1) a contradiction between the lifespans of three
antediluvians (Jared, Methuselah, and Lamech) and the onset of the flood and
(2) the coexistence of all of the postdiluvian generations (including Noah and
Shem) during the lifetime of Abraham. The first problem was solved in the textual traditions ancestral to M, S, and G by three different strategies of revision
for the chronology of Gen 5:3–32. The second problem was solved in the textual traditions ancestral to S and G by two overlapping strategies of revision for
Gen 11:10–32; M shows no signs of revision in this chapter.

I have also argued that two other chronological problems derive from this
initial textual situation: (3) an apparent contradiction between Lamech's lifespan
and the implicit sense of the narrative sequence of 11:31–12:4 and (4) a contradiction between Shem's age at the birth of Arpachshad and the date of the
flood. The third problem was solved in proto-S by reducing Lamech's lifespan
so that he dies in the year of Abraham's journey (the problem is unresolved in M
and G). The fourth problem was solved by a redactor or scribe by an explicating
plus specifying that Arpachshad was born two years after the flood. This plus is
in all versions and therefore belongs to the archetype of Genesis, prior to the differentiation of the textual traditions of Genesis.

The identification of these chronological problems and their ancient solutions
has several implications for our understanding of the Genesis text. First, a
coherent reconstruction of the textual history of Genesis 5 and 11 allows us to
recover the archetype of the text with a high degree of plausibility. Second, the
textual history allows us to gain some perspective on the literary and redactional
history of Genesis 5–11, particularly regarding the redaction of the ספר תולדת
אדם into its literary context. Third, this analysis provides some perspective on
the relationships among M, S, and G and their ancestral textual traditions. It is
to this matter of textual relationships that we now turn.

One of the most complex and contested issues in biblical textual criticism in
the post-Qumran era has been the construction of an adequate theoretical model
for the textual relationships among the major versions. While I defer a con-

sideration of methodological problems (see §6.1), one particular issue is relevant to the chronological revisions in Genesis 5 and 11. A much-debated question is whether M, S, and G represent three different text-types in the Pentateuch (so Cross 1964, and most recently 1985 and 1992) or whether they are "just three texts of the O.T. similar to other texts which were current in the Second Temple period," with only the proto-S texts identifiable as a distinctive group (Tov 1982 [quote from p. 24], and most recently 1992a: 155–63 and 1995).

In the light of the textual history just reconstructed for the chronologies of Genesis 5 and 11, one important implication is that M, S, and G are each representative of a different recension of Genesis. While this insight is not new (see Roberts 1951: 191, cited in Tov 1982: 17 n. 27; Klein 1974a: 263), its significance has not been fully assimilated in recent discussions of the Pentateuchal text.

If a recension is defined as "a textual tradition which contains some sort of editing of earlier texts" (Tov 1992a: 155) or "an edition of an ancient text involving a more or less systematic revision of an earlier text form" (Cross 1985: 139), then it is clear that M, S, and G in Genesis 5 and 11 belong to three different recensions of Genesis. Tov is correct in stressing that M, S, and G are simply three texts and are not the "central texts" around which all other texts revolve. But the evidence of Genesis 5 and 11 indicates that the differences among these three texts are not chance differences among any three texts but are derived from three different revisions of Genesis. The particular texts in which these revisions were first incorporated are the hyparchetypes for M, S, and G.

Notably, these revised texts were produced some time after the inception of the textual transmission of Genesis, that is, after the "original text" had been produced by the writers and editors of Genesis, and after the time of the textual archetype ancestral to all extant texts of Genesis (on this periodization of textual history, see Tov 1992a: 171–77). These were not three literary editions that were incorporated successively into one or more scribal traditions (as in most other cases of multiple editions in the Bible) but revisions made in three different scribal traditions during the period of the textual transmission of Genesis. In the systematic revisions of the chronologies of Genesis 5 and 11, the scribes in the different traditions acted as "a minor partner in the creative literary process" (Talmon 1975: 381), but the result was not three successive editions of a book, as the word *edition* is generally understood, but three recensions of the book, created synchronically, as it were, in three different streams of textual transmission.

We are justified, therefore, in defining the relationships among M, S, and G in Genesis as that of three texts belonging to three different recensions of Genesis. None of these three texts is itself the hyparchetype of the recension; rather, each is a later text, as is shown by the instances of probable scribal error in each version of Genesis 5 and 11 (as noted previously).

It is possible, as Klein proposes, that the overlap in the strategies of revision in S and G of Genesis 11 indicates a common ancestor, a hyparchetype ancestral to two of the recensions. The common formula for raising the postdiluvian b's ($b + 100$ for Arpachshad to Serug; $b + 50$ for Nahor) may have been "added to a Hebrew archetype before the differentiation into the local texts" (1974a: 257–58). It is also possible that this strategy of revision could have occurred independently because raising the b's by 100 is a revision found in all three recensions at various points (proto-M uses this strategy for Jared and possibly Lamech). But the shared deviation in the formula in the case of Nahor is so specific that a common textual ancestor is very plausible. This coincidence of revision in S and G may be a small basis on which to posit a common ancestor, but it is worth considering, particularly if additional evidence can be found to support this possible history (see §5.2 and §6.2).

The combined testimony of the major versions, the minor versions, and the ancillary sources on Genesis 5 and 11 indicates that there is evidence for three recensions—no more, no less. This is perhaps surprising. If M, S, and G are the chance survivors of a plethora of ancient texts, it would seem odd that each represents a different recension of Genesis. Despite a theoretical possibility of a fourth or fifth recension of Genesis, there is no evidence in the versions or ancillary sources of Genesis 5 and 11 for them. The only possible testimony might be Jub or LAB in the postdiluvian chronology, but there may be other explanations for these numbers (including scribal error), and they are not derivable from any systematic revision. If there were only three recensions of Genesis and the surviving major versions represent each of the three, then this circumstance deserves some attention. This may be a purely random result of historical chance, or it might involve some deliberate choices by the individuals or groups who transmitted or adopted the various texts. Whatever the reason, it is notable that M, S, and G are distinctly separable on the matter of the chronologies into three different recensions, with no clear evidence from any other source of a trace of another recension.

CHAPTER FIVE

Harmonizing Tendencies in S and G

5.1 HARMONIZING THE TORAH

The harmonization of inconsistencies in the Bible has a long history in biblical exegesis and pedagogy. Philipp Melanchthon, in his inaugural lecture of 1518, expressed forcefully the modern distaste for such reader's aids: "Now away with so many frigid petty glosses, these harmonizings and 'disharmonies' and other hindrances to intelligence" (apud Hall 1963: 40). Yet, it is arguable that the practice of harmonization has been necessary in maintaining the vitality of the Bible in Judaism and Christianity for more than two millennia. Without the possibility of making sense of the innumerable inconsistencies or contradictions in the Bible, a coherent sense of the Bible's religious authority is perhaps impossible. Hence, we find that the study of the Bible itself is hedged about with restrictions in many periods of Jewish and Christian history, as illustrated by the Talmudic dictum: "Keep your sons from Scripture" (*B. Berakot* 28b; see Talmage 1987).

Harmonizations of the Bible are also found in the biblical books themselves, indicating that the practice of harmonization has its roots in the biblical period. A clear example is 2 Chron 35:13, where the Chronicler harmonized parallel laws concerning the Passover sacrifice (see recently Fishbane 1985: 135–36). According to Exod 12:8–9 the Passover sacrifice is to be roasted (צלי אש), not stewed (מבשל במים). According to Deut 16:7 it is to be stewed (ובשלת), in conformity with the usual method for cooking sacrificial meat (see Weinfeld 1972: 217). The Chronicler harmonized these two texts by writing, ויבשלו הפסח באש כמשפט, "they stewed the Passover sacrifice in fire, according to the law" (2 Chron 35:13). In this new formulation, the contradiction between the texts of Exodus and Deuteronomy is overcome, and the harmonization claims the status of law. Fishbane observes that "on the face of it, the logic of this ritual statement is absurd, since one does not boil meat *in* fire; and the attribution that the

81

ritual was done 'according to the law' is presumptuous, since there is no 'law' to which the preparation refers" (1985: 135). Yet, to the Chronicler, the oddity of the revision was apparently less important than the principle of harmonizing discrepant texts. This point is emphasized by Fishbane: "the Scriptural harmonization in 2 Chr 35:13 and its later—rabbinically inspired—one are clear corollaries of one and the same principle: that the Pentateuchal Torah of Moses is integral and indivisible" (1985: 136). By means of harmonization, the Torah's diversity is transmuted into unity.

These two parallel but contradictory Torah texts, which the Chronicler harmonized in his literary composition, were also harmonized in the proto-G textual tradition. In Deut 16:7 of G, there is a notable plus in the culinary instructions for the Passover sacrifice, και εψησεις και οπτησεις (= ובשלת וצלית), "You shall stew and roast." A scribe in the proto-G tradition accomplished in Deuteronomy what the Chronicler achieved in Chronicles: the accommodation of Exod 12:8–9 and Deut 16:7. In Deuteronomy, as in Genesis (see §2.2), the harmonizations in G are attributable to its Hebrew *Vorlage*, not to the interventions of the Greek translator (see Tov 1992b: 17–20). The testimony of the G Pentateuch, therefore, indicates that Hebrew texts of the Pentateuch with harmonizations of parallel verses were in circulation by the mid-third century B.C.E. Pentateuchal manuscripts from the second and first centuries B.C.E. with numerous harmonizations are also known from Qumran (e.g., 4QpaleoExod[m], 4QNum[b]; see Sanderson 1986; Jastram 1992; Tov 1992a: 85–100).

In an important article on harmonizations in biblical texts, Tov has clarified important aspects of this textual phenomenon. His definition is useful and precise: "The procedure of harmonization can be expressed schematically as the change, addition or omission of a detail in some MSS of text A according to a parallel text B" (1985: 10). To this definition as involving change, addition, or omission, he adds the following qualifications: "However, as expected, in biblical MSS harmonizing omissions occur very rarely, if at all. In biblical MSS, harmonizing additions are more frequent than harmonistic changes. This situation is easily understandable, as the degree of intervention in the text is more limited for additions than for changes" (1985: 11).

These remarks are borne out in the identifiable harmonizations in Genesis 1–11. Rarely does one find a harmonizing minus. Harmonizing changes are fairly common. But by far the largest category is harmonizing pluses. As Tov acutely observes, the addition of a word or phrase to make the text internally consistent was more acceptable in scribal circles than the deletion or alteration of existing text. Harmonization tends to be additive; it equalizes texts by filling in the gaps in parallel texts. The scope of scribal intervention was limited by this rule of scribal hermeneutics: one did not subtract from Scripture; one perfected it by means of strategic supplementation.

Tov's classification of the major types of textual harmonization (1985: 6–10) is helpful in illustrating the variety of harmonizations in the versions of Genesis 1–11.

1. Harmonization of syntactical incongruities. A good example is Gen 1:24, where the archaic form וחיתו ארץ (M) is revised to וחית הארץ (S) in harmony with the parallel phrase חית הארץ in v 25.

2. Harmonization of minor contextual differences. This is the largest category of harmonizations in Genesis 1–11. A typical example is Gen 1:14, where השמים (4QGen[bk] M S G) is filled out with להאיר על הארץ (S G) in harmony with the parallel phrase השמים להאיר על הארץ in vv 15 and 17.

3. Harmonization of command and fulfillment. This type is frequent in the creation and flood stories, where commands and fulfillments often differ in wording. For example, in Gen 1:11–12 of G, the command (v 11) and the fulfillment (v 12) are perfectly harmonized, while M and S preserve most of the variation of the original.

4. Harmonization of references to earlier statements. This type, where a passage refers to an earlier statement that is lacking in the text, does not occur in Genesis 1–11. For examples elsewhere in Genesis (31:11–13; 44:22; S supplies the earlier statements), see Tov 1985: 8.

5. Harmonization of differences in major details. This is a rare category, for as Tov notes, "there are too many major differences between the laws and stories in the Pentateuch, so that any attempt to harmonize between them would result in a major rewriting of the Bible" (1985: 9). This is precisely what occurs in the genre of the "rewritten Bible" (e.g., Jub, Ant, LAB). One harmonization of major differences occurs in S of Gen 10:19, where the borders of Canaan, "from Sidon toward Gerar, as far as Gaza, and toward Sodom, Gomorrah, Admah, and Zeboiim, as far as Lasha" (M G) are harmonized with the descriptions in Gen 15:18 and Deut 11:24 (= Deut 34:2), yielding a major harmonization: "from the river of Egypt to the great river, the river Euphrates, to the Western Sea" (S).

6. Harmonization of schematic descriptions. This type is found in the G version of Genesis 1 and in S and G of the postdiluvian genealogy. The transposition and interpolation of the phrases ויהי כן and וירא אלהים כי טוב yield a highly symmetrical literary structure in the creation story of G

(see §2.2 at Gen 1:6, 8, 20). In the postdiluvian genealogy of Genesis 11, S and G fill out the text in varying ways to harmonize with the structure of the antediluvian genealogy of Genesis 5 (see §4.3)

The exegetical background of these various types of textual harmonization lies in the desire to perfect God's word by correcting or smoothing over discrepancies in Scripture. Frankel refers to this tendency as "the effort to complete the text" ("das Streben den Text zu vervollständigen"; 1841: 78). Tov observes that "the scribes who inserted the harmonizations acted within a scribal-literary tradition which facilitated and promoted the insertion of harmonizing details" (1985: 15). As indicated in the lists in the next sections, this type of textual intervention was far more common in the proto-S and proto-G traditions than in the proto-M tradition. In Genesis 1–11, G has the greatest number of individual harmonizations, roughly 90. This accords with Frankel's observation that G of Genesis has 270–280 harmonizations, far more than any other Pentateuchal book (1841: 79). In Genesis 1–11, S has roughly 40 harmonizations, less than half the number of G. But the most extensive single harmonizing pluses are found in S (at 10:19 and 11:11–25). In contrast, M has a mere 6 harmonizations, all in minor details.

The differences in the degree of harmonization among these three textual traditions are striking and no doubt reflect the textual hermeneutics of the respective scribal groups. It is probably no coincidence that the Pentateuchal text of M has a more conservative (that is, earlier) orthography than S and its congeners; in these matters, the proto-M scribes, by the Hellenistic period, tolerated less intervention in the text than their counterparts in the other textual traditions.

Tov has suggested that the background for the harmonization of biblical texts lies in the influence of "rewritten Bible" texts such as 4QReworked Pentateuch (4Q158 + 4Q364–67). He posits that "harmonizing additions like those in the Sam. Pent. are not likely to have originated in a manuscript tradition. Rather, they originated in a *literary* environment of rewritten texts such as 4Q158" (1985: 18). Although the influence of such texts on scribal harmonizations in biblical manuscripts is certainly possible, I would suggest that Tov has drawn his lines of influence too sharply. Both types of textual production—harmonized biblical mss and "rewritten" literary texts—are marked by the desire to perfect the Torah by the process of harmonizing discrepancies. But it is difficult to say that texts like 4Q158 came first. As we have seen, the Chronicler in the Persian period is already harmonizing discrepant Pentateuchal texts. The testimony of G indicates that harmonized Pentateuchal manuscripts were in circulation by the mid-third century B.C.E. The chronology of known texts may indicate that the direction of influence is more likely the reverse of Tov's suggestion, namely, from scribal harmonizations in biblical manuscripts to full-blown literary rewritings and expansions in the "rewritten Bible" genre of the second century B.C.E. and later (see Alexander 1988b; Tov 1994b). Whatever their mutual influences may have been, and whatever their differences in degrees of textual intervention (see the careful formulation of Sanderson 1986: 270–76), both types of textual activity are foreshadowed by the interpretive work of the Chronicler, Ezra, and others (see Fishbane 1985) who were the first to "meditate on His Torah day and night" (Ps 1:2).

5.2 HARMONIZATIONS SHARED BY S AND G (≠ M)

Gen 1:14 השמים 4QGen[bk] M S G (του ουρανου)] + להאיר על הארץ S G (εις φαυσιν της γης)
  A harmonizing plus with להאיר על הארץ vv 15, 17; see §2.2.

Gen 2:4 שמים וארץ S Tg[N] Syr Vg; ארץ ושמים M] את השמים ואת הארץ G (τον ουρανον και την γην)
  A harmonization with השמים והארץ v 4; see §2.2.

Gen 2:23 מאיש M] מאישה S G (εκ του ανδρος αυτης) Tg[O] Jub 3:6
  Perhaps an explicating plus or a harmonization with לאישה 3:6.

Gen 2:24 והיו M G (εσονται)] + שניהם G (οι δυο) Tg[P] Syr Vg sim S (והיה משניהם)
  A harmonizing plus with ויהיו שניהם v 25.

Gen 7:2 איש ואשתו 1-2° M] זכר ונקבה 1-2° S G (αρσεν και θηλυ) Tg[OP] Syr Vg
  Harmonized with זכר ונקבה vv 3, 9; 6:19; 6:20 (G).

Gen 7:2 שנים M S G (δυο)] + שנים S G (δυο) Syr Vg
  A harmonizing plus with שנים שנים 7:9, 15; cf. 6:19–20 (G).

Gen 7:3 השמים M S G (του ουρανου)] + הטהור S G (των καθαρων) Syr[mss] LAB 3:4
  A harmonizing plus with הבהמה הטהורה v 2, and העוף הטהר 8:20.

Gen 8:3 מקצה M] מקץ S G (μετα)
  A harmonization with מקץ v 6, or a simple haplography with graphic confusion (ה/ח).

Gen 8:21 עוד לקלל M] לקלל עוד S G (ετι του καταρασασθαι) Syr Vg
A harmonization with the sequence of עוד להכות v 21.

Gen 9:2 נתנו M] נתתי S; נתתי G (δεδωκα) TgN
A harmonization with נתתי v 3.

Gen 10:32 נפרדו M S G (διεσπαρησαν)] + איי S G (νησοι)
A harmonizing plus with נפרדו איי הגוים v 5.

Gen 11:8 ואת המגדל M] ואת העיר ואת המגדל S G (την πολιν και τον πυργον) Jub
10:24
A harmonization with את העיר ואת המגדל v 5.

Gen 11:11–25 fin] + וימת S G (και απεθανεν)
A multiple harmonizing plus with וימת Gen 5:8, 11, 14, 17, 20, 27, 31, sim
5:5, 23, sim 11:32. This formulaic plus recurs in 11:13 (2× in G),15, 17,
19, 21, 23, 25; see §4.3.

5.3 HARMONIZATIONS SHARED BY S AND M (≠ G)

Gen 1:11 פרי 2° 4QGenᵇ M S G (καρπον)] + למינו 4QGenᵇ M S
Perhaps a harmonizing plus with למינהו 2° v 12; see §2.2.

Gen 4:26 ולשת M S G (και τω Σηθ)] + גם הוא M S (om G)
A harmonizing plus, cf. גם הוא ילדה v 22 and ילד גם הוא 10:21; see §3.2.

Gen 7:3 על M S G (επι)] + פני M S (om G, sim Tgᴶ)
A harmonizing plus with על פני כל הארץ 8:9; see §3.2.

Gen 7:6 היה M S G (εγενετο; ην Gᴬ)] + מים M S G (υδατος) (om Gᴬ)
A harmonizing plus with המבול מים על הארץ 6:17; see §3.2.

Gen 7:22 נשמת M S G (πνοην)] + רוח M S (om G Vg)
A harmonizing plus with רוח חיים v 15; 6:17; see §3.2.

Gen 8:17 אתך 2° M S G (μετα σεαυτου)] + ושרצו בארץ M S (om G)
A harmonizing plus with שרצו בארץ 9:7; see §3.2.

5.4 HARMONIZATIONS IN S ALONE (≠ M G)

Gen 1:24 וחית הארץ M] וחיתו ארץ S
A linguistic modernization and/or harmonization with חית הארץ v 25.

Gen 3:16 בעצב M [בעצבון S
A harmonization with עצבונך v 16.

Gen 4:25 ותקרא M [ויקרא S 11QJub 1:2 (= Jub 4:7)
A harmonization with ויקרא את שמו v 26.

Gen 6:20 רמש M [אשר רמש על S; הרמש הרמש על G (τωυ ερπετωυ τωυ
ερποντωυ επι)
S: a harmonizing plus with אשר רמש על האדמה 7:8; G: a harmonizing plus
with הרמש הרמש על הארץ 8:17 (listed in §5.5).

Gen 7:16 זכר ונקבה M S G (αρσευ και θηλυ)] + זכר ונקבה S
A dittography or perhaps a harmonizing plus with שנים שנים v 15.

Gen 9:15 חיה M S G (ζωσης)] + אשר אתכם S Syr
A harmonizing plus with חיה אשר אתכם v 12.

Gen 10:19 מצידן באכא גררה עד עזה באכה סדמה ועמרה ואדמה וצבים עד לשע M G
(απο Σιδωνος . . . εως Λασα) [מנהר מצרים עד הנהר הגדול נהר פרת
ועד הים האחרון S
A harmonization with מנהר מצרים עד הנהר הגדול נהר פרת Gen 15:18, and
עד הים האחרון Deut 11:24 = Deut 34:2 (boundaries of promised land).

Gen 11:11–25 fin] + מאות שנה (#) (PN) ויהיו כל ימי S
A multiple harmonizing plus with ויהיו כל ימי (PN) (#) מאות שנה Gen 5:8,
11, 14, 17, 20, 27, 31; sim 5:5, 23; sim 11:32. This formulaic plus recurs in
vv 13, 15, 17, 19, 21, 23, 25; see §4.3.

Gen 11:14 וישלח חי M [ויחי שלח S
A harmonization with the clause-initial word order of vv 15–26 (12 times).

Gen 11:31 שרי M S G (Σαραυ)] + ואת מלכה S
A harmonizing plus with שרי . . . . מלכה v 29.

Gen 11:31 כלתו M G (την υυμφην αυτου)] כלותו S
A harmonization of number; see previous entry.

Gen 11:31 אברם M S G (Αβραμ)] + ונחור S
A harmonizing plus with אברם ונחור v 29.

Gen 11:31 בנו M G (του υιου αυτου)] בניו S
A harmonization of number; see previous entry.

5.5 HARMONIZATIONS IN G ALONE (≠ M S)

Gen 1:6   fin] + ויהי כן G (και εγενετο ουτος)
   Transposed from v 7; a harmonization with ויהי כן vv 9, 11, 15, 24, 30; cf.
   v 3; cf. 1:20 (G); see §2.2.

Gen 1:8   שמים 4QGen[b#g#] M S G (ουρανον)] + וירא אלהים כי טוב G (και ειδεν
   ο θεος οτι καλον)
   A harmonizing plus with וירא אלהים כי טוב vv 10, 12, 18, 21, 25, sim vv 4,
   31; see §2.2.

Gen 1:11   זרע 4QGen[b] M S G (σπερμα)] + למינהו G (κατα γενος και καθ'
   ομοιοτητα) Syr
   A harmonizing plus with זרע למינהו v 12; note the double translation in both
   vv; see §2.2.

Gen 1:11   בו 4QGen[b] M S G (εν αυτw)] + למינהו G (κατα γενος)
   A harmonizing plus with בו למינהו v 12; see §2.2.

Gen 1:12   ועץ M S G (και ξυλον)] + פרי G (καρπιμον) Tg[P]
   A harmonizing plus with ועץ פרי v 11; see §2.2.

Gen 1:12   למינהו 2° 4QGen[b] M S G (κατα γενος)] + על הארץ G (επι της γης)
   A harmonizing plus with על הארץ v 11; see §2.2.

Gen 1:20   fin] + ויהי כן G (και εγενετο ουτος)
   A harmonizing plus; cf. 1:6 (G); see §2.2.

Gen 1:28   ויאמר להם אלהים M S] לאמר G (λεγων)
   A harmonization with לאמר v 22; see §2.2.

Gen 1:28   ובכל הבהמה ובכל הארץ ובכל הרמש הרמש M S] ובכל חיה הרמשת G
   (και παντων των κτηνων και πασης της γης και παντων των ερπετων
   των ερποντων)
   A harmonizing plus with ובבהמה ובכל הארץ ובכל הרמש v 26; see §2.2.

Gen 1:30   ולכל 3° M S G (και παντι)] + רמש G (ερπετw)
   A harmonizing plus with ובכל הרמש הרמש vv 26, 28 (G); see §2.2.

Gen 2:4   אלה M S] זה ספר G (Αυτη η βιβλος)
   A harmonization with זה ספר תולדת 5:1; see §2.2.

Gen 2:15   האדם 4QGen[b] M S G (τον ανθρωπον)] + אשר יצר G (ον επλασεν)
   A harmonizing plus with האדם אשר יצר v 8.

Gen 2:17 תאכל 4QGen^b# M S] תאכלו G (φαγεσθε)
A harmonization with תאכלו ממנו 3:3.

Gen 2:17 תמות M S] תמותו G (αποθανεισθε)
A harmonization of number; see previous entry.

Gen 2:18 אעשה 4QGen^bh M S] נעשה G (ποιησωμεν) Vg Jub 3:4
A harmonization with נעשה 1:26.

Gen 3:2 מפרי M S G (απο καρπου)] + כל G^mss (παντος) Syr
A harmonizing plus; cf. מכל עץ v 1.

Gen 3:10 שמעתי M S G (ηκουσα)] + מתהלך G (περιπατουντος)
A harmonizing plus with מתהלך בגן v 8.

Gen 3:17 לאמר לא תאכל M S] לבלתי אכל G (τουτου μονου μη φαγειν)
A harmonization with לבלתי אכל v 11; note the emphatic translation in both instances.

Gen 4:18 מתושאל 1-2° M S] מתושלח 1-2° G (Μαθουσαλα)
A harmonization with מתושלח 5:21-27.

Gen 4:25 את 1° M S] + חוה G (Ευαν) Syr
A harmonizing plus with את חוה אשתו v 1.

Gen 4:25 אשתו M S G (την γυναικα αυτου)] + ותהר G (και συλλαβουσα) Syr
A harmonizing plus with אשתו ותהר ותלד v 1.

Gen 4:25 שת 1° M S G (Σηθ)] + לאמר G (λεγουσα) Vg sim Tg^ON(mg)J
A harmonizing plus with לאמר 5:29.

Gen 5:27 מתושלח M S G (Μαθουσαλα)] + אשר חי G (ας εζησεν)
A harmonizing plus with אשר חי v 5.

Gen 5:32 נח M S G (Νωε)] + שלשה בנים G (τρεις υιους) LAB 1:22
A harmonizing plus with נח שלשה בנים 6:10.

Gen 6:15 אתה M S] את התבה G (την κιβωτον)
A harmonization with תעשה את התבה v 14.

Gen 6:19 init] + ומכל הבהמה ומכל הרמש G (και απο παντων των κτηνων και απο παντων των ερπετων)
A harmonizing plus with ובבהמה ובכל הרמש 8:17 (exit from ark).

Gen 6:19 שנים M S G (δυο)] + שנים G (δυο) Syr
A harmonizing plus with שנים שנים 7:9, 15; cf. 6:20 (G) and 7:2 (S G).

Gen 6:20 מהעוף M S (מן העוף)] מכל העוף G (απο παντων των ορνεων των
πετεινων)
A harmonizing plus (with double translation) with וכל העוף למינהו 7:14; cf.
1:21 כל עוף כנף למינהו.

Gen 6:20 ומן M S] ומכל G (και απο παντων)
A harmonizing plus with ומכל הבהמה v 19 (G).

Gen 6:20 רמש M] אשר רמש על S; הרמש הרמש על G (των ερπετων των
ερποντων επι)
S: a harmonizing plus with אשר רמש על האדמה 7:8 (listed at §5.4); G: a
harmonizing plus with הרמש הרמש על הארץ 8:17.

Gen 6:20 שנים 6QpaleoGen M S G (δυο)] + שנים G (δυο) Syr
A harmonizing plus; cf. 6:19 (G) and 7:2 (S G).

Gen 6:20 להחיות M S G (τρεφεσθαι)] + אתך זכר ונקבה G (μετα σου αρσεν και
θηλυ)
A harmonizing plus with להחית אתך זכר ונקבה v 19.

Gen 7:2   מכל M S] מן G (απο) Syr
A harmonization with ומן הבהמה v 2.

Gen 7:3 ונקבה M S G (και θηλυ)] + ומעוף אשר לא טהור שנים שנים זכר ונקבה
G (και απο των πετεινων των μη καθαρων δυο δυο αρσεν και θηλυ)
A harmonizing plus with ומן הבהמה אשר לא טהרה היא שנים איש ואשתו v 2.

Gen 7:8   init] + ומן העוף G (και απο των πετεινον)
A harmonization with the sequence of 6:20.

Gen 7:9 אתו M S] את נח G (αυτω)
A harmonization with צוה אתו אלהים 6:22; cf. 7:16.

Gen 7:11 רבה M S 4QCommGenᵃ] om G
Perhaps a harmonization with 8:2.

Gen 7:13 אתם M S] אתו G (μετ᾽ αυτου) Tg^N(mg)J Syr
A harmonization with אתו אל התבה v 7.

Gen 7:16 אתו M S] את נח G (τω Nωε) (after אלהים)
A harmonizing or explicating plus; cf. את נח v 9.

Gen 7:17 יום M S G (ημερας)] + וארבעים לילה G (και τεσσαρακοντα νυκτας)
A harmonizing plus with וארבעים לילה v 12.

Gen 7:20 ויכסו M S G (και επεκαλυψεν)] + כל G (παντα)
A harmonizing plus with ויכסו כל v 19.

Gen 7:20 ההרים M S G (τα ορη)] + הגבהים G (τα υψηλα) Syr^mss Jub 5:26
A harmonizing plus with ההרים הגבהים v 19.

Gen 7:23 פני M S G (προσωπου)] + כל G (πασης)
A harmonizing plus with פני כל v 3.

Gen 7:24 ויגברו M S 4QCommGen^a] ויגבהו G (και υψωθη)
A reminiscence or harmonization with גבהו v 20, and/or perhaps graphic confusion (ר/ה).

Gen 8:1 הבהמה M S G (των κτηνων)] + וכל העוף וכל הרמש G (και παντων
των πετεινων και παντων των ερπετων); ואת כל העוף Syr
A harmonizing plus with וכל העוף וכל הרמש v 19 (exit from ark); cf. 6:19
(G).

Gen 8:7 הערב M S G (τον κορακα)] + לראות הקלו המים G (του ιδειν ει
κεκοπακεν το υδωρ)
A harmonizing plus with לראות הקלו המים v 8.

Gen 8:12 אחרים M S G (ετερας)] + ויסף G (παλιν)
A harmonizing plus with אחרים ויסף v 10.

Gen 8:13 שנה M S G (ετει)] + לחיי נח 4QCommGen^a G (εν τη ζωη του Νωε)
A harmonizing plus with לחיי נח 7:11.

Gen 8:13 התבה M S G (της κιβωτου)] + אשר עשה G (ην εποιησεν)
A harmonizing plus with התבה אשר עשה v 6.

Gen 8:13 חרבו 2° M S G (εξελιπεν)] + המים מעל G (το υδωρ απο)
A harmonizing plus with חרבו המים מעל v 13.

Gen 8:18 ואשתו ובניו M S] ובניו ואשתו G (και η γυνη αυτου και οι υιοι αυτου)
Syr
A harmonization with the sequence of v 16.

Gen 8:19 החיה M S G (τα θηρια)] + וכל הבהמה G (και παντα τα κτηνη) Syr
Vg
A harmonizing plus with החיה ואת כל הבהמה v 1.

Gen 8:21 האדם M S G (του ανθρωπου)] + רק G (επιμελως)
A harmonizing plus with רק רע 6:5.

Gen 8:21 כל M S G (πασαν)] + בשר G (σαρκα)
A harmonizing plus with כל בשר 9:11, 6:17, 19.

Gen 9:1 fin] + ורדו בה G (και κατακυριευσατε αυτης)
A harmonizing plus, cf. *ורדו בה v 7, and . . . ורדו ב 1:28.

Gen 9:7 שרצו בארץ M S] ומלאו את הארץ G (και πληρωσατε την γην) Vg
A harmonization with ומלאו את הארץ v 1 and 1:28.

Gen 9:11 מבול 2° M S G (κατακλυσμος)] + מים G (υδατος)
A harmonizing plus with מבול מים 6:17; cf. 7:6 (M); 9:15.

Gen 9:11 לשחת M G (του καταφθειραι)] להשחית S (also v 15); + כל G
(πασαν)
S: a linguistic modernization (Piel → Hiphil); G: a harmonizing plus with
לשחת כל v 15.

Gen 9:12 אלהים M S G (ο θεος)] + אל נח G (προς Νωε) Syr
An explicating or harmonizing plus with אלהים אל נח v 17.

Gen 9:14 הקשת M S] קשתי G (το τοξον μου) Vg LAB 3:12
A harmonization with קשתי v 13.

Gen 9:16 בין אלהים M S] ביני G (ανα μεσον εμου)
A harmonization with ביני v 15, sim vv 12, 17.

Gen 10:22 fin] + וקינן G (και Καιναν)
An editorial revision and harmonizing plus; cf. קינן Gen 5:9–14, following
entry at v 24, and 11:12 (G sim Jub 8:1); see §4.3.

Gen 10:24 ילד M S G (εγεννησεν)] + את קינן וקינן ילד G (τον Καιναν, και
Καιναν εγεννησεν)
An editoral revision and harmonizing plus; see previous entry and §4.3.

Gen 11:1 fin] + לכל G (πασιν)
A harmonizing plus with שפה אחת לכלם v 6.

Gen 11:31 מאור M S 4QCommGenᵃ] מארץ G (εκ της χωρας)
A reminiscence or harmonization with בארץ כשדים v 28 (G).

Gen 11:32 תרח 1° M S G (Θαρα)] + בחרן G (εν Χαρραν)
An anticipation or harmonizing plus with תרח בחרן v 32.

CHAPTER SIX

Toward the Textual History of Genesis

6.1 PROBLEMS OF METHOD

The first systematic attempt to construct a textual history of the Hebrew Bible, that of J. G. Eichhorn, states the nature of the task succinctly:

> A complete history of the Hebrew text would enumerate, with reference to causes and consequences, all the essential and accidental changes, whether for good or evil, which it has undergone in the process of thousands of years and in its passage through men's hands, from the time of its first composition down to the latest periods. (1888: 114 = German 3d ed., 1803)

If a textual history maps "all the essential and accidental changes" through time, then what we require first is a collection and analysis of the secondary readings. In this formulation, textual history is (to oversimplify only slightly) a history of error.

Modern methods for constructing textual histories have refined this view but generally affirm the significance of textual error in historical inquiry. In this area, "error" is used as a shorthand for "readings of secondary origin," including intentional changes as well as accidental (West 1973: 32). One difference between the procedures of textual history (*historia textus*) and textual criticism per se (*critica textus*) is that in the former errors are of primary importance and in the latter they are to be removed (see Chiesa 1992a: 264–67).

The dominant method in modern textual history is the stemmatic or genealogical method, which relies primarily on the identification of shared errors among texts. This method is most closely associated with the work of Karl Lachmann and others in the early nineteenth century (see Kenney 1974: 98–129) and is refined in the modern guides of Maas (1958) and West (1973). This procedure for determining the relationships among texts is succinctly summarized by West:

It will be possible to deduce their relationship from the pattern of agreements and disagreements among them; only it is important to realize that what is significant for this purpose is not agreement in true readings inherited from more ancient tradition, but agreement in readings of secondary origin, viz. corruptions and emendations, provided that they are not such as might have been produced by two scribes independently. (1973: 32)

Maas calls the shared secondary readings by which one can trace stemmatic relationships *Leitfehler* or "indicative errors," defined as "errors which can be utilized to make stemmatic inferences" (Maas 1985: 42–45, quote from p. 42). As West emphasizes, these are secondary readings unlikely to have been produced independently in different textual traditions. Hence, not all errors may serve as indicative errors. For example, many types of accidental error (including graphic confusion, word misdivision, haplographies, and other common types) are generally weak candidates for indicative errors because they are commonly produced in different texts independently. One requires distinctive errors in order to construct a reliable textual history.

Where indicative errors are shared by two texts, they serve as "conjunctive errors," indicating a degree of filiation between the texts. Where indicative errors are not shared, they serve as "separative errors," distinguishing different branches of the textual stemma (Maas 1958: 42–43). It is also common to find cross-contamination or "horizontal transmission" of readings, where one text has been revised by readings from a text in a different branch of the stemma (West 1973: 14, 38). The possibility of horizontal transmission complicates the use of indicative errors because, in any given case, the stemmatic relationship indicated may be horizontal rather than vertical. This is a major methodological problem for some works (e.g., Eusebius's *Ecclesiastica Historia*) for which the majority of manuscripts have been affected by horizontal transmission (Kenney 1974: 138–39). A degree of horizontal transmission is indicated by the pattern of indicative errors in S, as we will see later.

The major alternative to the use of indicative errors to determine textual relationships is the statistical method, whereby one catalogues all agreements and disagreements among texts, irrespective of whether the readings are primary or secondary (see West 1973: 46–47; Metzger 1992: 163–69; Polak 1992). The advantage of this approach is the elimination of the subjective element in adjudicating between primary and secondary readings. All variants are counted, and a statistical profile is generated for the percentages of agreements and disagreements among texts. Although the statistical method may have some advantages over the genealogical method (primarily in its promise of objectivity), it also has some serious flaws. West observes:

The trouble with this kind of analysis is that it is not clear what useful conclusions can be drawn from it. Two manuscripts may be grouped together just because they show no particular tendency to agree with any manuscript more than any other, in other words because they are equally promiscuous, even if they have no special similarity with each other textually. In some cases it is evident that the taxa reflect real affinity-groups, in others it does not. (1973: 47)

Tov has recently expressed a similar criticism of a statistical method that counts all agreements and disagreements equally:

While in the past I was more inclined to give equal importance to agreements and disagreements, claiming that MSS cannot be closely related if they both agree and disagree much, I recently started to realize that two MSS can be closely related even if they disagree much. After all, in the putative stemma of the MSS there is room for differing readings if they occurred after the point at which the two sources separated from each other. (Tov 1992c: 19)

The chief problem with the statistical method is that it doesn't necessarily indicate textual filiation. The degree of relatedness may be obscured by statistics as much as clarified by them. Unique readings, in particular, are largely irrelevant for establishing filiation; as Tov notes, they occur after the point of branching from the closest allied text. Chiesa rightly emphasizes this point: "in order to prove the existence of a connection between two witnesses one has to discover at least one both monogenetic and one disjunctive error. The *lectiones singulares*, the unique readings, have no weight at all" (1992a: 267).

We may conclude that where massive horizontal transmission is unlikely and indicative errors are identifiable, the genealogical method is preferable to the statistical method. For constructing a textual history, the identification and analysis of indicative errors provide the best available method.

In recent work on the textual history of the Hebrew Bible, particularly that on the affinities of the Qumran biblical manuscripts, one finds advocates for both the genealogical and statistical methods of textual history and for eclectic mixtures of the two. In three important discussions of method presented at the Madrid Qumran Congress, Cross (1992), Tov (1992c), and Chiesa (1992a) presented converging arguments in favor of the genealogical method and the analytic priority of indicative errors. Cross draws an analogy from modern genetics:

Manuscripts have bad genes and good genes. Bad genes are secondary or corrupt readings which have been introduced into a manuscript by a scribe and copied and recopied by scribes in his vicinity or who otherwise had access to his manuscript or one of its descendants. A cluster or long list of bad genes—secondary readings and errors—held in common by two manuscripts require filiation as an explanation. . . .

Both good genes and bad genes have significance in writing the history of the text. However, primary data for establishing filiation is the sharing of a significant group of bad genes. (1992: 7, 8)

Tov notes that his current position essentially agrees with Cross's (1992c: 18–19), and Chiesa gives some valuable background on the history of this method and its application to biblical texts (1992a: 266–67).

This methodological position represents a departure from the primarily statistical methods used by Cross and Tov in earlier work, where they list statistics for all agreements and disagreements among the texts in order to infer relationships (e.g., Tov 1982: 21–22; Cross 1955: 171–72; 1995: 132–37 [unchanged from 1961 ed.]). Their recent emphasis on indicative errors and clusters of errors represents a methodological advance on this statistical approach. One notable result of their mutual refinement of method is that they now agree on the textual affinity of 4QSam[a] and G, an issue of long contention (Cross 1992: 6–7; Tov 1992b: 19; Tov 1992c: 30–33).

There remain advocates for the statistical method. Polak (1992) has made a thorough statistical analysis of the portions of Exodus, Leviticus, and Samuel that coincide with 4QpaleoExod[b], 11QpaleoLev, and 4QSam[a]. While I am unable to follow (or fully comprehend) the details of his statistical method, I would note that his attention to shared secondary readings in order to establish textual relationships makes his an eclectic method, incorporating aspects of "objective" statistical analysis and "subjective" genealogical analysis (1992: 256–57, 264–65). Davila (1993) has made a statistical analysis of the portions of Genesis and Exodus for which there are 4Q manuscripts, though he, too, distinguishes between agreements in primary and secondary readings and hence uses an eclectic method. In both cases, their method fails to discriminate among the secondary readings for indicative errors. As Chiesa rightly emphasizes, "In textual criticism what matters is not the *number* of agreements and disagreements between the various witnesses, but the *nature* of their variant readings and/or errors" (1992a: 267).

In the light of these methodological considerations, I propose to analyze a sizeable and clearly delineated set of indicative errors in Genesis 1–11 in order to ascertain the textual relationships among the versions. The most distinctive and abundant readings suitable for this task are the harmonizations (see chapter 5) and the chronological revisions (see chapter 4). Both of these groups of data consist of secondary readings with a strong claim to be indicative errors. Although some of the shared harmonizations or shared chronological revisions may have been produced independently, most seem sufficiently distinctive to be classified as indicative errors, suitable for making stemmatic inferences. In view of the possibility that a given error might not be indicative, I will proceed by analyzing the shared clusters of indicative errors in order to establish textual filiation.

6.2 STEMMATIC RELATIONSHIPS

The data for indicative errors among the harmonizations in Genesis 1–11 are as follows (compiled from §5.2–5):

M = S   6 instances
M = G   0 instances
S = G   13 instances

The figure for S = G includes the series of shared pluses in Gen 11:11–25 (+ וימת) as one error. If one were to count each repetition of this plus, the total would be 20 shared indicative errors for S and G.

These data indicate strongly that M and G belong to distinct branches of the textual stemma, with no shared indicative errors in this set. In contrast, the data indicate that S has affinities to both M and G, though the affinities to G are more pronounced (by a ratio of roughly two to one).

The stemmatic data for S require one of the following historical scenarios:

1. A common hyparchetype with M and horizontal transmission of readings from proto-G text(s).
2. A common hyparchetype with G and horizontal transmission of readings from proto-M text(s).
3. No common hyparchetype; derivation by horizontal transmission from proto-M and proto-G texts.
4. No common hyparchetype; derivation from proto-M text(s) and horizontal transmission of readings from proto-G text(s).
5. No shared hyparchetype; derivation from proto-G text(s) and horizontal transmission of readings from proto-M text(s).

On the basis of the data from the harmonizations, it is impossible to prefer one scenario to another.

The data from the editorial revisions of the chronologies in Genesis 5 and 11 allow us to refine this analysis. The data for indicative errors among the chronological revisions in Genesis 5 and 11 are as follows (compiled from §4.2–3):

M = S   0 instances
M = G   0 instances
S = G   7 instances

The figure for S = G consists of the seven shared secondary readings for the postdiluvian *b*'s (age at birth of son) from Arpachshad to Nahor. The agreements in this series are sufficiently distinctive, particularly in the shared change in revision for Nahor (see §4.4), to be likely candidates for indicative errors. The figure for M = G excludes the agreements of M and G for Jared's *b* and *r*; as argued previously (§4.2), these numbers are probably the result of independent strategies of revision and therefore have no stemmatic value.

The conjunction in seven instances of chronological revision for S and G, plausibly indicating a common source, does not in itself alter the implications derived from the data for harmonizations. But the results from our analysis of the chronological revisions in Genesis 5 and 11 (§4.4) make it possible to refine the historical picture and to limit the stemmatic possibilities. In view of the three distinctive, systematic revisions of these chronologies, it is reasonable to conclude that M, S, and G in Genesis are representatives of three distinct recensions. Further, the seven shared revisions in S and G suggest the possibilitiy of a common hyparchetype for the proto-S and proto-G recensions. The demonstration that each revision has its own internal consistency and cannot be derived from either of the others (with the provision of a possible hyparchetype for the seven shared revisions in S and G) eliminates scenarios 3, 4, and 5 from the possible histories of proto-S. The chronological revisions in S are revisions of a text akin to the archetype and not revisions of the revisions in proto-M or proto-G.

Having excluded scenarios 3, 4, and 5 from the stemmatic possibilities, we turn to the relative merits of scenarios 1 and 2. One possibility, suggested by Klein (1974a: 257–58), is that the seven chronological revisions shared by S and G are attributable to a common ancestor and that the other systematic revisions in proto-S and proto-G are subsequent (and independent) recensional layers. This proposal is consistent with scenario 2. In this case, the indicative errors shared by S and M would be attributable to horizontal transmission, in which readings from proto-M text(s) were inserted into proto-S text(s) sometime during the histories of these two recensions. However, as noted before, this series of shared secondary readings may be too slim a basis on which to base such a solution. One would like more data to posit with confidence a common hyparchetype for G and S.

The plausibility of scenario 2 has been argued by many scholars, beginning with Gesenius's *De Pentateuchi Samaritani* in 1815 (see Waltke 1970: 228–32;

1992: 934; Tov 1981: 268–71). Since the discovery of the Qumran biblical manuscripts several scholars (esp. Cross, Waltke, Purvis, and Jastram) have defended this hypothesis. The best data come from 4QExod^b and 4QNum^b, which have affinities of varying degrees with G and S. Cross has argued that these two manuscripts stem from old Palestinian texts that were common ancestors of S and G (Cross 1964: 287; 1966: 84 n. 15). Although this position has yet to be fully detailed (see the recent editions of these two texts in DJD 12), this possibility for other books of the Pentateuch complements the possibility of a hyparchetype for proto-S and proto-G in Genesis.

Some other data relevant to this issue come from the chronologies in Jub. As noted before (§4.2–3), Jub has close affinities with S in Genesis 5 and shares the plus of Kenan II with G in Genesis 11. The hypothesis of a hyparchetype for proto-S and proto-G would make sense of this situation in Jub. It is possible that Jub preserves readings from a text descended from the proto-S hyparchetype that still preserved the old Palestinian plus of Kenan II. But there are also other possible histories that would explain the affinities of Jub (see later).

Although a clear picture of the textual history of the proto-S recension of Genesis remains underdetermined by the data, we have found some plausible reasons to prefer scenario 2. The horizontal transmission of readings from proto-M texts is historically plausible, as there is evidence for such horizontal transmission in the revisions of G toward proto-M texts in the first century B.C.E. and later (see Tov 1992a: 143–45; and §4.2 for Josephus). In a recent study of 4QNum^b, Jastram characterizes the extent of such horizontal transmission of readings:

> Though there is some evidence that the Samaritan text was revised toward the Masoretic at some point in its history, the evidence also shows that it was not revised toward the Masoretic text in such a way that its longer readings were excised. The Samaritan text, even after revision, still contained the major interpolations for which it is known. (1992: 180)

Revisions toward proto-M may have concentrated on small differences rather than large and were more likely sporadic than systematic.

Davila (1993) argues that M and S of Genesis belong to the same text-type, a position consistent with scenario 1. But his eclectic statistical method does not identify indicative errors and does not distinguish between vertical and horizontal transmission, and it is difficult to see how his method can be used to distinguish between scenarios 1 and 2. Moreover, his textual data do not include the chronologies in Genesis 5 and 11, in that Qumran manuscripts are lacking for these chapters. These are the chapters that establish most clearly the different recensional histories of M and S.

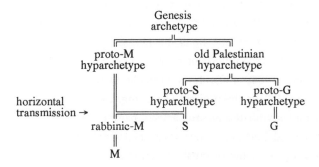

Figure 6-1: Stemmatic Model for Genesis 1–11

In adjudicating between scenarios 1 and 2 for the textual history of S in Genesis 1–11, it is reasonable to prefer scenario 2. Certainty is not possible, but there are more and better arguments for this scenario, given the parameters set by the pattern of indicative errors analyzed previously.

A plausible stemma for Genesis 1–11 may therefore be sketched, bearing in mind a residue of uncertainty (figure 6-1). Like all textual stemma, this one represents "a 'servicable' stemmatic relationship, meaning 'not necessarily historically exact'" (West 1973: 39). Although the reality was probably more complex, this is a minimal schema that plausibly represents parts of the reality. This is not history as it really happened but a model for history, a minimalist genealogy of errors.

There is at least one area in this stemma that is certain to have been more complex in history, that is, the cul-de-sac area between S, G, and the old Palestinian hyparchetype. Although we do not at present have evidence for more than two hyparchetypes at this level, texts such as Jub and LAB suggest the possibility of other branchings and occasions for horizontal transmission. The textual affinities of Jub have been the subject of two important studies by VanderKam (1977 and 1988), in which he notes the abundant affinities of Jub with both S and G. He has argued that "if there was a Palestinian family of texts of which the LXX and Sam are two representatives and Jubilees a third, then it must have been a very loose conglomeration of divergent texts" (1988: 84). I would differ with VanderKam's emphasis on unique readings and his primarily statistical method (see §6.1), but the picture of many Palestinian texts in circulation in the Second Temple period with varying degrees of affinity to S and G is very plausible. Horizontal transmission is always a factor where texts of different ancestry are in close proximity. As Cross emphasizes: "Recensionally distinct texts are fragile creations; one text, coming in contact with another, immediately dissolves into a mixed text. One set of corrections and centuries of development are destroyed in a twinkling" (1964: 299). There are doubtless more branchings and horizontal transmissions than we can document from the present state of the data. But I suspect that they would more likely fill in and complicate this stemma than erase it.

6.3 AFTER 70: RABBINIC-M AND THE MINOR VERSIONS

Among the Qumran texts, 4QGen[b] is our closest exemplar to the proto-M text(s) chosen by the Pharisees cum Rabbis to be their canonical Genesis. Of the roughly 300 words preserved in 4QGen[b], the consonantal text fits squarely within the minimal range of variation among our major M manuscripts (see §7.4). There are two orthographic variants among the major M manuscripts for these readings, and in both cases 4QGen[b] agrees with one or more M texts:

1:15   למארת 4QGen[b] V] למאורת C3 L
1:21   עוֹף 4QGen[b] C3 L] עֹף V

Sometime, somewhere, a Genesis text closely related to 4QGen[b] became the canonical text for rabbinic Judaism, the hyparchetype of all medieval texts of M. Concerning the circumstances of this choice, we are wholly ignorant (see Albrektson 1978; Goshen-Gottstein 1992b: 208–9), though it may be significant that all the biblical manuscripts found at other Dead Sea sites—including Genesis manuscripts from Murabbaʿat (DJD 2: 75-77) and thereabouts (Burchard 1966 [= Sdeir 1]; Puech 1980 [= Mur?])—are rabbinic-M texts.

We may infer something of the textual history of Genesis after the rise of rabbinic-M by attention to the testimony of the minor versions, Tgs, Syr, and Vg. We do not know the precise time when the archetypes of the Tgs and Syr were made (ca. first to second centuries C.E.; see Kaufman 1994; Brock 1992b: 794), but it is significant that many non-rabbinic-M readings are preserved in these versions. We do know when Jerome made his Vg translation of Genesis (ca. 400 C.E.), and numerous non-rabbinic-M readings are preserved in his work also. The data for the harmonizations in the minor versions of Genesis 1–11 that are shared with either S or G are as follows (compiled from §5.2–5):

Tg[O]   3 instances
Tg[N]   7 instances, including 2 from Tg[N(mg)]
Tg[J]   5 instances
Syr   20 instances
Vg   10 instances

In numerous instances, the harmonization in S, G, or both is shared by more than one of the minor versions or by a minor version and an ancillary source. These instances of multiple agreements are significant, as the chance reproduction of such readings is minimal. Clustered agreements in harmonizations occur in the following 13 cases:

Gen 2:4 G את השמים ואת הארץ ;Syr Vg Tg^N S שמים וארץ [M ארץ ושמים
(τον ουρανον και την γην)

Gen 2:18 אעשה 4QGen^{bh} M S] נעשה G (ποιησωμεν) Vg Jub 3:4

Gen 2:23 מאיש M [מאישה S G (εκ του ανδρος αυτης) Tg^O Jub 3:6

Gen 2:24 והיו M G (εσονται)] + שניהם G (οι δυο) Tg^P Syr Vg sim S (והיה
(משניהם

Gen 4:25 שת 1° M S G (Σηθ)] + לאמר G (λεγουσα) Vg sim Tg$^{ON(mg)J}$

Gen 7:2 איש ואשתו ° 1-2 M] זכר ונקבה °1-2 S G (αρσεν και θηλυ) Tg^{OP}
Syr Vg

Gen 7:2 שנים M S G (δυο)] + שנים S G (δυο) Syr Vg

Gen 7:3 השמים M S G (του ουρανου)] + הטהור S G (των καθαρων) Syr^{mss}
LAB 3:4

Gen 7:13 אתם M S] אתו G (μετ' αυτου) Tg$^{N(mg)J}$ Syr

Gen 7:20 ההרים M S G (τα ορη)] + הגבהים G (τα υψηλα) Syr^{mss} Jub 5:26

Gen 8:19 החיה M S G (τα θηρια)] + וכל הבהמה G (και παντα τα κτηνη)
Syr Vg

Gen 8:21 עוד לקלל M [לקלל עוד S G (ετι του καταρασασθαι) Syr Vg

Gen 9:14 הקשת M S] קשתי G (το τοξον μου) Vg LAB 3:12

In most of these instances, we can reasonably infer that the minor versions were translating Hebrew texts with non-rabbinic-M readings. There are other such instances in which the minor versions share readings with S or G against M, but those on this list are particularly notable as clusters of shared errors.

We may conclude that the history of non-rabbinic-M texts did not end at 70 C.E. (allowing, of course, for the persistence of S and G in their respective communities). Texts with varying affinities continued to circulate in the following generations, and their traces remain visible in numerous readings in the minor versions (for other examples, see Hendel, in press; Kedar 1988: 322). Other faint traces may survive in rabbinic exegetical literature (see Maori 1992). The survival of such texts is not historically surprising because rabbinic Judaism spread slowly after 70 C.E., attaining political and social dominance in Judea only in the third century C.E. or later. Synagogues, where Torah scrolls were read, may have come under rabbinic control as late as the seventh century C.E.

(Cohen 1987: 221–24). In view of this historical process, it is not surprising that some biblical texts preserved old readings that varied from rabbinic-M.

6.4 EXCURSUS: THE VOCALIZATION OF מסרת

The textual history of Genesis before the printing press era comes to completion with the work of the Tiberian Masoretes, who perfected a system for the vocalization and annotation of the biblical text (ca. 7th to 10th centuries C.E.). The traditional Hebrew text, M, owes its name to the בעלי המסרת, "Masters of the (textual) tradition." Perhaps ironically, scholars still disagree on the spelling and vocalization of the word מסרת, from which comes the name of the text. Sometimes M is the "Masoretic" text, from מָסֹרֶת; sometimes it is the "Massoretic" text, from מַסֹרֶת (for surveys of this issue, see Mulder 1988a: 105–6; Dotan 1971: 1418–19; Roberts 1951: 40–42). While the difference of ס ָ versus ס ַ in these words may seem inconsequential, the labors of the בעלי המסרת were often over just such minutiae, and attention to this detail may therefore be fitting tribute to their work.

Wilhelm Bacher argued more than a century ago that "the pronunciation מַסֹורֶת has no historical justification" (1891: 790). Bacher's argument is compelling, though it has not been widely adopted. In the following, I will reformulate and refine his position and reexamine the relevant data.

In Rabbinic Hebrew, מסרת (usually *plene* מסורת) means "tradition." The most famous example, and one of the earliest, is *M. ʾAbot* 3.13, מסרת סיג לתורה, "Tradition is a fence around the Torah." This saying, attributed to Rabbi ʿAqiba, is a response to one of the leitmotifs of the tractate, the saying of the Men of the Great Synagogue in *M. ʾAbot* 1.1, עשו סיג לתורה, "Make a fence around the Torah." Both sayings, in turn, implicitly refer to the authoritative exegetical traditions, which extend in an unbroken line back to Moses and Sinai (*M. ʾAbot* 1.1): משה קבל תורה מסיני ומסרה, "Moses received the Torah from Sinai and transmitted it . . . ." The verb "transmit, hand down" is מסר (for the semantic history of this verb, see Ben-Ḥayyim 1965: 211–13). Clearly, according to the logic of the tractate, the noun מסרת refers to that which has been transmitted (מסר) from Moses and Sinai (cf. Neusner 1994: 674–75). The same meaning for מסר is found in Qumran Hebrew, as in the intriguing parallel to *M. ʾAbot* 1.1 in the Damascus Document (CD 3.3), where Abraham transmits God's commandments to his heirs, וימסור לישהק וליעקב, "he transmitted [God's commandments] to Isaac and Jacob."

The grammatical question concerning מסרת in this context is not its meaning, which is unambiguous, but its form. There are many nominal patterns available for a noun related to the Qal verb מסר. The pattern *qātōlet* is not one of them, however, as it is the pattern for the infinitive absolute, and the pattern *qattōlet* is exceedingly rare (only פָּרֹכֶת, כַּפֹּרֶת, בְּצֹרֶת in Biblical Hebrew) and is unproductive in postbiblical Hebrew (Bacher 1891: 788 n. 1). What possible reason could there be for "tradition" to be written מסרת?

The only plausible reason is that there was a noun already of this form that was taken to mean "tradition." This noun is מסרת in Ezek 20:37, a hapax legomenon. The sentence reads (with Masoretic vocalization), וְהֵבֵאתִי אֶתְכֶם בְּמָסֹרֶת הַבְּרִית. Translations of this sentence vary. Greenberg renders it "I will lead you into the obligation of the covenant," which is almost certainly correct (1983a: 362; 1983b: 38–41). The form of the noun מָסֹרֶת is explicable by a derivation from √אסר, "to bind," with the attenuation of the א and compensatory lengthening of the preceding vowel. Hence, the development of the form is **ma'sōret* → *māsōret*, from the nominal pattern *maqtōlet*. (There are seven other nouns of this pattern in the Hebrew Bible; see JM §88Lj.) This analysis has been accepted by many grammarians from the 10th century C.E. to the present (Greenberg 1983b: 38–39). For most Jewish readers, however, this word was thought to mean "tradition." The Theodotionic revision of G translates מסרת as παραδόσει, "tradition." (Compare Aquila, who literalistically or etymologically translates as δεσμοῖς, "bonds.") Targum Jonathan and Rashi also concur in understanding this word in Ezekiel as "tradition." Because there is no dissenting view in rabbinic literature, the concurrence of Theodotion, the Targum, and Rashi indicates that the standard view in rabbinic Judaism was that מסרת in Ezek 20:37 meant "tradition." Bacher states this argument clearly: "the Targum, when it is unopposed by any other explanation in the literature of tradition, is sufficiently convincing, expecially as its translation is supported by Theodotion, and as Rashi gives evidence for the maintenance of the traditional view" (1891: 788).

The key question is whether the בעלי המסרת of Tiberias believed that מסרת in Ezek 20:37 meant "tradition." From the vocalization of מָסֹרֶת, we may infer an etymology from √אסר, thereby accounting for the peculiar form. But even if from √אסר, could it still be taken to mean "tradition"? Greenberg has noted a saying in the Talmud that in two instances uses the word מסרת and in two others uses the word שבועה, "oath" (1983b: 40). He uses this case of synonymity to argue that מסרת may be read here as "oath," as is its probable original meaning in Ezek 20:37. But it is probably more likely that this synonymity indicates that מסרת as "tradition" could also be taken as "binding tradition," and therefore

שבועה, "oath," could be a natural alternative. The semantic range indicated by this synonymity suggests that מסרת in Ezek 20:37 could easily be derived from אסר, as the vocalization indicates, and still be semantically informed by מסר, as the use of the word in rabbinic Judaism indicates.

We are therefore warranted to conclude that מָסֹרֶת is the Masoretic vocalization of the noun מסרת, meaning "tradition," with the extended meanings "binding, authoritative tradition" and "(Masoretic) textual tradition." There is no evidence before the 17th century for any other vocalization of מסרת, and reason enough to believe that the Masoretes, like their peers, read the phrase מָסֹרֶת הַבְּרִית in Ezek 20:37 as "tradition of the covenant" or the like. To posit an unrelated noun מַסֹרֶת meaning "tradition," from √מסר, has no linguistic or historical basis, as Bacher pointed out. It is linguistically preferable, and far more economical, to see מסרת in Ezek 20:37 as the parent of the Rabbinic Hebrew מסרת, "tradition" (which was understood to be related to √מסר by synchronic reanalysis), rather than to separate the two and derive the latter from an unproductive nominal pattern in postbiblical Hebrew.

Etymology does not restrict semantic development in Hebrew words. As Barr observes regarding the vocabulary of Qumran Hebrew, "we find old words of the Bible, probably long archaic, reused with senses which have come to be attached to them through exegetical tradition" (1989b: 90). Once we allow for this process of exegetical cum semantic development, the etymological objection to Bacher's argument vanishes (pace GKC §3b n. 1; GKB 1. §3d; JM §16 n. 2).

The linguistic and historical evidence suggests that the Masoretic vocalization of מסרת is given in Ezek 20:37. In M, the word is vocalized מָסֹרֶת. There is no cogent reason to think that this was not the noun for "tradition" at the time of the בעלי המסרת. These textual scholars were therefore the בַּעֲלֵי הַמָּסֹרֶת, and their biblical version (M) is the Masoretic text.

Part II

Critical Edition

וכשאתה מלמד את בנך למדהו בספר מוגה

And when you teach your son,
teach him from a corrected scroll.

B. Talmud, *Pesaḥim* 112a

CHAPTER SEVEN

Introduction to the Critical Edition

7.1 RATIONALE FOR A CRITICAL (ECLECTIC) EDITION

Outside the field of Hebrew Bible, there is little doubt concerning the purpose of textual criticism. Maas states unequivocally, "The business of textual criticism is to produce a text as close as possible to the original (*constitutio textus*)" (1958: 1). The current article in the *Encyclopaedia Britannica* begins, "The technique of restoring texts as nearly as possible to their original form is called textual criticism" (Kenney 1992: 614). The production of critical texts by means of the analysis of manuscripts, the adjudication among variant readings, and, when necessary, the reconstruction or conjecture of better or original readings is the purpose of textual criticism. Aside from this goal, there is little justification for the labors of the textual critic.

In the field of the textual criticism of the Hebrew Bible, few scholars adhere to this goal. The exceptions are notable. Against Goshen-Gottstein's claim that "the reconstruction of the *Urtext* is not the supreme goal" (1965: 12), Cross contends that "the supreme goal, or rather the only goal of textual criticism is the reconstruction of the *Urtext*, however slowly or cautiously we may be required to move forward in its pursuit" (1979: 51). More recently, Borbone (1990) and Chiesa (1992a and 1992b) have reiterated this position. Yet, such statements are uncommon. More often, one finds that the critic's aim is to produce diplomatic editions of M, as is the case for *BHS* (and its future replacement, *BHQ*), HUBP, and other projects. For the massive HUBP edition, Goshen-Gottstein states that the object is "to present nothing but the facts" (1965: 7). This is a curiously positivistic goal for an activity that calls itself criticism, which by definition involves making judgments in evaluating the evidence. A critic, from Greek κριτικός, is one "able to discern and decide." The textual critic is one who exercises an educated judgment concerning the textual data, not an antiquarian collector presenting the reader with a bewildering plethora of "facts."

In his *Textual Criticism of the Hebrew Bible*, Tov presents a detailed consideration of the theoretical and practical problems involved in making fully
critical editions of the Hebrew Bible. Tov admits that "textual criticism aims at
the 'original' form of the biblical books" (1992a: 288), defining the original
form for this purpose as "the copy (or textual tradition) that contained the finished literary product and which stood at the beginning of the process of textual
transmission" (1992a: 171). He qualifies this aim as follows: "Even if this aim
can be accomplished in only a few details, it would at least appear to be correct
on a theoretical level, and must therefore be adhered to" (1992a: 180). Thus far,
Tov is in agreement with the goals and procedures of textual criticism generally,
namely, "textual critics aim at establishing critical or eclectic editions of texts"
(Tov 1992a: 289).

But Tov further claims that there is an essential difference in the textual
criticism of the Hebrew Bible, precluding the production of fully critical texts
and editions. He gives both theoretical and practical reasons for this unique
situation:

> It is evident that the textual criticism of the Hebrew Bible differs from the textual
> criticism of other compositions, for there have been relatively few attempts to
> reconstruct the original text of a biblical book, for theoretical as well as practical
> reasons: the Hebrew *Vorlage* of the ancient translations cannot be reconstructed
> satisfactorily, and often it is impossible to make a decision with regard to the
> originality of readings. Because of these problems, most of the existing critical edi-
> tions are diplomatic. . . . In these diplomatic editions the exegete should not expect
> to find a finished product comprising the conclusions of text-critical scholars, but
> rather, the raw materials which will aid him to form his own opinion based upon the
> available textual evidence. (1992a: 289)

Let us examine these reasons individually.

First, Tov observes that there have been relatively few attempts to make fully
critical editions of biblical texts. This historical fact does seem to make the
Hebrew Bible unique among ancient texts. A notable exception is Borbone's
recent edition of Hosea (1990), in which he admirably carries out the text-
critical task for this textually challenged book. Tov notes, however, that most
modern commentaries include a "virtual" critical text in their translations and
notes and that numerous scholars have produced critical texts for individual units
or pericopes of the Hebrew Bible (1992a: 372 n. 2). The exceptions to the rule
are therefore sufficiently numerous to raise doubts about its necessity or
desirability. Cross accounts for the lack of work in this area to "the prestige of
the *textus receptus*" and, more important, to "the inertia which slows scholars
from changing methods . . . which have grown habitual in their scholarly prac-

tice" (1979: 50). In other words, the fact that critical editions have not been made in great number in the past does not mean that this situation is warranted. In light of the availability of the Qumran manuscripts and the important methodological advances made in the field in recent decades, one could easily argue that the production of critical texts is a glaring desideratum in the field.

Second, Tov gives as the theoretical reason for this state of affairs: "the Hebrew *Vorlage* of the ancient translations cannot be reconstructed satisfactorily." It may be somewhat ironic that this statement comes from Tov's pen, for he has been instrumental in the formulation of sound procedures for the reconstruction of the *Vorlage* of G in books where the translation technique is sufficiently literal to permit such reconstruction (see 1981 and most recently 1992b). As long as one adheres to the methodological prescriptions and cautions propounded by Tov, one is warranted to examine G as a source for authentic textual variants. And, as Tov has shown extensively, in many instances this can be done satisfactorily. This theoretical difficulty, therefore, which may have been profound in the pre-Qumran era, has been clarified to the point that it has become part of the task of textual criticism, not an insoluble problem that necessarily precludes that task.

Third, Tov gives a practical obstacle for the production of critical texts: "often it is impossible to make a decision with regard to the originality of readings." This is true. But I would note that this is the case for any ancient work, whether Homer, Sophocles, the New Testament, or Genesis. The difficulty of adjudicating among variant readings is, in its very essence, the difficulty of textual criticism. That is why it is called textual criticism and not textual inventory. Textual criticism involves "the necessity of judging variant readings and forms of a text on their intrinsic merits in the light of the information available" (Kenney 1992: 619). Where a decision on the basis of intrinsic merits is impossible, the critic as a general rule may prefer the reading that has the best extrinsic merit, that is, the reading from the best manuscript. We have shown that in the case of Genesis this is M. I have argued previously that where a reasonable decision cannot be made, the M reading is the prudent default position (see §1.2). Reynolds and Wilson nicely articulate this principle, along with an apt definition of "best manuscript": "Since the best manuscript is that which gives the greatest number of correct readings in passages where there are rational grounds for decision, it is more likely than the others to give the correct reading in passages where no such grounds exist" (1974: 195). Instances where a decision is impossible are not unique to the textual criticism of the Hebrew Bible. A textual critic learns to deal prudently with these situations.

I have pointed out some of the chief deficiencies in the reasons—historical, theoretical, and practical—adduced by Tov to justify the view that "textual criticism of the Hebrew Bible differs from the textual criticism of other compositions" when it comes to the production of critical texts and editions. Chiesa is quite right to insist that "it seems quite unnecessary to postulate an *ad hoc* status for the Biblical writings alone" (1992a: 265). It may be relatively harder to produce critical texts for the Hebrew Bible than for the New Testament or Homer, in part because of the limitations involved in retroverting G, but, in books where G has a reliably literal translation technique, the degree of difficulty is within our means.

Some books of the Hebrew Bible are more amenable to the production of critical texts than others. The books of the Pentateuch have the greatest abundance of textual resources, given the reliability of the G translation technique and the existence of S. The Qumran texts in the Pentateuch are valuable not only in themselves but in the light they shed on the textual value of S and G. The minor versions and ancillary sources are also valuable in the Pentateuch, particularly for corroborating variants in S and G. In other parts of the Hebrew Bible, the textual resources are not as rich, and the problems for producing critical texts and editions are relatively greater.

In light of the increase of evidence and the advances in method in the post-Qumran era, Cross observes that "many barriers hindering the practice of a genuine eclectic criticism have fallen in our day" (1979: 51). Fully critical editions, by which I mean critical texts with critical apparatuses that document the judgments made in constituting the text, are justifiable and desirable for books of the Hebrew Bible, particularly for Genesis and the other Pentateuchal books. Many scholars will continue to follow the view that "the student of the Bible text must be content to deal with facts" (Goshen-Gottstein 1992b: 206). Genuine textual criticism of the Hebrew Bible must discriminate among the facts, which implies (by definition) the production of fully critical editions.

7.2 THE CRITICAL TEXT

Wevers nicely defines the nature of a critical text is his comments on his edition of G: "The printing of a critical text . . . is the presentation by an editor after weighing all the textual evidence at his disposal of the earliest reconstruction of the text possible, an approximation to the original insofar as that is reasonable" (1974: 186). The concept of the "original," of which the critical text is an approximation, requires some careful unpacking. An allied concept, necessary for delimiting the textual nature of the "original," is the "archetype."

The archetype is the "earliest inferable textual state" (Kenney 1992: 616). As Tov notes, there is always a "possibility of a large interval of time between the date of the archetype, reconstructed from the existing evidence, and the original composition" (1992a: 167). The archetype of Genesis is the state of the text that we try to infer by adjudicating among the variants of the extant versions. But sometimes the archetype does not preserve the readings of the original. Where this is detectable, one can resort only to conjecture to cure the error and approximate the original. In the critical text presented here I have adopted diagnostic conjectures, that is, readings not inferable from the existing readings, in two places (at Gen 4:22 and 10:5). There are, no doubt, other places where the archetype differs from the original, but these cases are either undetectable or insufficiently strong to warrant diagnostic conjectures. There are probably instances where a gloss or explicating plus exists in the archetype that was not in the original (the explicating דמו in Gen 9:4 might be an example), but the margin of uncertainty is sufficiently large that it is best to include these in the critical text. The critical text, while it approximates the original, more nearly approximates the archetype. It is impossible to say how close or distant the archetype is to the original; by definition, we lack the textual data to tell. An optimist would hope that the archetype of Genesis was a good text, itself approximating the original.

Although the archetype is, in theory, achievable by text-critical methods, the original is an ideal goal, which is to say that it is an abstract and logically unachievable goal. As in the method of calculus, it is the limit toward which one strives but never completely reaches. The critical text is an approximation of the ideal, but it is never finished; it is necessarily a work in progress. As the Mishnah notes of Torah study generally: לא עליך המלאכה לגמור, "it is not given to you to complete the work" (*M. 'Abot* 2.20). This is clearly the case for the production of critical texts.

The original—the ideal goal behind the critical text—is admirably defined by Tov as "the copy (or textual tradition) that contained the finished literary product and which stood at the beginning of the process of textual transmission" (1992a: 171). Although, as Wellhausen noted, "it is difficult to find the boundary where literary history ends and textual criticsm begins" (apud Albrektson 1994: 31), Tov's definition serves well to pinpoint the historical situation at which textual criticism aims. The original text, for the purpose of textual criticism, is a text that once existed and that we attempt to reconstitute by removing the accumulation of scribal errors and changes. The critical text is a "reconstruction of what no longer exists" (Kenney 1992: 614), which is to say that it is a work of historical inquiry, guided by historical method.

In the case of the Hebrew Bible, the ideal of the original text is often complicated by issues of canon. Barthélemy makes a distinction between literary authenticity and canonical authenticity, the former belonging to the "original" text and the latter belonging to "the most ancient text . . . that functioned as a sacred book for a community" (1982: *77). Tov makes a comparable distinction when he states that the aim is to reconstitute the original text, but in the form or edition that was canonized in the Jewish *Tanakh* (1992a: 177-79). Although such issues may be relevant in the books for which there are multiple editions preserved among the textual versions, therefore requiring decisions about *which* original text to reconstitute (see Ulrich 1992; Sanders 1991; Tov 1992a: 313-49), these problems arguably do not bear on Genesis.

In fact, it may be possible to specify the point at which the original text of Genesis emerges into view in literary and canonical form. With all the requisite caveats concerning our understanding of the literary history of the Pentateuch, it is arguable that the publication of the Pentateuch—that is, the point when it was made public (and authoritative)—is narrated in Nehemiah 8 (see Fishbane 1985: 107-29; Williamson 1987: 90-98):

> On the first day of the seventh month, Ezra the priest brought the Torah (התורה) to the congregation—the men, women, and all who could understand. He read it aloud in the public square before the Water Gate from dawn to midday, to the men, women, and those who could understand. The ears of all the people were attentive to the Book of the Torah. (Neh 8:2-3)

Fishbane (1985: 108) notes that, given a few assumptions, the date for this event can be specified as October 2, 458 B.C.E. While I would not press the point too strongly, this event of the publication of the Torah to the people of Jerusalem may serve as a literary approximation of the original text that no longer exists but serves as our ideal for textual criticism. This is the biblical image of the text that "contained the finished literary product and which stood at the beginning of the process of textual transmission." It is also canonically "the most ancient text . . . that functioned as a sacred book for a community." This is the picture of what Freedman calls "the earliest Bible" (1987).

From the understanding of the nature of the archetype and the original text of Genesis that I have sketched, the status of the critical text as "an approximation to the original insofar as that is reasonable" should be clear. Although it is conventional to regard such a critical text as an "eclectic" text in that the readings adopted come from a variety of manuscripts, from a historical perspective it is more correct to regard the manuscripts as eclectic and the critical text as an attempt to reverse the eclectic agglomeration of primary and secondary readings. As Borbone nicely observes in his critical edition of Hosea: "This text—except of course for the erroneous evaluations of the writer, which the benevolent reader can remedy using the apparatus—will be more certain and less 'eclectic' than the text of a single ms" (1990: 26).

In the critical text, I have retained the Masoretic vocalization for readings preserved in M (see §7.4). Primary readings not in M are unvocalized, making them easily recognizable. Other notations included in the critical text are paragraph markers (from ms C3) and chapter and verse numbers. Masoretic accents are not included in the critical text because of the technical limitations of my computer software and the minimal pragmatic value of such variants (see Goshen-Gottstein 1965: 42).

7.3 APPARATUS I: SIGNIFICANT TEXTUAL VARIANTS

Variants from the critical text are catalogued and commented upon in Apparatus I, on the page facing the Hebrew text. Only significant variants are included. A cursory comparison of M and S will show many more variations in spelling, in the presence or absence of conjuctive וֹ- or the particle אֵת, and other minor textual changes. By limiting the variants listed, I am exercising editorial subjectivity, but the alternative is to overwhelm the reader with minor variants. In this choice, I am following the advice of Goshen-Gottstein in his discussion of the textual data germane to a critical apparatus (1965: 23). As an additional limit on the clutter of the apparatus, I have listed the testimony of the minor versions only where they diverge from M (see §1.3). Hence, the default or unmarked value for the minor versions is agreement with M. By use of this convention, the apparatus is made less bulky with no loss of information.

Text-critical comments on the secondary reading(s) follow the semicolon. The language of the comments is necessarily terse, but I have tried to make them explanatory, not cryptic. Fuller discussions of many secondary readings are found in part I, particularly in §2.2 (Gen 1:1–2:4), §3.2 (secondary readings in M), and §4.2–3 (chronologies of Genesis 5 and 11). No apology is necessary for including comments on the secondary readings, as this is the essence of the text-critical task. Even Goshen-Gottstein, with his avowed purpose of producing a critical edition that "present[s] nothing but the facts" (1965: 7), produced apparatuses thoroughly informed by his text-critical judgment. Though he states that "the 'comment' is part of the fact-finding process" (1965: 25), it clearly represents his evaluation of the facts, to the limited degree he allows himself. The text-critical comments are *in nuce* the justification for the readings included in the critical text. Hence, they are the core of the enterprise.

In the instances where the reading in the critical text is a reconstruction (see §1.2), the reading is signaled in the apparatus by an asterisk *. Nine reconstructions are included in the critical text. Of these, four consist of a single letter (4:7 [3×]; 9:7), one consists of two letters (5:3), and four are numbers in the chronologies (5:19, 26, 28, 30). There are also two diagnostic conjectures included in the critical text (see §1.2), both widely accepted in the scholarly literature (4:22; 10:5). The two diagnostic conjectures are marked in the apparatus and in the critical text by brackets < >.

The abbreviations and sigla used in Apparatus I have been selected from those used in the DJD editions of biblical texts, the Göttingen Septuagint, the HUBP, and Maas (1958). The format for the apparatus derives largely from the DJD style. Parentheses are used to enclose relevant data (such as the Greek of G) following the siglum for that text. The only serious departure from these standard works is my use of ordinary type for the abbreviations of the major and minor versions. The major versions, M, S, G, and Q, are represented by abbreviations of a single capital letter, and the minor versions, Tgs (Tg^O, Tg^N, Tg^J; Tg^P = Tg^N + Tg^J), Syr, and Vg, are represented by abbreviations of two or three letters. The ancillary sources, Jub, Ant, and LAB, are represented by abbreviations (or acronyms) of three letters. These typographical decisions lend some clarity and order to the citation of the textual evidence and eliminate the needless obscurity of Gothic letters and other sigla.

7.4 APPARATUS II: MASORETIC VARIANTS

Variants in spelling, punctuation, and vocalization among the major Masoretic sources from the 10th and 11th centuries C.E. are catalogued in Apparatus II, below the Hebrew text. Where the critical text diverges from M, the apparatus still lists all variations among the Masoretic texts (e.g., at 4:18; 5:25, 26). Collation of the major texts shows that the variations are minimal, limited almost exclusively to *plene* versus *defectiva* spelling, the use or nonuse of *dageš*, and the use or nonuse of *ḥaṭep* vowels.

The use of Masoretic manuscripts in a critical text requires a somewhat different strategy than is available for the other major versions. As Orlinsky observed, "There never was, and there never can be, a single fixed masoretic text of the Bible" (1966: xviii). The idea of a critical Masoretic text runs into insuperable problems, such as the variations in *dageš* and *ḥaṭep* vowels just mentioned and in the differences in paragraphing among all the major Masoretic manuscripts. The decision of the HUBP to use the Aleppo Codex as the best text of M is also not available for Genesis; since the fire in the Aleppo synagogue in 1948, only a photograph of a page of Genesis remains (Wickes 1887: frontispiece).

For my Masoretic sources, I have collated all the available M manuscripts dated to the 11th century C.E. and earlier as our oldest and best exemplars of the Tiberian Masoretic tradition(s) (see the descriptions in Yeivin 1980: 12–30; Tov 1992a: 46–47). The manuscripts collated are:

C3   Cairo Pentateuch Codex, ca. 10th century C.E.
L   St. Petersburg (formerly Leningrad) Codex, ca. 1009 C.E.
S   Damascus (formerly Sassoon) Pentateuch Codex, ca. 10th century
      C.E. (extant from Gen 9:26)

In addition, I have collated the printed edition of the Second Rabbinic Bible (V, printed in Venice in 1524–25), from which derives the traditional *textus receptus* (see Goshen-Gottstein 1992a: 221–26). According to Penkower's dissertation, this edition was "based upon Sephardic manuscripts that were close to the text of the accurate Tiberian manuscripts such as L and A" (Tov 1992a: 78). I have also included variants from the list of differences between Ben Asher (bA) and Ben Naphtali (bN) compiled by Mishael Ben Uzziel in the 10th or early 11th century (Lipschütz 1962).

Where the Masoretic sources diverge, I have given preference to C3, a recently rediscovered Pentateuch codex corrected and authorized by Mishael Ben Uzziel (see Penkower 1988). In the absence of A in Genesis, C3 is probably our best representative of the Ben Asher tradition. In that Mishael Ben Uzziel was a Masoretic authority, I think it reasonable to accept this text as a close approximation to the Tiberian ideal. Where it is discernible, I have also included the testimony of the original (uncorrected) text of C3, designated as C3[pm]; this text shows affinities with the Ben Naphtali tradition (Penkower 1988: 69–72). The corrected text of C3 is consistently close to A in the portions preserved in both (Deut 28:17–34:12), although there are minor differences, most notably in the Masorah and in the general nonuse of *ḥaṭep* vowels under nonguttural consonants (Penkower 1988: 66–67).

To illustrate this minor difference, I have catalogued the variations in use of *ḥaṭep* vowels among C3, L, S, and A in Gen 26:34–27:30 (the section of A preserved in the photograph in Wickes 1887). The variants are found in the Piel of √*brk*:

27:19   תברכני C3 S] רְ A L
27:23   ויברכהו C3 S L] רְ A
27:27   ויברכהו C3 S] רְ A L
27:29   ומברכך C3 S] רְ A L

In these instances, C3 and S preserve the earlier system in which nongutturals with vocal *šewa³* are not marked with a *ḥaṭep* vowel, whereas A (consistently) and L (three out of four) reflect the more developed system (see Yeivin 1980: 282–84; but cf. Apparatus II at Gen 2:14). As a point of reference, the Cairo Prophets Codex (C), pointed by Aaron Ben Asher's father, Moshe, consistently writes these forms with a simple *šewa³* (Yeivin 1968: 39).

Concerning the placement of furtive *pataḥ*, C3 and L tend to place it under the letter preceding the guttural where it is a *mater lectionis*, as in רָקִיעַ or שֵׂיחַ, but under the guttural where it is not, as in נֹחַ. This practice in C3 and L agrees with that in A (Yeivin 1968: 21–22). In my edition, I have adopted the familiar typographic convention of placing the furtive *pataḥ* below the guttural.

Where C3 contains an obvious error, I have preferred the unanimous reading of the other sources (note the superfluous *dageš* in C3 of 8:9 and 8:10). Even the best Masoretes made mistakes (note the superfluous *dageš* in A of 5:18; listed in Ofer 1989: 316). In the many areas of C3 with erasures and corrections, the presence or absence of *dageš* or *maqqep* is often difficult to discern; hence, my collation of these details is not exact.

For the designation of open (פתוחה) and closed (סתומה) paragraphs in the critical text, I have also followed C3. They are marked in C3 with often-elaborate rectangular designs. I have indicated these divisions by a series of squares with the type of paragraph division indicated in brackets, □□[פ]□□ or □□[ס]□□. Following the precedent of HUBP, I have not burdened the apparatus with the numerous variations among the Masoretic manuscripts in paragraphing. All of the major Masoretic manuscripts diverge, and no sound basis is available for preferring one set to another (see Tov 1992a: 50–51).

The sigla for the Masoretic texts are from Yeivin (1980: 15–21; similarly Tov 1992a: 46–47), and the format for Apparatus II is generally drawn from the Masoretic apparatus of HUBP. I have retained the well-entrenched siglum L for the text still commonly called the Leningrad Codex or *Leningradensis* (cf. Barthélemy [1992: vii–viii], who uses siglum F for Firkovitch). In deference to recent history, I urge that textual critics refer to this important text by its correct toponym, St. Petersburg, hence the St. Petersburg Bible Codex. This was its designation for nearly half a century from its first description in 1875 (see Strack 1902: 728). Stalin renamed the city Leningrad in 1924 (it was Petrograd from 1914), but it is St. Petersburg once more.

CHAPTER EIGHT

Critical Text and Apparatuses

1 5 יום 1° M S G (ημεραν)] יומם 4QGen^g Tg^OP Syr; dittography (מם) or prps explication (יומם = "daytime"), cf 8:22

6   fin] + ויהי כן G (και εγενετο ουτος); transposed from v 7, harmonization with ויהי כן vv 9, 11, 15, 24, 30, cf v 3, cf below v 20

7   ויבדל 4QGen^b#g M S G (και διεχωρισεν)] + אלהים G (ο θεος); explicating plus

ויהי כן 4QGen^bg M S] om G; transposed to v 6

8   שמים 4QGen^b#g# M S G (ουρανον)] + וירא אלהים כי טוב G (και ειδεν ο θεος οτι καλον); harmonizing plus with וירא אלהים כי טוב vv 10, 12, 18, 21, 25, sim vv 4, 31

9   יקוו 4QGen^b M S G (συναχθητω)] יקאו 4QGen^g; parablepsis

השמים 1° 4QGen^b M S] לשמים 4QGen^g Tg^J; linguistic modernization (LBH construction: ל–תחת)

מקוה 4QGen^h G (συναγωγην)] מקום 4QGen^b M S Jub 2:5 LAB 15:6; prps graphic confusion (ה/ם)

(ותרא היב[שה]) 4QGen^k# ויקוו המים מתחת השמים אל מקויהם ותרא היבשה G (και συνηχθη το υδωρ το υποκατω του ουρανου εις τας συναγωγας αυτων και ωφθη η ξηρα) sim Jub 2:6] om 4QGen^bg M S; haplography by homoioarkton (ויק– ∩ ויק–) or prps homoioteleuton (היבשה ∩ היבשה)

11 זרע 4QGen^b M S G (σπερμα)] + למינהו G (κατα γενος και καθ´ ομοιοτητα) Syr; harmonizing plus with זרע למינהו v 12, note double translation in both vv

ועץ S G (και ξυλον) Tg^J Syr Vg] עץ 4QGen^b M; parablepsis

פרי 2° 4QGen^b M S G (καρπον)] + למינו 4QGen^b M S; prps harmonizing plus with למינהו 2 ° v 12, cf next entry

בו 4QGen^b M S G (εν αυτω)] + למינהו G (κατα γενος); harmonizing plus with בו למינהו v 12, cf previous entry

12 ועץ M S G (και ξυλον)] + פרי G (καρπιμον) Tg^P; harmonizing plus with ועץ פרי v 11

למינהו 2° 4QGen^b M S G (κατα γενος)] + על הארץ G (επι της γης); harmonizing plus with על הארץ v 11

14 השמים 4QGen^bk M S G (του ουρανου)] + להאיר על הארץ S G (εις φαυσιν της γης); harmonizing plus with השמים להאיר על הארץ vv 15, 17

ולש[נים] 4QGen^k G (και εις ενιαυτους) Syr] ושנים M S; parablepsis

20 ישרצו 4QGen^b M S] יש[רוצו] 1QGen; dialectal variant (Qimron 1986: 50–53)

1 ¹ בְּרֵאשִׁית בָּרָא אֱלֹהִים אֵת הַשָּׁמַיִם וְאֵת הָאָרֶץ: ² וְהָאָרֶץ הָיְתָה
תֹהוּ וָבֹהוּ וְחֹשֶׁךְ עַל־פְּנֵי תְהוֹם וְרוּחַ אֱלֹהִים מְרַחֶפֶת עַל־פְּנֵי הַמָּיִם:
³ וַיֹּאמֶר אֱלֹהִים יְהִי אוֹר וַיְהִי־אוֹר: ⁴ וַיַּרְא אֱלֹהִים אֶת־הָאוֹר כִּי־טוֹב וַיַּבְדֵּל
אֱלֹהִים בֵּין הָאוֹר וּבֵין הַחֹשֶׁךְ: ⁵ וַיִּקְרָא אֱלֹהִים לָאוֹר יוֹם וְלַחֹשֶׁךְ קָרָא
לָיְלָה וַיְהִי־עֶרֶב וַיְהִי־בֹקֶר יוֹם אֶחָד: □□[פ]□□ ⁶ וַיֹּאמֶר אֱלֹהִים יְהִי
רָקִיעַ בְּתוֹךְ הַמָּיִם וִיהִי מַבְדִּיל בֵּין מַיִם לָמָיִם: ⁷ וַיַּעַשׂ אֱלֹהִים אֶת־הָרָקִיעַ
וַיַּבְדֵּל בֵּין הַמַּיִם אֲשֶׁר מִתַּחַת לָרָקִיעַ וּבֵין הַמַּיִם אֲשֶׁר מֵעַל לָרָקִיעַ וַיְהִי־כֵן:
⁸ וַיִּקְרָא אֱלֹהִים לָרָקִיעַ שָׁמָיִם וַיְהִי־עֶרֶב וַיְהִי־בֹקֶר יוֹם שֵׁנִי: □□[פ]□□
⁹ וַיֹּאמֶר אֱלֹהִים יִקָּווּ הַמַּיִם מִתַּחַת הַשָּׁמַיִם אֶל־מָקוֹם אֶחָד וְתֵרָאֶה הַיַּבָּשָׁה
וַיְהִי־כֵן ויקוו המים מתחת השמים אל מקויהם ותרא היבשה: ¹⁰ וַיִּקְרָא
אֱלֹהִים לַיַּבָּשָׁה אֶרֶץ וּלְמִקְוֵה הַמַּיִם קָרָא יַמִּים וַיַּרְא אֱלֹהִים כִּי־טוֹב:
¹¹ וַיֹּאמֶר אֱלֹהִים תַּדְשֵׁא הָאָרֶץ דֶּשֶׁא עֵשֶׂב מַזְרִיעַ זֶרַע וְעֵץ פְּרִי עֹשֶׂה פְּרִי
אֲשֶׁר זַרְעוֹ־בוֹ עַל־הָאָרֶץ וַיְהִי־כֵן: ¹² וַתּוֹצֵא הָאָרֶץ דֶּשֶׁא עֵשֶׂב מַזְרִיעַ זֶרַע
לְמִינֵהוּ וְעֵץ עֹשֶׂה־פְּרִי אֲשֶׁר זַרְעוֹ־בוֹ לְמִינֵהוּ וַיַּרְא אֱלֹהִים כִּי־טוֹב:
¹³ וַיְהִי־עֶרֶב וַיְהִי־בֹקֶר יוֹם שְׁלִישִׁי: □□[פ]□□ ¹⁴ וַיֹּאמֶר אֱלֹהִים יְהִי
מְאֹרֹת בִּרְקִיעַ הַשָּׁמַיִם לְהַבְדִּיל בֵּין הַיּוֹם וּבֵין הַלָּיְלָה וְהָיוּ לְאֹתֹת וּלְמוֹעֲדִים
וּלְיָמִים וְשָׁנִים: ¹⁵ וְהָיוּ לִמְאוֹרֹת בִּרְקִיעַ הַשָּׁמַיִם לְהָאִיר עַל־הָאָרֶץ
וַיְהִי־כֵן: ¹⁶ וַיַּעַשׂ אֱלֹהִים אֶת־שְׁנֵי הַמְּאֹרֹת הַגְּדֹלִים אֶת־הַמָּאוֹר הַגָּדֹל
לְמֶמְשֶׁלֶת הַיּוֹם וְאֶת־הַמָּאוֹר הַקָּטֹן לְמֶמְשֶׁלֶת הַלַּיְלָה וְאֵת הַכּוֹכָבִים: ¹⁷ וַיִּתֵּן
אֹתָם אֱלֹהִים בִּרְקִיעַ הַשָּׁמָיִם לְהָאִיר עַל־הָאָרֶץ: ¹⁸ וְלִמְשֹׁל בַּיּוֹם וּבַלַּיְלָה
וּלֲהַבְדִּיל בֵּין הָאוֹר וּבֵין הַחֹשֶׁךְ וַיַּרְא אֱלֹהִים כִּי־טוֹב: ¹⁹ וַיְהִי־עֶרֶב
וַיְהִי־בֹקֶר יוֹם רְבִיעִי: □□[פ]□□ ²⁰ וַיֹּאמֶר אֱלֹהִים יִשְׁרְצוּ הַמַּיִם

1 3 יְהִי V [יְהִי L C3 ‖ 9 יִקָּווּ V L [וּ C3 (see Yeivin 1968: 49; 1980:
285-86) ‖ 12 עֹשֶׂה V C3 [עשׂה L ‖ 14 הַשָּׁמַיִם L C3 [מָ V ‖
L [לֶ V C3 ‖ 18 וּלֲהַבְדִּיל L C3 [למארת V ‖ 15 למאורת L

1 20　fin] + ויהי כן G (και εγενετο ουτος); harmonizing plus, cf above v 6

22　לאמר 4QGen^{b#d} M S G (λεγων)] ויאמר להם Syr; harmonizing plus with
　　ויאמר להם v 28, cf below v 28 (G)

　　ירב 4QGen^b M] ירבה 4QGen^g S; linguistic modernization (jussive form
　　→ imperfect form, frequent in S)

24　וחיתו ארץ M] וחית הארץ S; linguistic modernization and/or harmoniza-
　　tion with חית הארץ v 25

26　ובבהמה M S G (και των κτηνων)] + ובכל הארץ M S G (και πασης της
　　γης); + ובכל חית הארץ Syr; corrupt phrase, prps haplography (ה -ל ∩
　　ל-ה); Syr adds harmonization with חית הארץ v 25; correct phrase fol-
　　lows (ובכל . . . הארץ)

27　בצלמו M S] om G; haplography by homoioarkton (בצל- ∩ בצל-)

28　ויאמר להם אלהים M S] לאמר G (λεγων); harmonization with לאמר v 22,
　　cf above v 22 (Syr)

　　השמים M S G (του ουρανου)] + ובבהמה Syr; harmonizing plus with
　　השמים ובבהמה v 26

　　ובכל הבהמה ובכל הארץ ובכל הרמש הרמש M S] ובכל חיה הרמשת G (και
　　παντων των κτηνων και πασης της γης και παντων των ερπετων των
　　ερποντων); harmonizing plus with ובבהמה ובכל הארץ ובכל הרמש v 26

29　עשב זרע M S G (χορτον σποριμον)] + מזריע? G (σπειρον); harmonizing
　　plus with עשב מזריע זרע vv 11–12, or prps dittography (זרע זרע)

　　פרי M S G (καρπον)] + עץ M S (om G); prps anticipation of פרי עץ 3:2
　　and 3:3

30　ולכל 3 ° M S G (και παντι)] + רמש G (ερπετω); harmonizing plus with
　　ובכל הרמש הרמש vv 26, 28 (G)

2 2　הששי S G (τη εκτη) Syr Jub 2:16] השביעי M; anticipation of השביעי v 2
　　by anticipation, note similar phraseology in both halves of v 2 (. . . ביום
　　מלאכתו אשר עשה)

4　זה ספר תולדת אלה M S] זה ספר G (Αυτη η βιβλος); harmonization with
　　5:1

4　יהוה אלהים M S] אלהים G (ο θεος); (mult) prps harmonization with
　　divine name of 1:1–2:4a; frequent but not consistent in G, see below 4:1

　　את השמים ואת הארץ M] שמים וארץ S Tg^N Syr Vg; ארץ ושמים G (τον
　　ουρανον και την γην); harmonization with השמים והארץ v 4

9　אלהים M S G (ο θεος)] + עוד G (ετι); explicating plus, cf 1:11–12, sim
　　2:19

שֶׁרֶץ נֶפֶשׁ חַיָּה וְעוֹף יְעוֹפֵף עַל־הָאָרֶץ עַל־פְּנֵי רְקִיעַ הַשָּׁמָיִם: 21 וַיִּבְרָא
אֱלֹהִים אֶת־הַתַּנִּינִם הַגְּדֹלִים וְאֵת כָּל־נֶפֶשׁ הַחַיָּה הָרֹמֶשֶׂת אֲשֶׁר שָׁרְצוּ הַמַּיִם
לְמִינֵהֶם וְאֵת כָּל־עוֹף כָּנָף לְמִינֵהוּ וַיַּרְא אֱלֹהִים כִּי־טוֹב: 22 וַיְבָרֶךְ אֹתָם
אֱלֹהִים לֵאמֹר פְּרוּ וּרְבוּ וּמִלְאוּ אֶת־הַמַּיִם בַּיַּמִּים וְהָעוֹף יִרֶב בָּאָרֶץ:
23 וַיְהִי־עֶרֶב וַיְהִי־בֹקֶר יוֹם חֲמִישִׁי: ‪ ‬‪□□[פ]□□‬ 24 וַיֹּאמֶר אֱלֹהִים
תּוֹצֵא הָאָרֶץ נֶפֶשׁ חַיָּה לְמִינָהּ בְּהֵמָה וָרֶמֶשׂ וְחַיְתוֹ־אֶרֶץ לְמִינָהּ וַיְהִי־כֵן:
25 וַיַּעַשׂ אֱלֹהִים אֶת־חַיַּת הָאָרֶץ לְמִינָהּ וְאֶת־הַבְּהֵמָה לְמִינָהּ וְאֵת כָּל־רֶמֶשׂ
הָאֲדָמָה לְמִינֵהוּ וַיַּרְא אֱלֹהִים כִּי־טוֹב: 26 וַיֹּאמֶר אֱלֹהִים נַעֲשֶׂה אָדָם
בְּצַלְמֵנוּ כִּדְמוּתֵנוּ וְיִרְדּוּ בִדְגַת הַיָּם וּבְעוֹף הַשָּׁמַיִם וּבַבְּהֵמָה וּבְכָל־הָאָרֶץ
הָרֹמֵשׂ עַל־הָאָרֶץ: 27 וַיִּבְרָא אֱלֹהִים אֶת־הָאָדָם בְּצַלְמוֹ בְּצֶלֶם אֱלֹהִים בָּרָא
אֹתוֹ זָכָר וּנְקֵבָה בָּרָא אֹתָם: 28 וַיְבָרֶךְ אֹתָם אֱלֹהִים וַיֹּאמֶר לָהֶם אֱלֹהִים פְּרוּ
וּרְבוּ וּמִלְאוּ אֶת־הָאָרֶץ וְכִבְשֻׁהָ וּרְדוּ בִּדְגַת הַיָּם וּבְעוֹף הַשָּׁמַיִם וּבְכָל־חַיָּה
הָרֹמֶשֶׂת עַל־הָאָרֶץ: 29 וַיֹּאמֶר אֱלֹהִים הִנֵּה נָתַתִּי לָכֶם אֶת־כָּל־עֵשֶׂב זֹרֵעַ זֶרַע
אֲשֶׁר עַל־פְּנֵי כָל־הָאָרֶץ וְאֶת־כָּל־הָעֵץ אֲשֶׁר־בּוֹ פְרִי־עֵץ זֹרֵעַ זָרַע לָכֶם יִהְיֶה
לְאָכְלָה: 30 וּלְכָל־חַיַּת הָאָרֶץ וּלְכָל־עוֹף הַשָּׁמַיִם וּלְכֹל רוֹמֵשׂ עַל־הָאָרֶץ
אֲשֶׁר־בּוֹ נֶפֶשׁ חַיָּה אֶת־כָּל־יֶרֶק עֵשֶׂב לְאָכְלָה וַיְהִי־כֵן: 31 וַיַּרְא אֱלֹהִים
אֶת־כָּל־אֲשֶׁר עָשָׂה וְהִנֵּה־טוֹב מְאֹד וַיְהִי־עֶרֶב וַיְהִי־בֹקֶר יוֹם הַשִּׁשִּׁי:
‪□□[פ]□□‬

2 1 וַיְכֻלּוּ הַשָּׁמַיִם וְהָאָרֶץ וְכָל־צְבָאָם: 2 וַיְכַל אֱלֹהִים בַּיּוֹם הַשְּׁבִיעִי
מְלַאכְתּוֹ אֲשֶׁר עָשָׂה וַיִּשְׁבֹּת בַּיּוֹם הַשְּׁבִיעִי מִכָּל־מְלַאכְתּוֹ אֲשֶׁר עָשָׂה:
3 וַיְבָרֶךְ אֱלֹהִים אֶת־יוֹם הַשְּׁבִיעִי וַיְקַדֵּשׁ אֹתוֹ כִּי בוֹ שָׁבַת מִכָּל־מְלַאכְתּוֹ
אֲשֶׁר־בָּרָא אֱלֹהִים לַעֲשׂוֹת: ‪ ‬‪□□[פ]□□‬ 4 אֵלֶּה תוֹלְדוֹת הַשָּׁמַיִם
וְהָאָרֶץ בְּהִבָּרְאָם בְּיוֹם עֲשׂוֹת יְהֹוָה אֱלֹהִים אֶרֶץ וְשָׁמָיִם: 5 וְכֹל שִׂיחַ הַשָּׂדֶה
טֶרֶם יִהְיֶה בָאָרֶץ וְכָל־עֵשֶׂב הַשָּׂדֶה טֶרֶם יִצְמָח כִּי לֹא הִמְטִיר יְהֹוָה אֱלֹהִים
עַל־הָאָרֶץ וְאָדָם אַיִן לַעֲבֹד אֶת־הָאֲדָמָה: 6 וְאֵד יַעֲלֶה מִן־הָאָרֶץ וְהִשְׁקָה
אֶת־כָּל־פְּנֵי־הָאֲדָמָה: 7 וַיִּיצֶר יְהֹוָה אֱלֹהִים אֶת־הָאָדָם עָפָר מִן־הָאֲדָמָה וַיִּפַּח
בְּאַפָּיו נִשְׁמַת חַיִּים וַיְהִי הָאָדָם לְנֶפֶשׁ חַיָּה: 8 וַיִּטַּע יְהֹוָה אֱלֹהִים גַּן־בְּעֵדֶן
מִקֶּדֶם וַיָּשֶׂם שָׁם אֶת־הָאָדָם אֲשֶׁר יָצָר: 9 וַיַּצְמַח יְהֹוָה אֱלֹהִים מִן־הָאֲדָמָה

‪V ‖‬ הַגְּדֹלִים ‪C3 L] ג‬ ‪V ‖‬ 21 עוֹף ‪C3 L] עֹף‬ ‪V ‖‬ 25 הַבְּהֵמָה ‪C3 L] ב‬ ‪V ‖‬ 21
28 ורדו ‪C3 L] ד‬ ‪V ‖‬ 2 3 כִּי ‪C3 L] כ‬ ‪V ‖‬ 4 יְהֹוָה ‪C3 (not consistently‬
‪thereafter) V S (from 9:26)] ו L ‖‬ 6 פְנֵי־ ‪L] פֵּנִי־‬ ‪V‬

2 11 חוילה S^{mss} G (Ευιλατ)] החוילה M S; prps dittography with graphic confusion (ה/ח)

12 ההיא M^Q S Tg^P Syr] ההוא M^K Tg^O; (mult; Gen 2:12; 3:12; 3:20; 4:22; 10:11; 10:12, etc.) graphic confusion (ו/י), frequent in Pentateuch: *qĕrê perpetuum*

טוב M S G (καλον)] + מאד S; exegetical plus

14 ושם M S] om G; haplography by homoioteleuton (שהם– ∩ שם–) reminiscence of ושם הנהר v 13

חדקל 4QGen^b M] הדקל S; weakening of guttural

15 האדם 4QGen^b M S G (τον ανθρωπον)] + אשר יצר G (ον επλασεν); harmonizing plus with האדם אשר יצר v 8

ה– (2×: לעבדה ולשמרה)] ה– (2×) M; older orthography of final ה for -ô, vocalized in M as -â, cf below 4:7, 9:21

17 תאכל 4QGen^{b#} M S] תאכלו G (φαγεσθε); harmonization with תאכלו 3:3

תמות 4QGen^b M S] תמותו G (αποθανεισθε); harmonization of number, see previous entry

18 אעשה 4QGen^{bh} M S] נעשה G (ποιησωμεν) Vg Jub 3:4; harmonization with נעשה 1:26

19 אלהים 4QGen^b M S G (ο θεος)] + עוד S G (ετι); explicating plus, cf 1:24-25, sim 2:9

20 ולכל עוף G (και πασιν τοις πετεινοις) Tg^J Syr Vg] ולעוף M S; haplography by homoioteleuton (ל– ∩ ל–)

23 מאיש M] מאישה S G (εκ του ανδρος αυτης) Tg^O Jub 3:6; prps explicating plus, or harmonization with לאישה 3:6

לקחה M S G (ελημφθη)] + זאת M S (om G Syr); explicating plus

24 והיו M G (εσονται)] + שניהם G (οι δυο) Tg^P Syr Vg sim S (והיה משניהם); harmonizing plus with ויהיו שניהם v 25

3 1 ויאמר 4QGen^{k#} M S G (και ειπεν)] + הנחש G (ο οφις) Syr; explicating plus

אף M S] האף 4QGen^k; linguistic modernization or dittography (ה–ה–)

2 מפרי M S G (απο καρπου)] + כל G^{mss} (παντος) Syr; harmonizing plus, cf מכל עץ v 1

3 העץ M S G (του ξυλου)] + הזה S; explicating plus

6 ונחמד M S G (και ωραιον)] + העץ M S (om G Vg); explicating or harmonizing plus with העץ v 6

ויאכל M] ויאכלו S G (εφαγον); explicating or harmonizing plus with תאכלו vv 1, 3 (cf 2:17, G), or dittography (ו–ו–)

כָּל־עֵץ נֶחְמָד לְמַרְאֶה וְטוֹב לְמַאֲכָל וְעֵץ הַחַיִּים בְּתוֹךְ הַגָּן וְעֵץ הַדַּעַת טוֹב
וָרָע: 10 וְנָהָר יֹצֵא מֵעֵדֶן לְהַשְׁקוֹת אֶת־הַגָּן וּמִשָּׁם יִפָּרֵד וְהָיָה לְאַרְבָּעָה
רָאשִׁים: 11 שֵׁם הָאֶחָד פִּישׁוֹן הוּא הַסֹּבֵב אֵת כָּל־אֶרֶץ הַחֲוִילָה אֲשֶׁר־שָׁם
הַזָּהָב: 12 וּזֲהַב הָאָרֶץ הַהִיא טוֹב שָׁם הַבְּדֹלַח וְאֶבֶן הַשֹּׁהַם: 13 וְשֵׁם־הַנָּהָר
הַשֵּׁנִי גִּיחוֹן הוּא הַסּוֹבֵב אֵת כָּל־אֶרֶץ כּוּשׁ: 14 וְשֵׁם הַנָּהָר הַשְּׁלִישִׁי חִדֶּקֶל
הוּא הַהֹלֵךְ קִדְמַת אַשּׁוּר וְהַנָּהָר הָרְבִיעִי הוּא פְרָת: 15 וַיִּקַּח יְהוָה אֱלֹהִים
אֶת־הָאָדָם וַיַּנִּחֵהוּ בְגַן־עֵדֶן לְעָבְדָהּ וּלְשָׁמְרָהּ: 16 וַיְצַו יְהוָה אֱלֹהִים
עַל־הָאָדָם לֵאמֹר מִכֹּל עֵץ־הַגָּן אָכֹל תֹּאכֵל: 17 וּמֵעֵץ הַדַּעַת טוֹב וָרָע לֹא
תֹאכַל מִמֶּנּוּ כִּי בְּיוֹם אֲכָלְךָ מִמֶּנּוּ מוֹת תָּמוּת: 18 וַיֹּאמֶר יְהוָה אֱלֹהִים
לֹא־טוֹב הֱיוֹת הָאָדָם לְבַדּוֹ אֶעֱשֶׂה־לּוֹ עֵזֶר כְּנֶגְדּוֹ: 19 וַיִּצֶר יְהוָה אֱלֹהִים
מִן־הָאֲדָמָה כָּל־חַיַּת הַשָּׂדֶה וְאֵת כָּל־עוֹף הַשָּׁמַיִם וַיָּבֵא אֶל־הָאָדָם לִרְאוֹת
מַה־יִּקְרָא־לוֹ וְכֹל אֲשֶׁר יִקְרָא־לוֹ הָאָדָם נֶפֶשׁ חַיָּה הוּא שְׁמוֹ: 20 וַיִּקְרָא
הָאָדָם שֵׁמוֹת לְכָל־הַבְּהֵמָה וּלְעוֹף הַשָּׁמַיִם וּלְכֹל חַיַּת הַשָּׂדֶה וּלְאָדָם
לֹא־מָצָא עֵזֶר כְּנֶגְדּוֹ: 21 וַיַּפֵּל יְהוָה אֱלֹהִים תַּרְדֵּמָה עַל־הָאָדָם וַיִּישָׁן וַיִּקַּח
אַחַת מִצַּלְעֹתָיו וַיִּסְגֹּר בָּשָׂר תַּחְתֶּנָּה: 22 וַיִּבֶן יְהוָה אֱלֹהִים אֶת־הַצֵּלָע
אֲשֶׁר־לָקַח מִן־הָאָדָם לְאִשָּׁה וַיְבִאֶהָ אֶל־הָאָדָם: 23 וַיֹּאמֶר הָאָדָם זֹאת הַפַּעַם
עֶצֶם מֵעֲצָמַי וּבָשָׂר מִבְּשָׂרִי לְזֹאת יִקָּרֵא אִשָּׁה כִּי מֵאִישׁ לֻקֳחָה: 24 עַל־כֵּן
יַעֲזָב־אִישׁ אֶת־אָבִיו וְאֶת־אִמּוֹ וְדָבַק בְּאִשְׁתּוֹ וְהָיוּ לְבָשָׂר אֶחָד: 25 וַיִּהְיוּ
שְׁנֵיהֶם עֲרוּמִּים הָאָדָם וְאִשְׁתּוֹ וְלֹא יִתְבֹּשָׁשׁוּ:

3 1 וְהַנָּחָשׁ הָיָה עָרוּם מִכֹּל חַיַּת הַשָּׂדֶה אֲשֶׁר עָשָׂה יְהוָה אֱלֹהִים
וַיֹּאמֶר אֶל־הָאִשָּׁה אַף כִּי־אָמַר אֱלֹהִים לֹא תֹאכְלוּ מִכֹּל עֵץ הַגָּן: 2 וַתֹּאמֶר
הָאִשָּׁה אֶל־הַנָּחָשׁ מִפְּרִי עֵץ־הַגָּן נֹאכֵל: 3 וּמִפְּרִי הָעֵץ אֲשֶׁר בְּתוֹךְ־הַגָּן אָמַר
אֱלֹהִים לֹא תֹאכְלוּ מִמֶּנּוּ וְלֹא תִגְּעוּ בּוֹ פֶּן־תְּמֻתוּן: 4 וַיֹּאמֶר הַנָּחָשׁ
אֶל־הָאִשָּׁה לֹא־מוֹת תְּמֻתוּן: 5 כִּי יֹדֵעַ אֱלֹהִים כִּי בְּיוֹם אֲכָלְכֶם מִמֶּנּוּ וְנִפְקְחוּ
עֵינֵיכֶם וִהְיִיתֶם כֵּאלֹהִים יֹדְעֵי טוֹב וָרָע: 6 וַתֵּרֶא הָאִשָּׁה כִּי טוֹב הָעֵץ
לְמַאֲכָל וְכִי תַאֲוָה־הוּא לָעֵינַיִם וְנֶחְמָד הָעֵץ לְהַשְׂכִּיל וַתִּקַּח מִפִּרְיוֹ וַתֹּאכַל וַתִּתֵּן
גַּם־לְאִישָׁהּ עִמָּהּ וַיֹּאכַל: 7 וַתִּפָּקַחְנָה עֵינֵי שְׁנֵיהֶם וַיֵּדְעוּ כִּי עֵירֻמִּם הֵם
וַיִּתְפְּרוּ עֲלֵה תְאֵנָה וַיַּעֲשׂוּ לָהֶם חֲגֹרֹת: 8 וַיִּשְׁמְעוּ אֶת־קוֹל יְהוָה אֱלֹהִים

14 הָרְבִיעִי C3 V ר] L V || 18 אעשה C3 V] ה L || 18 כנגדו C3 L] ד V ||
23 לקחה C3] קֳ L V || 5 ידע C3 L V] בתוך bN || בתוך C3 L V bA] 3 3 ||
V יודע || 5 אכלכם C3 L] כֶ V

3 9   לוֹ M S G (αυτω)] + אדם G (Αδαμ) Syr; explicating plus

10   ויאמר M S G (και ειπεν)] + לוֹ G (αυτω); explicating plus

שמעתי M S G (ηκουσα)] + מתהלך G (περιπατουντος); harmonizing plus
with מתהלך בגן v 8

11   ויאמר M S G (και ειπεν)] + לוֹ G (αυτω); + לוֹ יהוה Syr; explicating
plus

עירם M] ערום 1QGen ([ער]וֹם) S; linguistic modernization, sim vv 7, 10
(S)

15   ישופך M S] ישכך G (τηρησει); graphic confusion (פ/כ), see next entry

תשופנו M S] תשוכנו G (τηρησεις); graphic confusion (פ/כ), see previous
entry

16   והרנך M S (והריונך]] והגיונך G (και στεναγμον σου) Jub 3:24; exegetical
revision, or prps graphic confusion (ר/ג)?

בעצב M] בעצבון S; harmonization with עצבונך v 16

תשוקתך M S] תשובתך G (η αποστροφη σου) TgON Syr Jub 3:24; exegetical revision, or prps graphic confusion (ק/ב)?, sim 4:7

17   לבלתי אכל M S] לאמר לא תאכל G (τουτου μονου μη φαγειν); harmonization with לבלתי אכל v 11, note emphatic translation in both instances

בעבודך M S] בעבודך G (εν τοις εργοις σου) Vg; graphic confusion
(ד/ר), cf below 8:21

19   לחם M S] לחמך G (τον αρτον σου); explicating plus

עפר 2° M G (γην)] עפרך S; explicating plus, or prps dittography with
graphic confusion (ר/ך)

22   ולקח M S G (και λαβη)] + גם M S (om G Syrmss); explicating plus, cf
ותקח מפריו 3:6

24   וישכן M S G (και κατωκισεν)] + אתו G (αυτον); explicating or exegetical
plus, see next entry

עדן M S G (τρυφης)] + וישם G (και εταξεν); explicating or exegetical
plus, note the variant distribution of objects with verbs

4 1   יהוה M S] אלהים G (θεου); (mult) frequent in G, see above 2:4

מִתְהַלֵּךְ בַּגָּן לְר֣וּחַ הַיּ֑וֹם וַיִּתְחַבֵּ֨א הָֽאָדָ֜ם וְאִשְׁתּ֗וֹ מִפְּנֵי֙ יְהוָ֣ה אֱלֹהִ֔ים בְּת֖וֹךְ עֵ֥ץ
הַגָּֽן: 9 וַיִּקְרָ֛א יְהוָ֥ה אֱלֹהִ֖ים אֶל־הָֽאָדָ֑ם וַיֹּ֥אמֶר ל֖וֹ אַיֶּֽכָּה: 10 וַיֹּ֕אמֶר אֶת־קֹלְךָ֥
שָׁמַ֖עְתִּי בַּגָּ֑ן וָאִירָ֛א כִּֽי־עֵירֹ֥ם אָנֹ֖כִי וָאֵחָבֵֽא: 11 וַיֹּ֕אמֶר מִ֚י הִגִּ֣יד לְךָ֔ כִּ֥י עֵירֹ֖ם
אָ֑תָּה הֲמִן־הָעֵ֗ץ אֲשֶׁ֧ר צִוִּיתִ֛יךָ לְבִלְתִּ֥י אֲכָל־מִמֶּ֖נּוּ אָכָֽלְתָּ: 12 וַיֹּ֖אמֶר הָֽאָדָ֑ם
הָֽאִשָּׁה֙ אֲשֶׁ֣ר נָתַ֣תָּה עִמָּדִ֔י הִ֛וא נָֽתְנָה־לִּ֥י מִן־הָעֵ֖ץ וָאֹכֵֽל: 13 וַיֹּ֨אמֶר יְהוָ֧ה
אֱלֹהִ֛ים לָאִשָּׁ֖ה מַה־זֹּ֣את עָשִׂ֑ית וַתֹּ֙אמֶר֙ הָֽאִשָּׁ֔ה הַנָּחָ֥שׁ הִשִּׁיאַ֖נִי וָאֹכֵֽל:
14 וַיֹּאמֶר֩ יְהוָ֨ה אֱלֹהִ֥ים ׀ אֶֽל־הַנָּחָשׁ֮ כִּ֣י עָשִׂ֣יתָ זֹּאת֒ אָר֤וּר אַתָּה֙ מִכָּל־הַבְּהֵמָ֔ה
וּמִכֹּ֖ל חַיַּ֣ת הַשָּׂדֶ֑ה עַל־גְּחֹנְךָ֣ תֵלֵ֔ךְ וְעָפָ֥ר תֹּאכַ֖ל כָּל־יְמֵ֥י חַיֶּֽיךָ: 15 וְאֵיבָ֣ה ׀
אָשִׁ֗ית בֵּֽינְךָ֙ וּבֵ֣ין הָֽאִשָּׁ֔ה וּבֵ֥ין זַרְעֲךָ֖ וּבֵ֣ין זַרְעָ֑הּ ה֚וּא יְשׁוּפְךָ֣ רֹ֔אשׁ וְאַתָּ֖ה
תְּשׁוּפֶ֥נּוּ עָקֵֽב: ☐☐[ס]☐☐ 16 אֶֽל־הָאִשָּׁ֣ה אָמַ֗ר הַרְבָּ֤ה אַרְבֶּה֙ עִצְּבוֹנֵ֣ךְ
וְהֵֽרֹנֵ֔ךְ בְּעֶ֖צֶב תֵּֽלְדִ֣י בָנִ֑ים וְאֶל־אִישֵׁךְ֙ תְּשׁ֣וּקָתֵ֔ךְ וְה֖וּא יִמְשָׁל־בָּֽךְ:
☐☐[ס]☐☐ 17 וּלְאָדָ֣ם אָמַ֗ר כִּֽי־שָׁמַעְתָּ֮ לְק֣וֹל אִשְׁתֶּךָ֒ וַתֹּ֙אכַל֙ מִן־הָעֵ֔ץ אֲשֶׁ֤ר
צִוִּיתִ֙יךָ֙ לֵאמֹ֔ר לֹ֥א תֹאכַ֖ל מִמֶּ֑נּוּ אֲרוּרָ֤ה הָֽאֲדָמָה֙ בַּֽעֲבוּרֶ֔ךָ בְּעִצָּבוֹן֙ תֹּֽאכֲלֶ֔נָּה כֹּ֖ל
יְמֵ֥י חַיֶּֽיךָ: 18 וְק֥וֹץ וְדַרְדַּ֖ר תַּצְמִ֣יחַֽ לָ֑ךְ וְאָכַלְתָּ֖ אֶת־עֵ֥שֶׂב הַשָּׂדֶֽה: 19 בְּזֵעַ֤ת
אַפֶּ֙יךָ֙ תֹּ֣אכַל לֶ֔חֶם עַ֤ד שֽׁוּבְךָ֙ אֶל־הָ֣אֲדָמָ֔ה כִּ֥י מִמֶּ֖נָּה לֻקָּ֑חְתָּ כִּֽי־עָפָ֣ר אַ֔תָּה
וְאֶל־עָפָ֖ר תָּשֽׁוּב: 20 וַיִּקְרָ֧א הָֽאָדָ֛ם שֵׁ֥ם אִשְׁתּ֖וֹ חַוָּ֑ה כִּ֛י הִ֥וא הָֽיְתָ֖ה אֵ֥ם כָּל־חָֽי:
21 וַיַּעַשׂ֩ יְהוָ֨ה אֱלֹהִ֜ים לְאָדָ֧ם וּלְאִשְׁתּ֛וֹ כָּתְנ֥וֹת ע֖וֹר וַיַּלְבִּשֵֽׁם: ☐☐[פ]☐☐
22 וַיֹּ֣אמֶר ׀ יְהוָ֣ה אֱלֹהִ֗ים הֵ֤ן הָֽאָדָם֙ הָיָה֙ כְּאַחַ֣ד מִמֶּ֔נּוּ לָדַ֖עַת ט֣וֹב וָרָ֑ע וְעַתָּ֣ה ׀
פֶּן־יִשְׁלַ֣ח יָד֗וֹ וְלָקַח֙ גַּ֚ם מֵעֵ֣ץ הַֽחַיִּ֔ים וְאָכַ֖ל וָחַ֥י לְעֹלָֽם: 23 וַֽיְשַׁלְּחֵ֛הוּ יְהוָ֥ה אֱלֹהִ֖ים
מִגַּן־עֵ֑דֶן לַֽעֲבֹד֙ אֶת־הָ֣אֲדָמָ֔ה אֲשֶׁ֥ר לֻקַּ֖ח מִשָּֽׁם: 24 וַיְגָ֖רֶשׁ אֶת־הָֽאָדָ֑ם וַיַּשְׁכֵּ֡ן
מִקֶּ֩דֶם֩ לְגַן־עֵ֨דֶן אֶת־הַכְּרֻבִ֜ים וְאֵ֣ת לַ֤הַט הַחֶ֙רֶב֙ הַמִּתְהַפֶּ֔כֶת לִשְׁמֹ֕ר אֶת־דֶּ֖רֶךְ עֵ֥ץ
הַֽחַיִּֽים: ☐☐[ס]☐☐

4 וְהָ֣אָדָ֔ם יָדַ֖ע אֶת־חַוָּ֣ה אִשְׁתּ֑וֹ וַתַּ֙הַר֙ וַתֵּ֣לֶד אֶת־קַ֔יִן וַתֹּ֕אמֶר קָנִ֥יתִי
אִ֖ישׁ אֶת־יְהוָֽה: 2 וַתֹּ֣סֶף לָלֶ֔דֶת אֶת־אָחִ֖יו אֶת־הָ֑בֶל וַֽיְהִי־הֶ֙בֶל֙ רֹ֣עֵה צֹ֔אן וְקַ֕יִן
הָיָ֖ה עֹבֵ֥ד אֲדָמָֽה: 3 וַֽיְהִ֖י מִקֵּ֣ץ יָמִ֑ים וַיָּבֵ֨א קַ֜יִן מִפְּרִ֧י הָֽאֲדָמָ֛ה מִנְחָ֖ה לַֽיהוָֽה:
4 וְהֶ֨בֶל הֵבִ֥יא גַם־ה֛וּא מִבְּכֹר֥וֹת צֹאנ֖וֹ וּמֵֽחֶלְבֵהֶ֑ן וַיִּ֣שַׁע יְהוָ֔ה אֶל־הֶ֖בֶל
וְאֶל־מִנְחָתֽוֹ: 5 וְאֶל־קַ֥יִן וְאֶל־מִנְחָת֖וֹ לֹ֣א שָׁעָ֑ה וַיִּ֤חַר לְקַ֙יִן֙ מְאֹ֔ד וַֽיִּפְּל֖וּ פָּנָֽיו:
6 וַיֹּ֥אמֶר יְהוָ֖ה אֶל־קָ֑יִן לָ֚מָּה חָ֣רָה לָ֔ךְ וְלָ֖מָּה נָֽפְל֥וּ פָנֶֽיךָ: 7 הֲל֤וֹא אִם־תֵּיטִיב֙

4 7   לנתח] M S לפתח? G (διελης); prps graphic confusion (פ/נ)?

רבץ] 4QGen^{b#} M S G (ησυχασον); simple haplography (תת) תרבץ*

(תשוקתו) 4QGen^b (only בו) M S; תשוקתה, בה :×2)] תֹ- (בו :×2) -הָ,*
orthographic modernization: older orthography for final -â (also for final
-ô) revised to newer orthography for final -ô

תשוקתו 4QGen^{b#} M S] תשובתו G (η αποστροφη σου) Tg^O Syr; exegetical
revision, or prps graphic confusion (ק/ב)?, sim 3:16

8   נלכה השדה S G (Διελθωμεν εις το πεδιον) Tg^P Syr Vg] om 4QGen^b M;
parablepsis, prps by anticipation of similar sequence in following clause:
. . . קין אל הבל אחיו ויה

10   ויאמר 4QGen^{b#} M S G (και ειπεν)] + אלהים G (ο θεος); + לו יהוה Syr;
explicating plus

דמי M] דם S G (αιματος) Tg^{ON} Syr Jub 4:3; linguistic modernization or
revision, see next two entries

צעקים 4QGen^{b#} M] צעק S G (βοα) Syr; linguistic revision, see previous
entry

11   דמי M] דם S G (αιμα) Tg^{ON} Syr; linguistic revision, see v 10

15   לכן M S] לא כן G (Ουχ ουτως) Syr Vg; linguistic or exegetical revision

16   נוד M S (נד)] ניד G? (Ναιδ); prps graphic confusion (י/ו)

18   עירד 1-2° M S] עידר G (Γαιδαδ); עידר Syr; graphic confusion (ד/ר), cf
ירד 5:18-20

מחייאל 1° cf M (מחייאל 2°) S (מחיאל) G (Μαιηλ) and vocalic pattern of
Vg (Maviahel)] מחויאל M; graphic confusion (י/ו), prps by anticipation
of vocalic pattern of מתושאל v 18

מתושאל 1-2° M S] מתושלח G (Μαθουσαλα); harmonization with
מתושלח 5:21-27

20   אהלי מקנה M S] אהל ומקנה G? (εν σκηναις κτηνοτροφων); prps word
misdivision with graphic confusion (י/ו), cf אהלי מקנה 2 Chron 14:14

22   <אבי כל>] om M S G; parablepsis, cf Tg^O (הוא הוה רבהון דכל) and Tg^J
(רב לכל)

תובל קין 2° M S] תובל 2° G (θοβελ) LAB 2:9; corruption of name, cf
תובל קין 1° rendered in G as θοβελ και ην

25   אדם M S G (Αδαμ)] + עוד M S (om G); explicating plus with v 1, see
next two entries

שְׂאֵת וְאִם לֹא תֵיטִיב לַפֶּתַח חַטָּאת רֹבֵץ וְאֵלֶיךָ תְּשׁוּקָתוֹ וְאַתָּה תִּמְשָׁל־בּוֹ: 8 וַיֹּאמֶר קַיִן אֶל־הֶבֶל אָחִיו נֵלְכָה הַשָּׂדֶה וַיְהִי בִּהְיוֹתָם בַּשָּׂדֶה וַיָּקָם קַיִן אֶל־הֶבֶל אָחִיו וַיַּהַרְגֵהוּ: 9 וַיֹּאמֶר יְהוָֹה אֶל־קַיִן אֵי הֶבֶל אָחִיךָ וַיֹּאמֶר לֹא יָדַעְתִּי הֲשֹׁמֵר אָחִי אָנֹכִי: 10 וַיֹּאמֶר מֶה עָשִׂיתָ קוֹל דְּמֵי אָחִיךָ צֹעֲקִים אֵלַי מִן־הָאֲדָמָה: 11 וְעַתָּה אָרוּר אָתָּה מִן־הָאֲדָמָה אֲשֶׁר פָּצְתָה אֶת־פִּיהָ לָקַחַת אֶת־דְּמֵי אָחִיךָ מִיָּדֶךָ: 12 כִּי תַעֲבֹד אֶת־הָאֲדָמָה לֹא־תֹסֵף תֵּת־כֹּחָהּ לָךְ נָע וָנָד תִּהְיֶה בָאָרֶץ: 13 וַיֹּאמֶר קַיִן אֶל־יְהוָֹה גָּדוֹל עֲוֹנִי מִנְּשֹׂא: 14 הֵן גֵּרַשְׁתָּ אֹתִי הַיּוֹם מֵעַל פְּנֵי הָאֲדָמָה וּמִפָּנֶיךָ אֶסָּתֵר וְהָיִיתִי נָע וָנָד בָּאָרֶץ וְהָיָה כָל־מֹצְאִי יַהַרְגֵנִי: 15 וַיֹּאמֶר לוֹ יְהוָֹה לָכֵן כָּל־הֹרֵג קַיִן שִׁבְעָתַיִם יֻקָּם וַיָּשֶׂם יְהוָֹה לְקַיִן אוֹת לְבִלְתִּי הַכּוֹת־אֹתוֹ כָּל־מֹצְאוֹ: 16 וַיֵּצֵא קַיִן מִלִּפְנֵי יְהוָֹה וַיֵּשֶׁב בְּאֶרֶץ־נוֹד קִדְמַת־עֵדֶן: 17 וַיֵּדַע קַיִן אֶת־אִשְׁתּוֹ וַתַּהַר וַתֵּלֶד אֶת־חֲנוֹךְ וַיְהִי בֹּנֶה עִיר וַיִּקְרָא שֵׁם הָעִיר כְּשֵׁם בְּנוֹ חֲנוֹךְ: 18 וַיִּוָּלֵד לַחֲנוֹךְ אֶת־עִירָד וְעִירָד יָלַד אֶת־מְחוּיָאֵל וּמְחִיָּיאֵל יָלַד אֶת־מְתוּשָׁאֵל וּמְתוּשָׁאֵל יָלַד אֶת־לָמֶךְ: 19 וַיִּקַּח־לוֹ לֶמֶךְ שְׁתֵּי נָשִׁים שֵׁם הָאַחַת עָדָה וְשֵׁם הַשֵּׁנִית צִלָּה: 20 וַתֵּלֶד עָדָה אֶת־יָבָל הוּא הָיָה אֲבִי יֹשֵׁב אֹהֶל וּמִקְנֶה: 21 וְשֵׁם אָחִיו יוּבָל הוּא הָיָה אֲבִי כָּל־תֹּפֵשׂ כִּנּוֹר וְעוּגָב: 22 וְצִלָּה גַם־הִיא יָלְדָה אֶת־תּוּבַל קַיִן ‹אֲבִי כָל־› לֹטֵשׁ כָּל־חֹרֵשׁ נְחֹשֶׁת וּבַרְזֶל וַאֲחוֹת תּוּבַל־קַיִן נַעֲמָה: 23 וַיֹּאמֶר לֶמֶךְ לְנָשָׁיו עָדָה וְצִלָּה שְׁמַעַן קוֹלִי נְשֵׁי לֶמֶךְ הַאְזֵנָּה אִמְרָתִי כִּי אִישׁ הָרַגְתִּי לְפִצְעִי וְיֶלֶד לְחַבֻּרָתִי: 24 כִּי שִׁבְעָתַיִם יֻקַּם־קָיִן וְלֶמֶךְ שִׁבְעִים וְשִׁבְעָה: 25 וַיֵּדַע אָדָם

4 25 את 1° M S] + חוה G (Ευαν) Syr; harmonizing plus with את חוה אשתו v
1

אשתו M S G (την γυναικα αυτου)] + ותהר G (και συλλαβουσα) Syr;
harmonizing plus with אשתו ותהר ותלד v 1

ותקרא M] ויקרא S 11QJub 1.2 (= Jub 4:7); harmonization with ויקרא את
שמו v 26

שת 1° M S G (Σηθ)] + לאמר G (λεγουσα) Vg sim Tg^ON(mg)J; harmonizing plus with לאמר 5:29

26 ולשת M S G (και τω Σηθ)] + גם הוא M S (om G); harmonizing plus, cf
גם הוא ילדה v 22 and ילד גם הוא 10:21

זה G (ουτος) Tg^P Syr Vg 11QJub^M 3.2 (= Jub 4:12)] אז M S; parablepsis, prps with simple haplography (-ה ה-)

החל S Syr cf 11QJub^M 3.2 ([ריאש]ון) (= Jub 4:12)] הוחל M G (ηλπισεν,
from √יחל); parablepsis, cf construction: (inf. cst.) לHCHL 6:1; 10:8

5 3 130 M S] 230 G; revision of chronology

*בן] om M S G; haplography by homoioarkton (ב- ∩ -ב)

4 800 M S] 700 G; revision of chronology

6 105 M S] 205 G; revision of chronology

7 807 M S] 707 G; revision of chronology

9 90 M S] 190 G; revision of chronology

10 815 M S] 715 G; revision of chronology

12 70 M S] 170 G; revision of chronology

13 840 M S] 740 G; revision of chronology

15 65 M S] 165 G; revision of chronology

16 830 M S] 730 G; revision of chronology

18 62 S] 162 M G; revision of chronology

19 *900] 800 M G; 785 S; revision of chronology

20 962 M G] 847 S; revision of chronology

21 65 M S] 165 G; revision of chronology

22 300 M S] 200 G; revision of chronology

23 ויהיו S G (και εγενοντο)] ויהי M; simple haplography with graphic confusion (ו/י), cf below v 31

25 67 S] 187 M; 167 G; revision of chronology

אֶת־אִשְׁתּוֹ וַתֵּלֶד בֵּן וַתִּקְרָא אֶת־שְׁמוֹ שֵׁת כִּי שָׁת־לִי אֱלֹהִים זֶרַע אַחֵר תַּחַת
הֶבֶל כִּי הֲרָגוֹ קָיִן: 26 וּלְשֵׁת גַּם־הוּא יֻלַּד בֵּן וַיִּקְרָא אֶת־שְׁמוֹ אֱנוֹשׁ אָז הוּחַל לִקְרֹא
בְּשֵׁם יְהֹוָה: □□[פ]□□

5 1 זֶה סֵפֶר תּוֹלְדֹת אָדָם בְּיוֹם בְּרֹא אֱלֹהִים אָדָם בִּדְמוּת אֱלֹהִים עָשָׂה
אֹתוֹ: 2 זָכָר וּנְקֵבָה בְּרָאָם וַיְבָרֶךְ אֹתָם וַיִּקְרָא אֶת־שְׁמָם אָדָם בְּיוֹם הִבָּרְאָם:
3 וַיְחִי אָדָם שְׁלֹשִׁים וּמְאַת שָׁנָה וַיּוֹלֶד בִּדְמוּתוֹ כְּצַלְמוֹ וַיִּקְרָא אֶת־שְׁמוֹ
שֵׁת: 4 וַיִּהְיוּ יְמֵי־אָדָם אַחֲרֵי הוֹלִידוֹ אֶת־שֵׁת שְׁמֹנֶה מֵאֹת שָׁנָה וַיּוֹלֶד בָּנִים
וּבָנוֹת: 5 וַיִּהְיוּ כָּל־יְמֵי אָדָם אֲשֶׁר־חַי תְּשַׁע מֵאוֹת שָׁנָה וּשְׁלֹשִׁים שָׁנָה וַיָּמֹת:
□□[ס]□□ 6 וַיְחִי־שֵׁת חָמֵשׁ שָׁנִים וּמְאַת שָׁנָה וַיּוֹלֶד אֶת־אֱנוֹשׁ:
7 וַיְחִי־שֵׁת אַחֲרֵי הוֹלִידוֹ אֶת־אֱנוֹשׁ שֶׁבַע שָׁנִים וּשְׁמֹנֶה מֵאוֹת שָׁנָה וַיּוֹלֶד
בָּנִים וּבָנוֹת: 8 וַיִּהְיוּ כָּל־יְמֵי־שֵׁת שְׁתֵּים עֶשְׂרֵה שָׁנָה וּתְשַׁע מֵאוֹת שָׁנָה
וַיָּמֹת: □□[ס]□□ 9 וַיְחִי אֱנוֹשׁ תִּשְׁעִים שָׁנָה וַיּוֹלֶד אֶת־קֵינָן: 10 וַיְחִי
אֱנוֹשׁ אַחֲרֵי הוֹלִידוֹ אֶת־קֵינָן חֲמֵשׁ עֶשְׂרֵה שָׁנָה וּשְׁמֹנֶה מֵאוֹת שָׁנָה וַיּוֹלֶד
בָּנִים וּבָנוֹת: 11 וַיִּהְיוּ כָּל־יְמֵי אֱנוֹשׁ חָמֵשׁ שָׁנִים וּתְשַׁע מֵאוֹת שָׁנָה וַיָּמֹת:
□□[פ]□□ 12 וַיְחִי קֵינָן שִׁבְעִים שָׁנָה וַיּוֹלֶד אֶת־מַהֲלַלְאֵל: 13 וַיְחִי קֵינָן
אַחֲרֵי הוֹלִידוֹ אֶת־מַהֲלַלְאֵל אַרְבָּעִים שָׁנָה וּשְׁמֹנֶה מֵאוֹת שָׁנָה וַיּוֹלֶד בָּנִים
וּבָנוֹת: 14 וַיִּהְיוּ כָּל־יְמֵי קֵינָן עֶשֶׂר שָׁנִים וּתְשַׁע מֵאוֹת שָׁנָה וַיָּמֹת:
□□[ס]□□ 15 וַיְחִי מַהֲלַלְאֵל חָמֵשׁ שָׁנִים וְשִׁשִּׁים שָׁנָה וַיּוֹלֶד אֶת־יָרֶד:
16 וַיְחִי מַהֲלַלְאֵל אַחֲרֵי הוֹלִידוֹ אֶת־יֶרֶד שְׁלֹשִׁים שָׁנָה וּשְׁמֹנֶה מֵאוֹת שָׁנָה
וַיּוֹלֶד בָּנִים וּבָנוֹת: 17 וַיִּהְיוּ כָּל־יְמֵי מַהֲלַלְאֵל חָמֵשׁ וְתִשְׁעִים שָׁנָה וּשְׁמֹנֶה
מֵאוֹת שָׁנָה וַיָּמֹת: □□[ס]□□ 18 וַיְחִי־יֶרֶד שְׁתַּיִם וְשִׁשִּׁים שָׁנָה וּמְאַת שָׁנָה וַיּוֹלֶד
אֶת־חֲנוֹךְ: 19 וַיְחִי־יֶרֶד אַחֲרֵי הוֹלִידוֹ אֶת־חֲנוֹךְ שְׁמֹנֶה מֵאוֹת שָׁנָה וַיּוֹלֶד בָּנִים
וּבָנוֹת: 20 וַיִּהְיוּ כָּל־יְמֵי־יֶרֶד שְׁתַּיִם וְשִׁשִּׁים שָׁנָה וּתְשַׁע מֵאוֹת שָׁנָה וַיָּמֹת:
□□[ס]□□ 21 וַיְחִי חֲנוֹךְ חָמֵשׁ וְשִׁשִּׁים שָׁנָה וַיּוֹלֶד אֶת־מְתוּשָׁלַח:
22 וַיִּתְהַלֵּךְ חֲנוֹךְ אֶת־הָאֱלֹהִים אַחֲרֵי הוֹלִידוֹ אֶת־מְתוּשֶׁלַח שְׁלֹשׁ מֵאוֹת שָׁנָה
וַיּוֹלֶד בָּנִים וּבָנוֹת: 23 וַיְהִי כָּל־יְמֵי חֲנוֹךְ חָמֵשׁ וְשִׁשִּׁים שָׁנָה וּשְׁלֹשׁ מֵאוֹת
שָׁנָה: 24 וַיִּתְהַלֵּךְ חֲנוֹךְ אֶת־הָאֱלֹהִים וְאֵינֶנּוּ כִּי־לָקַח אֹתוֹ אֱלֹהִים:
□□[פ]□□ 25 וַיְחִי מְתוּשֶׁלַח שֶׁבַע וּשְׁמֹנִים שָׁנָה וַיּוֹלֶד אֶת־לָמֶךְ: 26 וַיְחִי

5 4 מאת C3 L V] מאות C3ᵖᵐ ‖ 18 ויחי C3 L V] הֵ A (Ofer 1989: 316) ‖
25 ושמנים C3 L] ושמונים V

5 26   *902] 782 M; 653 S; 802 G; revision of chronology

27   מתושלח M S G (Μαθουσαλα)] + אשר חי G (ας εζησεν); harmonizing plus with אשר חי v 5

         969 M G] 720 S; revision of chronology

28   *88] 182 M; 53 S; 188 G; revision of chronology, with scribal errors in M and S; M: *188 → 182 by reminiscence of שתים ושמונים שנה v 26; S: *88 → 53 by anticipation of שלש וחמשים שנה v 31

29   ינחמנו M S] ינ(י)חנו G (διαναπαυσει) LAB 1:20; simple haplography with graphic confusion (מ/נ), or exegetical revision (note √נחם and √עצב in 5:28 and 6:6)

30   *665] 595 M; 600 S; 565 G; revision of chronology, with M affected by scribal errors in vv 28, 31

31   ויהיו S G (εγενοντο)] ויהי M; simple haplography with graphic confusion (י/ו), cf above v 23

         753 G] 777 M; 653 S; revision of chronology, with scribal error in M; M: *753 → 777 by reminiscence of שבעים ושבעה in 4:24 (Song of Lamech)

32   נח M S G (Νωε)] + שלשה בנים G (τρεις υιους) LAB 1:22; harmonizing plus with נח שלשה בנים 6:10

6 1   פני M S] om G Vg; parablepsis

3   ידון M S] ידור 4QCommGenª G (καταμεινη) Tg⁰ Syr Vg Jub 5:8; linguistic modernization, or prps graphic confusion (ר/ן)

         אדם M S G (ανθρωποις)] + הזה G (τουτοις) sim Tg⁰; explicating plus

4   וילדו M] ויולידו S; linguistic modernization (Qal → Hiphil, frequent in S)

7   עד 2° M S] ‑ומ G (και απο) Vg; linguistic modernization, cf unmodernized 7:23 (G)

14   עשה M S G (ποιησεν)] + לכן? G (ουν); explicating plus, or dittography with parablepsis (לכן לך)

15   אתה M S] את התבה G (την κιβωτον); harmonization with תעשה את התבה v 14

16   ופתח M S G (την δε θυραν)] + התבה M S (om G); explicating plus

מְתוּשֶׁלַח אַחֲרֵי הוֹלִידוֹ אֶת־לֶמֶךְ שְׁתַּיִם שְׁנִים וּתְשַׁע מֵאוֹת שָׁנָה וַיּוֹלֶד בָּנִים

וּבָנוֹת: 27 וַיִּהְיוּ כָּל־יְמֵי מְתוּשֶׁלַח תֵּשַׁע וְשִׁשִּׁים שָׁנָה וּתְשַׁע מֵאוֹת שָׁנָה

וַיָּמֹת: □□[ס]□□ 28 וַיְחִי־לֶמֶךְ שְׁמֹנֶה וּשְׁמֹנִים שָׁנָה וַיּוֹלֶד בֵּן:

29 וַיִּקְרָא אֶת־שְׁמוֹ נֹחַ לֵאמֹר זֶה יְנַחֲמֵנוּ מִמַּעֲשֵׂנוּ וּמֵעִצְּבוֹן יָדֵינוּ מִן־הָאֲדָמָה

אֲשֶׁר אֵרְרָהּ יְהֹוָה: □□[ס]□□ 30 וַיְחִי־לֶמֶךְ אַחֲרֵי הוֹלִידוֹ אֶת־נֹחַ

חָמֵשׁ וְשִׁשִּׁים שָׁנָה וַחֲמֵשׁ מֵאֹת שָׁנָה וַיּוֹלֶד בָּנִים וּבָנוֹת: 31 וַיִּהְיוּ

כָּל־יְמֵי־לֶמֶךְ שֶׁבַע וְשִׁבְעִים שָׁנָה וּשְׁבַע מֵאוֹת שָׁנָה וַיָּמֹת: □□[ס]□□

32 וַיְהִי־נֹחַ בֶּן־חֲמֵשׁ מֵאוֹת שָׁנָה וַיּוֹלֶד נֹחַ אֶת־שֵׁם אֶת־חָם וְאֶת־יָפֶת:

6 1 וַיְהִי כִּי־הֵחֵל הָאָדָם לָרֹב עַל־פְּנֵי הָאֲדָמָה וּבָנוֹת יֻלְּדוּ לָהֶם:

2 וַיִּרְאוּ בְנֵי־הָאֱלֹהִים אֶת־בְּנוֹת הָאָדָם כִּי טֹבֹת הֵנָּה וַיִּקְחוּ לָהֶם נָשִׁים מִכֹּל

אֲשֶׁר בָּחָרוּ: 3 וַיֹּאמֶר יְהֹוָה לֹא־יָדוֹן רוּחִי בָאָדָם לְעֹלָם בְּשַׁגַּם הוּא בָשָׂר

וְהָיוּ יָמָיו מֵאָה וְעֶשְׂרִים שָׁנָה: 4 הַנְּפִלִים הָיוּ בָאָרֶץ בַּיָּמִים הָהֵם וְגַם

אַחֲרֵי־כֵן אֲשֶׁר יָבֹאוּ בְּנֵי הָאֱלֹהִים אֶל־בְּנוֹת הָאָדָם וְיָלְדוּ לָהֶם הֵמָּה הַגִּבֹּרִים

אֲשֶׁר מֵעוֹלָם אַנְשֵׁי הַשֵּׁם: □□[ס]□□ 5 וַיַּרְא יְהֹוָה כִּי רַבָּה רָעַת

הָאָדָם בָּאָרֶץ וְכָל־יֵצֶר מַחְשְׁבֹת לִבּוֹ רַק רַע כָּל־הַיּוֹם: 6 וַיִּנָּחֶם יְהֹוָה

כִּי־עָשָׂה אֶת־הָאָדָם בָּאָרֶץ וַיִּתְעַצֵּב אֶל־לִבּוֹ: 7 וַיֹּאמֶר יְהֹוָה אֶמְחֶה

אֶת־הָאָדָם אֲשֶׁר־בָּרָאתִי מֵעַל פְּנֵי הָאֲדָמָה מֵאָדָם עַד־בְּהֵמָה עַד־רֶמֶשׂ

וְעַד־עוֹף הַשָּׁמָיִם כִּי נִחַמְתִּי כִּי עֲשִׂיתִם: 8 וְנֹחַ מָצָא חֵן בְּעֵינֵי יְהֹוָה:

□□[פ]□□ 9 אֵלֶּה תּוֹלְדֹת נֹחַ נֹחַ אִישׁ צַדִּיק תָּמִים הָיָה בְּדֹרֹתָיו

אֶת־הָאֱלֹהִים הִתְהַלֶּךְ־נֹחַ: 10 וַיּוֹלֶד נֹחַ שְׁלֹשָׁה בָנִים אֶת־שֵׁם אֶת־חָם

וְאֶת־יָפֶת: 11 וַתִּשָּׁחֵת הָאָרֶץ לִפְנֵי הָאֱלֹהִים וַתִּמָּלֵא הָאָרֶץ חָמָס: 12 וַיַּרְא

אֱלֹהִים אֶת־הָאָרֶץ וְהִנֵּה נִשְׁחָתָה כִּי־הִשְׁחִית כָּל־בָּשָׂר אֶת־דַּרְכּוֹ עַל־הָאָרֶץ:

□□[ס]□□ 13 וַיֹּאמֶר אֱלֹהִים לְנֹחַ קֵץ כָּל־בָּשָׂר בָּא לְפָנַי כִּי־מָלְאָה הָאָרֶץ

חָמָס מִפְּנֵיהֶם וְהִנְנִי מַשְׁחִיתָם אֶת־הָאָרֶץ: 14 עֲשֵׂה לְךָ תֵּבַת עֲצֵי־גֹפֶר קִנִּים

תַּעֲשֶׂה אֶת־הַתֵּבָה וְכָפַרְתָּ אֹתָהּ מִבַּיִת וּמִחוּץ בַּכֹּפֶר: 15 וְזֶה אֲשֶׁר תַּעֲשֶׂה

אֹתָהּ שְׁלֹשׁ מֵאוֹת אַמָּה אֹרֶךְ הַתֵּבָה חֲמִשִּׁים אַמָּה רָחְבָּהּ וּשְׁלֹשִׁים אַמָּה

קוֹמָתָהּ: 16 צֹהַר תַּעֲשֶׂה לַתֵּבָה וְאֶל־אַמָּה תְּכַלֶּנָּה מִלְמַעְלָה וּפֶתַח בְּצִדָּהּ

תָּשִׂים תַּחְתִּיִּם שְׁנִיִּם וּשְׁלִשִׁים תַּעֲשֶׂהָ: 17 וַאֲנִי הִנְנִי מֵבִיא אֶת־הַמַּבּוּל מַיִם

---

26 וּשְׁמוֹנִים C3 L] צ V || 29 וּמֵעִצָּבוֹן C3 L] צ V || 29 וּשְׁמֹנִים C3pm V C3 L] אֵרְרָה
C3 L V] רֶ V || 63 בְּשַׁגַּם C3 L] גַ V || 4 הָהֵם C3 L] הֶ V || 16 תְּכַלֶּנָּה
L] לֶ C3 V

6 17   לשחת M] להשחית S; linguistic modernization (Piel → Hiphil)

19   init] + ומכל הבהמה ומכל הרמש G (και απο παντων των κτηνων και απο παντων των ερπετων); harmonizing plus with ובבהמה ובכל הרמש 8:17 (exit from ark)

שנים M S G (δυο)] + שנים G (δυο) Syr; harmonizing plus with שנים שנים 7:9, 15; cf below 6:20, 7:2

יהיו M G (εσονται)] והיה S; parablepsis with graphic confusion (ו/י)

20   מהעוף M] מן העוף S; מכל העוף G (απο παντων των ορνεων των πετεινων); S: linguistic modernization; G: harmonizing plus (with double translation) with 1:21 כל עוף כנף למינהו 7:14, cf וכל העוף למינהו; G: harmonizing

ומן M S] ומכל G (και απο παντων); harmonizing plus with ומכל הבהמה v 19 (G)

ומכל S G (και απο παντων) TgO(mss)P Syr Vg] מכל M; parablepsis, prps anticipation of מכל 2°

רמש M] אשר רמש על S; הרמש הרמש על G (των ερπετων των ερποντων επι); S: harmonizing plus with אשר רמש על האדמה 7:8; G: harmonizing plus with הרמש הרמש על הארץ 8:17

למינהו 2° M] למיניהם 6QpaleoGen (ל[מי]ניהם) S G? (κατα γενος αυτων); linguistic revision, see previous entry, cf construction of 1:21

שנים 6QpaleoGen M S G (δυο)] + שנים G (δυο) Syr; harmonizing plus, see above v 19

להחיות M S G (τρεφεσθαι)] + אתך זכר ונקבה G (μετα σου αρσεν και θηλυ); harmonizing plus with v 19 להחית אתך זכר ונקבה

7 1   יהוה M] אלהים S Syr; יהוה אלהים G (κυριος ο θεος); infrequent in S, cf below v 9 (S), and above 4:1 (G)

2   מכל M S] מן G (απο) Syr; harmonization with ומן הבהמה v 2

2   איש ואשתו 1-2° M] זכר ונקבה 1-2° S G (αρσεν και θηλυ) TgOP Syr Vg; harmonization with זכר ונקבה vv 3, 9, 6:19, 6:20 (G)

2   לא טהרה M S G (μη καθαρων)] + היא M (הוא) S (om G); explicating plus

שנים M S G (δυο)] + שנים S G (δυο) Syr Vg; harmonizing plus, cf 6:19

3   השמים M S G (του ουρανου)] + הטהור S G (των καθαρων) Syrmss LAB 3:4; harmonizing plus with הבהמה הטהורה v 2, and העוף הטהר 8:20

G ומעוף אשר לא טהור שנים שנים זכר ונקבה M S G (και θηλυ)] + ונקבה (και απο των πετεινων των μη καθαρων δυο δυο αρσεν και θηλυ); harmonizing plus with ומן הבהמה אשר לא טהרה היא שנים איש ואשתו v 2

על M S G (επι)] + פני M S (om G, sim TgJ); harmonizing plus with על פני כל הארץ 8:9

עַל־הָאָרֶץ לְשַׁחֵת כָּל־בָּשָׂר אֲשֶׁר־בּוֹ רוּחַ חַיִּים מִתַּחַת הַשָּׁמָיִם כֹּל
אֲשֶׁר־בָּאָרֶץ יִגְוָע: 18 וַהֲקִמֹתִי אֶת־בְּרִיתִי אִתָּךְ וּבָאתָ אֶל־הַתֵּבָה אַתָּה וּבָנֶיךָ
וְאִשְׁתְּךָ וּנְשֵׁי־בָנֶיךָ אִתָּךְ: 19 וּמִכָּל־הָחַי מִכָּל־בָּשָׂר שְׁנַיִם מִכֹּל תָּבִיא
אֶל־הַתֵּבָה לְהַחֲיֹת אִתָּךְ זָכָר וּנְקֵבָה יִהְיוּ: 20 מֵהָעוֹף לְמִינֵהוּ וּמִן־הַבְּהֵמָה
לְמִינָהּ וּמִכֹּל רֶמֶשׂ הָאֲדָמָה לְמִינֵהוּ שְׁנַיִם מִכֹּל יָבֹאוּ אֵלֶיךָ לְהַחֲיוֹת:
21 וְאַתָּה קַח־לְךָ מִכָּל־מַאֲכָל אֲשֶׁר יֵאָכֵל וְאָסַפְתָּ אֵלֶיךָ וְהָיָה לְךָ וְלָהֶם
לְאָכְלָה: 22 וַיַּעַשׂ נֹחַ כְּכֹל אֲשֶׁר צִוָּה אֹתוֹ אֱלֹהִים כֵּן עָשָׂה: □□[פ]□□
7 1 וַיֹּאמֶר יְהוָה לְנֹחַ בֹּא־אַתָּה וְכָל־בֵּיתְךָ אֶל־הַתֵּבָה כִּי־אֹתְךָ רָאִיתִי
צַדִּיק לְפָנַי בַּדּוֹר הַזֶּה: 2 מִכֹּל הַבְּהֵמָה הַטְּהוֹרָה תִּקַּח־לְךָ שִׁבְעָה שִׁבְעָה
אִישׁ וְאִשְׁתּוֹ וּמִן־הַבְּהֵמָה אֲשֶׁר לֹא טְהֹרָה הִוא שְׁנַיִם אִישׁ וְאִשְׁתּוֹ: 3 גַּם מֵעוֹף
הַשָּׁמַיִם שִׁבְעָה שִׁבְעָה זָכָר וּנְקֵבָה לְחַיּוֹת זֶרַע עַל־פְּנֵי כָל־הָאָרֶץ: 4 כִּי לְיָמִים
עוֹד שִׁבְעָה אָנֹכִי מַמְטִיר עַל־הָאָרֶץ אַרְבָּעִים יוֹם וְאַרְבָּעִים לָיְלָה וּמָחִיתִי
אֶת־כָּל־הַיְקוּם אֲשֶׁר עָשִׂיתִי מֵעַל פְּנֵי הָאֲדָמָה: 5 וַיַּעַשׂ נֹחַ כְּכֹל אֲשֶׁר־צִוָּהוּ

19 להחית [C3 L V להחיות C3ᵖᵐ ‖ 20 להחית [C3 L V להחיות C3ᵖᵐ ‖
7 2 הטהורה [C3 L V הטהרה C3ᵖᵐ

7 6   היה M S G (εγενετο; ην G^A)] + מים M S G (υδατος) (om G^A); harmonizing plus with המבול מים על הארץ 6:17

8   init] + ומן העוף G (και απο των πετεινον); harmonization with sequence of 6:20, see next entry

ומן העוף M S] om G; transposed to init v 8

9   אלהים M G (θεος)] יהוה S; cf above v 1

את נח M S] אתו G (αυτω); harmonization with צוה אתו אלהים 6:22, cf v 16

11   עשר יום M S Jub 5:23] עשרים G (εικαδι); word misdivision with simple haplography and graphic confusion (ו/י), sim 8:4, 14

רבה M S 4QCommGen^a] om G; prps harmonization with 8:2

13   אתם M S] אתו G (μετ´ αυτου) Tg^N(mg)J Syr; harmonization with אתו אל התבה v 7

14   init] + המה M S (הם) (om G); explicating plus

fin] + כל צפור כל כנף M S (om G); explicating plus, cf כל צפור כל כנף Ezek 17:23

16   זכר ונקבה M S G (αρσεν και θηλυ)] + זכר ונקבה S; dittography, or prps harmonizing plus with שנים שנים v 15

16   אתו M S] את נח G (τω Νωε) (after אלהים); harmonizing or explicating plus, cf את נח v 9

fin] + את התבה G (την κιβωτον) sim Tg^J, cf Tg^N; explicating plus

17   יום M S G (ημερας)] + וארבעים לילה G (και τεσσαρακοντα νυκτας); harmonizing plus with וארבעים לילה v 12

20   גבהו G (υψωθη)] גברו M S; reminiscence of המים גברו v 19, cf ויגברו המים vv 18, 24, or prps graphic confusion (ר/ה)?

ויכסו M S G (και επεκαλυψεν)] + כל G (παντα); harmonizing plus with ויכסו כל v 19

ההרים M S G (τα ορη)] + הגבהים G (τα υψηλα) Syr^mss Jub 5:26; harmonizing plus with ההרים הגבהים v 19

22   נשמת M S G (πνοην)] + רוח M S (om G Vg); harmonizing plus with רוח חיים v 15, 6:17

23   פני M S G (προσωπου)] + כל G (πασης); harmonizing plus with פני כל v 3

24   ויגברו M S 4QCommGen^a] ויגבהו G (και υψωθη); reminiscence or harmonization with גבהו v 20, and/or prps graphic confusion (ה/ר)

8 1   הבהמה M S G (των κτηνων)] + וכל העוף וכל הרמש G (και παντων των πετεινων και παντων των ερπετων); ואת כל העוף Syr; harmonizing pluses with וכל העוף וכל הרמש v 19 (exit from ark), cf above 6:19 (G)

יְהֹוָה: ⁶ וְנֹחַ בֶּן־שֵׁשׁ מֵאוֹת שָׁנָה וְהַמַּבּוּל הָיָה עַל־הָאָרֶץ: ⁷ וַיָּבֹא נֹחַ וּבָנָיו
וְאִשְׁתּוֹ וּנְשֵׁי־בָנָיו אִתּוֹ אֶל־הַתֵּבָה מִפְּנֵי מֵי הַמַּבּוּל: ⁸ מִן־הַבְּהֵמָה הַטְּהוֹרָה
וּמִן־הַבְּהֵמָה אֲשֶׁר אֵינֶנָּה טְהֹרָה וּמִן־הָעוֹף וְכֹל אֲשֶׁר־רֹמֵשׂ עַל־הָאֲדָמָה:
⁹ שְׁנַיִם שְׁנַיִם בָּאוּ אֶל־נֹחַ אֶל־הַתֵּבָה זָכָר וּנְקֵבָה כַּאֲשֶׁר צִוָּה אֱלֹהִים אֶת־נֹחַ:
¹⁰ וַיְהִי לְשִׁבְעַת הַיָּמִים וּמֵי הַמַּבּוּל הָיוּ עַל־הָאָרֶץ: ¹¹ בִּשְׁנַת שֵׁשׁ־מֵאוֹת שָׁנָה
לְחַיֵּי־נֹחַ בַּחֹדֶשׁ הַשֵּׁנִי בְּשִׁבְעָה־עָשָׂר יוֹם לַחֹדֶשׁ בַּיּוֹם הַזֶּה נִבְקְעוּ כָּל־מַעְיְנֹת
תְּהוֹם רַבָּה וַאֲרֻבֹּת הַשָּׁמַיִם נִפְתָּחוּ: ¹² וַיְהִי הַגֶּשֶׁם עַל־הָאָרֶץ אַרְבָּעִים יוֹם
וְאַרְבָּעִים לָיְלָה: ¹³ בְּעֶצֶם הַיּוֹם הַזֶּה בָּא נֹחַ וְשֵׁם־וְחָם וָיֶפֶת בְּנֵי־נֹחַ וְאֵשֶׁת
נֹחַ וּשְׁלֹשֶׁת נְשֵׁי־בָנָיו אִתָּם אֶל־הַתֵּבָה: ¹⁴ וְכָל־הַחַיָּה לְמִינָהּ וְכָל־הַבְּהֵמָה
לְמִינָהּ וְכָל־הָרֶמֶשׂ הָרֹמֵשׂ עַל־הָאָרֶץ לְמִינֵהוּ וְכָל־הָעוֹף לְמִינֵהוּ: ¹⁵ וַיָּבֹאוּ
אֶל־נֹחַ אֶל־הַתֵּבָה שְׁנַיִם שְׁנַיִם מִכָּל־הַבָּשָׂר אֲשֶׁר־בּוֹ רוּחַ חַיִּים: ¹⁶ וְהַבָּאִים
זָכָר וּנְקֵבָה מִכָּל־בָּשָׂר בָּאוּ כַּאֲשֶׁר צִוָּה אֹתוֹ אֱלֹהִים וַיִּסְגֹּר יְהֹוָה בַּעֲדוֹ:
¹⁷ וַיְהִי הַמַּבּוּל אַרְבָּעִים יוֹם עַל־הָאָרֶץ וַיִּרְבּוּ הַמַּיִם וַיִּשְׂאוּ אֶת־הַתֵּבָה וַתָּרָם
מֵעַל הָאָרֶץ: ¹⁸ וַיִּגְבְּרוּ הַמַּיִם וַיִּרְבּוּ מְאֹד עַל־הָאָרֶץ וַתֵּלֶךְ הַתֵּבָה עַל־פְּנֵי
הַמָּיִם: ¹⁹ וְהַמַּיִם גָּבְרוּ מְאֹד מְאֹד עַל־הָאָרֶץ וַיְכֻסּוּ כָּל־הֶהָרִים הַגְּבֹהִים
אֲשֶׁר־תַּחַת כָּל־הַשָּׁמָיִם: ²⁰ חֲמֵשׁ עֶשְׂרֵה אַמָּה מִלְמַעְלָה גָּבְרוּ הַמָּיִם וַיְכֻסּוּ
הֶהָרִים: ²¹ וַיִּגְוַע כָּל־בָּשָׂר הָרֹמֵשׂ עַל־הָאָרֶץ בָּעוֹף וּבַבְּהֵמָה וּבַחַיָּה
וּבְכָל־הַשֶּׁרֶץ הַשֹּׁרֵץ עַל־הָאָרֶץ וְכֹל הָאָדָם: ²² כֹּל אֲשֶׁר נִשְׁמַת־חַיִּים בְּאַפָּיו
מִכֹּל אֲשֶׁר בֶּחָרָבָה מֵתוּ: ²³ וַיִּמַח אֶת־כָּל־הַיְקוּם אֲשֶׁר עַל־פְּנֵי הָאֲדָמָה
מֵאָדָם עַד־בְּהֵמָה עַד־רֶמֶשׂ וְעַד־עוֹף הַשָּׁמַיִם וַיִּמָּחוּ מִן־הָאָרֶץ וַיִּשָּׁאֶר אַךְ־נֹחַ
וַאֲשֶׁר אִתּוֹ בַּתֵּבָה: ²⁴ וַיִּגְבְּרוּ הַמַּיִם עַל־הָאָרֶץ חֲמִשִּׁים וּמְאַת יוֹם:
8 ¹ וַיִּזְכֹּר אֱלֹהִים אֶת־נֹחַ וְאֵת כָּל־הַחַיָּה וְאֶת־כָּל־הַבְּהֵמָה אֲשֶׁר אִתּוֹ
בַּתֵּבָה וַיַּעֲבֵר אֱלֹהִים רוּחַ עַל־הָאָרֶץ וַיָּשֹׁכּוּ הַמָּיִם: ² וַיִּסָּכְרוּ מַעְיְנֹת תְּהוֹם

6 שש C3 L] שֵׁשׁ־ V ‖ 8 הטהורה C3pm הַטְּהוֹרָה C3 L V] הַטְּהֹרָה C3pm ‖ 11 מעינת C3
L V] מַעְיְנוֹת C3pm ‖ 23 וישאר C3 V] ◌ֵ L ‖ 23 ◌ַ V] מ◌ַ C3 L] וימח

8 2   ויכל M] ויכלא S; linguistic modernization or revision

3   הלוך ושוב M G (πορευομενον . . . ενεδιδου)] הלכו ושבו S; linguistic modernization (inf. abs. → perfect, frequent in S), sim vv 5, 7

     מקצה M] מקץ S G (μετα); harmonization with מקץ v 6, or simple haplography with graphic confusion (ה/ח),

4   עשר יום M S sim 4QCommGen^a (עשר)] עשרים G (εικαδι) Vg; word misdivision with simple haplography and graphic confusion (ו/י), sim 7:11, 8:14

     אררט M G (Αραραατ)] הררט S 4QCommGen^a (הוררט); weakening of guttural, prps with assimilation to הרי

5   הלוך וחסור M G (πορευομενον ηλαττονουτο) 4QCommGen^a] הלכו וחסרו S; linguistic modernization, cf vv 3, 7

     בעשירי M S G] + באחד G (εν δε τω ενδεκατω); dittography (באחד/באחד)

7   הערב M S G (τον κορακα)] + לראות הקלו המים G (του ιδειν ει κεκοπακεν το υδωρ); harmonizing plus with לראות הקלו המים v 8

7   יצוא ושוב M] יצא ושב S; linguistic modernization, cf vv 3, 5

9   על M S G (επι)] + כל G (παντι); anticipation of כל v 9

10   וייחל G (και επισχων)] ויחל M S (also v 12) 4QCommGen^a; simple haplography (יי), cf וייחל v 12

12   אחרים M S G (ετερας)] + ויסף G (παλιν); harmonizing plus with אחרים ויסף v 10

13   שנה M S G (ετει)] + לחיי נח 4QCommGen^a G (εν τη ζωη του Νωε); harmonizing plus with לחיי נח 7:11

     התבה M S G (της κιβωτου)] + אשר עשה G (ην εποιησεν); harmonizing plus with התבה אשר עשה v 6

     חרבו 2° M S G (εξελιπεν)] + המים מעל G (το υδωρ απο); harmonizing plus with חרבו המים מעל v 13

14   עשר יום 4QCommGen^a Jub 5:31] ועשרים יום M S; ועשרים G (εικαδι); G: word misdivision with simple haplography and graphic confusion (ו/י); M S: same, with prior dittography (יום יום) or secondary correction of יום, cf 7:11, 8:4

15   וידבר M S] ויאמר G (και ειπεν); harmonization with ויאמר אלהים 9:8

וַאֲרֻבֹּת הַשָּׁמַיִם וַיִּכָּלֵא הַגֶּשֶׁם מִן־הַשָּׁמָיִם: 3 וַיָּשֻׁבוּ הַמַּיִם מֵעַל הָאָרֶץ הָלוֹךְ וָשׁוֹב וַיַּחְסְרוּ הַמַּיִם מִקְצֵה חֲמִשִּׁים וּמְאַת יוֹם: 4 וַתָּנַח הַתֵּבָה בַּחֹדֶשׁ הַשְּׁבִיעִי בְּשִׁבְעָה־עָשָׂר יוֹם לַחֹדֶשׁ עַל הָרֵי אֲרָרָט: 5 וְהַמַּיִם הָיוּ הָלוֹךְ וְחָסוֹר עַד הַחֹדֶשׁ הָעֲשִׂירִי בָּעֲשִׂירִי בְּאֶחָד לַחֹדֶשׁ נִרְאוּ רָאשֵׁי הֶהָרִים: 6 וַיְהִי מִקֵּץ אַרְבָּעִים יוֹם וַיִּפְתַּח נֹחַ אֶת־חַלּוֹן הַתֵּבָה אֲשֶׁר עָשָׂה: 7 וַיְשַׁלַּח אֶת־הָעֹרֵב וַיֵּצֵא יָצוֹא וָשׁוֹב עַד־יְבֹשֶׁת הַמַּיִם מֵעַל הָאָרֶץ: 8 וַיְשַׁלַּח אֶת־הַיּוֹנָה מֵאִתּוֹ לִרְאוֹת הֲקַלּוּ הַמַּיִם מֵעַל פְּנֵי הָאֲדָמָה: 9 וְלֹא־מָצְאָה הַיּוֹנָה מָנוֹחַ לְכַף־רַגְלָהּ וַתָּשָׁב אֵלָיו אֶל־הַתֵּבָה כִּי־מַיִם עַל־פְּנֵי כָל־הָאָרֶץ וַיִּשְׁלַח יָדוֹ וַיִּקָּחֶהָ וַיָּבֵא אֹתָהּ אֵלָיו אֶל־הַתֵּבָה: 10 וַיָּחֶל עוֹד שִׁבְעַת יָמִים אֲחֵרִים וַיֹּסֶף שַׁלַּח אֶת־הַיּוֹנָה מִן־הַתֵּבָה: 11 וַתָּבֹא אֵלָיו הַיּוֹנָה לְעֵת עֶרֶב וְהִנֵּה עֲלֵה־זַיִת טָרָף בְּפִיהָ וַיֵּדַע נֹחַ כִּי־קַלּוּ הַמַּיִם מֵעַל הָאָרֶץ: 12 וַיִּיָּחֶל עוֹד שִׁבְעַת יָמִים אֲחֵרִים וַיְשַׁלַּח אֶת־הַיּוֹנָה וְלֹא־יָסְפָה שׁוּב־אֵלָיו עוֹד: 13 וַיְהִי בְּאַחַת וְשֵׁשׁ־מֵאוֹת שָׁנָה בָּרִאשׁוֹן בְּאֶחָד לַחֹדֶשׁ חָרְבוּ הַמַּיִם מֵעַל הָאָרֶץ וַיָּסַר נֹחַ אֶת־מִכְסֵה הַתֵּבָה וַיַּרְא וְהִנֵּה חָרְבוּ פְּנֵי הָאֲדָמָה: 14 וּבַחֹדֶשׁ הַשֵּׁנִי בְּשִׁבְעָה וְעֶשְׂרִים יוֹם לַחֹדֶשׁ יָבְשָׁה הָאָרֶץ: ▯▯[פ]▯▯ 15 וַיְדַבֵּר אֱלֹהִים אֶל־נֹחַ לֵאמֹר: 16 צֵא מִן־הַתֵּבָה אַתָּה וְאִשְׁתְּךָ וּבָנֶיךָ וּנְשֵׁי־בָנֶיךָ אִתָּךְ:

8 17 הוצא M^K] היצה M^Q; הוציה S; M^Q: graphic confusion (ו/י); S: linguistic modernization (jussive form → imperfect form, frequent in S)

אתך 2° M S G (μετα σεαυτου)] + ושרצו בארץ M S (om G); harmonizing plus with שרצו בארץ 9:7

18 ובניו ובניו ואשתו M S] ואשתו G (και η γυνη αυτου και οι υιοι αυτου) Syr; harmonization with sequence of v 16

19 החיה M S G (τα θηρια)] + וכל הבהמה G (και παντα τα κτηνη) Syr Vg cf LAB 3:4; harmonizing plus with החיה ואת כל הבהמה v 1

וכל העוף וכל הרמש ה- S G (και παν πετεινον και παν ερπετον) Syr] וכל העוף וכל הרמש כל M; om וכל העוף Vg; M: metathesis of וכל העוף and כל הרמש, with additional כל; Vg: haplography by homoioteleuton (וכל ∩ וכל)

21 עוד לקלל M] עוד לקלל עוד S G (ετι του καταρασασθαι) Syr Vg; harmonization with sequence of אסף עוד להכות v 21

בעבור M S] בעבור G (δια τα εργα); graphic confusion (ד/ר), cf 3:17

האדם M S G (του ανθρωπου)] + רק G (επιμελως); harmonizing plus with רק רע 6:5

21 כל M S G (πασαν)] + בשר G (σαρκα); harmonizing plus with כל בשר 6:17, 19

22 init] + עד M S (om G Vg); explicating plus

22 ויום M G (ημεραν)] יומם S; dittography (ממ) or explication, cf 1:5

9 1 fin] + ורדו בה G (και κατακυριευσατε αυτης); harmonizing plus, cf ורדו ב- v 7, and ורדו בה* 1:28

2 נתנו M] נתתיו S; נתתי G (δεδωκα) Tg^N; harmonization with נתתי v 3

5 init] + ואך M G (και γαρ) (om S); reminiscence of אך v 4

ואך M G (και γαρ)] om S; prps haplography by homoioarkton (את ∩ אך)

ומיד האדם M S] om G; haplography by homoioteleuton (ומיד ∩ מיד)

6 באדם M S] om G Vg; haplography by homoioteleuton (האדם ∩ באדם)

7 שרצו בארץ M S] ומלאו את הארץ G (και πληρωσατε την γην) Vg; harmonization with ומלאו את הארץ v 1 and 1:28

ורדו* cf G^mss (κατακυριευσατε)] ורבו M S G (και πληθυνεσθε); reminiscence of ורבו v 7, cf ורדו 1:28

10 הארץ M S G (της γης)] + אתכם M S (om G Vg); explicating plus

fin] + לכל חית הארץ M S (om G); explicating plus, cf ובכל חית הארץ v 10

‫17 כָּל־הַחַיָּה אֲשֶׁר־אִתְּךָ מִכָּל־בָּשָׂר בָּעוֹף וּבַבְּהֵמָה וּבְכָל־הָרֶמֶשׂ הָרֹמֵשׂ‬
‫עַל־הָאָרֶץ הוצא אִתָּךְ וּפָרוּ וְרָבוּ עַל־הָאָרֶץ: 18 וַיֵּצֵא נֹחַ וּבָנָיו וְאִשְׁתּוֹ‬
‫וּנְשֵׁי־בָנָיו אִתּוֹ: 19 כָּל־הַחַיָּה וְכָל הָעוֹף וְכֹל הרמש הרומש עַל־הָאָרֶץ‬
‫לְמִשְׁפְּחֹתֵיהֶם יָצְאוּ מִן־הַתֵּבָה: 20 וַיִּבֶן נֹחַ מִזְבֵּחַ לַיהוָה וַיִּקַּח מִכֹּל הַבְּהֵמָה‬
‫הַטְּהֹרָה וּמִכֹּל הָעוֹף הַטָּהֹר וַיַּעַל עֹלֹת בַּמִּזְבֵּחַ: 21 וַיָּרַח יְהוָה אֶת־רֵיחַ‬
‫הַנִּיחֹחַ וַיֹּאמֶר יְהוָה אֶל־לִבּוֹ לֹא־אֹסִף לְקַלֵּל עוֹד אֶת־הָאֲדָמָה בַּעֲבוּר הָאָדָם‬
‫כִּי יֵצֶר לֵב הָאָדָם רַע מִנְּעֻרָיו וְלֹא־אֹסִף עוֹד לְהַכּוֹת אֶת־כָּל־חַי כַּאֲשֶׁר‬
‫עָשִׂיתִי: 22 כָּל־יְמֵי הָאָרֶץ זֶרַע וְקָצִיר וְקֹר וָחֹם וְקַיִץ וָחֹרֶף וְיוֹם וָלַיְלָה לֹא‬
‫יִשְׁבֹּתוּ:‬

‫9 1 וַיְבָרֶךְ אֱלֹהִים אֶת־נֹחַ וְאֶת־בָּנָיו וַיֹּאמֶר לָהֶם פְּרוּ וּרְבוּ וּמִלְאוּ‬
‫אֶת־הָאָרֶץ: 2 וּמוֹרַאֲכֶם וְחִתְּכֶם יִהְיֶה עַל כָּל־חַיַּת הָאָרֶץ וְעַל כָּל־עוֹף‬
‫הַשָּׁמַיִם בְּכֹל אֲשֶׁר תִּרְמֹשׂ הָאֲדָמָה וּבְכָל־דְּגֵי הַיָּם בְּיֶדְכֶם נִתָּנוּ: 3 כָּל־רֶמֶשׂ‬
‫אֲשֶׁר הוּא־חַי לָכֶם יִהְיֶה לְאָכְלָה כְּיֶרֶק עֵשֶׂב נָתַתִּי לָכֶם אֶת־כֹּל: 4 אַךְ־בָּשָׂר‬
‫בְּנַפְשׁוֹ דָמוֹ לֹא תֹאכֵלוּ: 5 וְאַךְ אֶת־דִּמְכֶם לְנַפְשֹׁתֵיכֶם אֶדְרֹשׁ מִיַּד כָּל־חַיָּה‬
‫אֶדְרְשֶׁנּוּ וּמִיַּד הָאָדָם מִיַּד אִישׁ אָחִיו אֶדְרֹשׁ אֶת־נֶפֶשׁ הָאָדָם: 6 שֹׁפֵךְ דַּם‬
‫הָאָדָם בָּאָדָם דָּמוֹ יִשָּׁפֵךְ כִּי בְּצֶלֶם אֱלֹהִים עָשָׂה אֶת־הָאָדָם: 7 וְאַתֶּם פְּרוּ‬
‫וּרְבוּ שִׁרְצוּ בָאָרֶץ וּרְדוּ־בָהּ: ☐☐[פ]☐☐ 8 וַיֹּאמֶר אֱלֹהִים אֶל־נֹחַ‬
‫וְאֶל־בָּנָיו אִתּוֹ לֵאמֹר: 9 וַאֲנִי הִנְנִי מֵקִים אֶת־בְּרִיתִי אִתְּכֶם וְאֶת־זַרְעֲכֶם‬
‫אַחֲרֵיכֶם: 10 וְאֵת כָּל־נֶפֶשׁ הַחַיָּה אֲשֶׁר אִתְּכֶם בָּעוֹף בַּבְּהֵמָה וּבְכָל־חַיַּת‬
‫הָאָרֶץ מִכֹּל יֹצְאֵי הַתֵּבָה: 11 וַהֲקִמֹתִי אֶת־בְּרִיתִי אִתְּכֶם וְלֹא־יִכָּרֵת כָּל־בָּשָׂר‬

18 וַיֵּצֵא [L C3 V וַיֹּצֵא] L ‖ 20 הַטְּהֹרָה [C3 V הַטְּהוֹרָה] L ‖ L ‖ 20 הַטָּהֹר [C3 L הַטָּהוֹר] V
‖ 21 לֹא־ 1° [C3 L לֹא] V

9 11   מבול 2° M S G (κατακλυσμος)] + מים G (υδατος); harmonizing plus
with מבול מים 6:17, cf 7:6 (M), 9:15

לשחת M G (του καταφθειραι)] להשחית S (also v 15); + כל G (πασαν);
S: linguistic modernization (Piel → Hiphil); G: harmonizing plus with
לשחת כל v 15

12   אלהים M S G (ο θεος)] + אל נח G (προς Νωε) Syr; explicating or harmonizing plus with אלהים אל נח v 17

14   הקשת M S] קשתי G (το τοξον μου) Vg LAB 3:12; harmonization with
קשתי v 13

15   חיה M S G (ζωσης)] + אשר אתכם S Syr; harmonizing plus with חיה אשר
אתכם v 12

16   לזכר M G (του μνησθηναι)] לאזכרה S TgO Syr; linguistic revision

בין אלהים M S] ביני G (ανα μεσον εμου); harmonization with ביני v 15,
sim vv 12, 17

21   אהלה MK] אהלו MQ S; orthographic modernization

22   אביו M S G (του πατρος αυτου)] + ויצא G (και εξελθων) Vg; explicating plus

10 2   ויון M S G (και Ιωναν)] + אלישה G (και Ελισα); anticipation of יון
אלישה v 4

3   דיפת 1 Chron 1:6 cf Syr (דיפר)] ריפת M S G (Ριφαθ); graphic confusion
(ר/ד), cf Persian *dahyu-pati*

4   תרשיש M S G (θαρσις)] תרשישה 1 Chron 1:7; reminiscence of preceding word-final ה of אלישה; note reverse process (anticipation of -∅) in
S: אליש תרשיש

דדנים M; דורנים Syr; רדנים S (רודנים) G (Ροδιοι) 1 Chron 1:7 (רודנים)]
graphic confusion (ר/ד), prps (in M) with anticipation of דדן v 7

5   <אלה בני יפת>] om M S G; parablepsis, cf. vv 20, 31

7   סבתה M S] סבתא 1 Chron 1:9; assimilation to word-final א of סבא,
שבא, סבתכא v 7, see next entry

רעמה 1–2° M S] רעמא 1–2° 1 Chron 1:9; see previous entry

8   הוליד M] ילד S; linguistic modernization (Qal → Hiphil, frequent in S)

עוֹד מִמֵּי הַמַּבּוּל וְלֹא־יִהְיֶה עוֹד מַבּוּל לְשַׁחֵת הָאָרֶץ: 12 וַיֹּאמֶר אֱלֹהִים זֹאת
אוֹת־הַבְּרִית אֲשֶׁר־אֲנִי נֹתֵן בֵּינִי וּבֵינֵיכֶם וּבֵין כָּל־נֶפֶשׁ חַיָּה אֲשֶׁר אִתְּכֶם
לְדֹרֹת עוֹלָם: 13 אֶת־קַשְׁתִּי נָתַתִּי בֶּעָנָן וְהָיְתָה לְאוֹת בְּרִית בֵּינִי וּבֵין הָאָרֶץ:
14 וְהָיָה בְּעַנְנִי עָנָן עַל־הָאָרֶץ וְנִרְאֲתָה הַקֶּשֶׁת בֶּעָנָן: 15 וְזָכַרְתִּי אֶת־בְּרִיתִי
אֲשֶׁר בֵּינִי וּבֵינֵיכֶם וּבֵין כָּל־נֶפֶשׁ חַיָּה בְּכָל־בָּשָׂר וְלֹא־יִהְיֶה עוֹד הַמַּיִם
לְמַבּוּל לְשַׁחֵת כָּל־בָּשָׂר: 16 וְהָיְתָה הַקֶּשֶׁת בֶּעָנָן וּרְאִיתִיהָ לִזְכֹּר בְּרִית עוֹלָם
בֵּין אֱלֹהִים וּבֵין כָּל־נֶפֶשׁ חַיָּה בְּכָל־בָּשָׂר אֲשֶׁר עַל־הָאָרֶץ: 17 וַיֹּאמֶר אֱלֹהִים
אֶל־נֹחַ זֹאת אוֹת־הַבְּרִית אֲשֶׁר הֲקִמֹתִי בֵּינִי וּבֵין כָּל־בָּשָׂר אֲשֶׁר עַל־הָאָרֶץ:
18 וַיִּהְיוּ בְנֵי־נֹחַ הַיֹּצְאִים מִן־הַתֵּבָה שֵׁם וְחָם וָיָפֶת וְחָם הוּא [ס]□□
אֲבִי כְנָעַן: 19 שְׁלֹשָׁה אֵלֶּה בְּנֵי־נֹחַ וּמֵאֵלֶּה נָפְצָה כָל־הָאָרֶץ: 20 וַיָּחֶל נֹחַ
אִישׁ הָאֲדָמָה וַיִּטַּע כָּרֶם: 21 וַיֵּשְׁתְּ מִן־הַיַּיִן וַיִּשְׁכָּר וַיִּתְגַּל בְּתוֹךְ אָהֳלֹה:
22 וַיַּרְא חָם אֲבִי כְנַעַן אֵת עֶרְוַת אָבִיו וַיַּגֵּד לִשְׁנֵי־אֶחָיו בַּחוּץ: 23 וַיִּקַּח שֵׁם
וָיֶפֶת אֶת־הַשִּׂמְלָה וַיָּשִׂימוּ עַל־שְׁכֶם שְׁנֵיהֶם וַיֵּלְכוּ אֲחֹרַנִּית וַיְכַסּוּ אֵת עֶרְוַת
אֲבִיהֶם וּפְנֵיהֶם אֲחֹרַנִּית וְעֶרְוַת אֲבִיהֶם לֹא רָאוּ: 24 וַיִּיקֶץ נֹחַ מִיֵּינוֹ וַיֵּדַע
אֵת אֲשֶׁר־עָשָׂה לוֹ בְּנוֹ הַקָּטָן: 25 וַיֹּאמֶר אָרוּר כְּנָעַן עֶבֶד עֲבָדִים יִהְיֶה
לְאֶחָיו: 26 וַיֹּאמֶר בָּרוּךְ יְהֹוָה אֱלֹהֵי שֵׁם וִיהִי כְנַעַן עֶבֶד לָמוֹ: 27 יַפְתְּ אֱלֹהִים
לְיֶפֶת וְיִשְׁכֹּן בְּאָהֳלֵי־שֵׁם וִיהִי כְנַעַן עֶבֶד לָמוֹ: 28 וַיְחִי־נֹחַ אַחַר הַמַּבּוּל שְׁלֹשׁ
מֵאוֹת שָׁנָה וַחֲמִשִּׁים שָׁנָה: 29 וַיִּהְיוּ כָּל־יְמֵי־נֹחַ תְּשַׁע מֵאוֹת שָׁנָה וַחֲמִשִּׁים
שָׁנָה וַיָּמֹת: □□[פ]□□
10 1 וְאֵלֶּה תּוֹלְדֹת בְּנֵי־נֹחַ שֵׁם חָם וָיָפֶת וַיִּוָּלְדוּ לָהֶם בָּנִים אַחַר
הַמַּבּוּל: 2 בְּנֵי יֶפֶת גֹּמֶר וּמָגוֹג וּמָדַי וְיָוָן וְתֻבָל וּמֶשֶׁךְ וְתִירָס: 3 וּבְנֵי גֹּמֶר
אַשְׁכְּנַז וְרִיפַת וְתֹגַרְמָה: 4 וּבְנֵי יָוָן אֱלִישָׁה וְתַרְשִׁישׁ כִּתִּים וְרֹדָנִים: 5 מֵאֵלֶּה
נִפְרְדוּ אִיֵּי הַגּוֹיִם <אלה בני יפת> בְּאַרְצֹתָם אִישׁ לִלְשֹׁנוֹ לְמִשְׁפְּחֹתָם
בְּגוֹיֵהֶם: 6 וּבְנֵי חָם כּוּשׁ וּמִצְרַיִם וּפוּט וּכְנָעַן: 7 וּבְנֵי כוּשׁ סְבָא וַחֲוִילָה
וְסַבְתָּה וְרַעְמָה וְסַבְתְּכָא וּבְנֵי רַעְמָה שְׁבָא וּדְדָן: 8 וְכוּשׁ יָלַד אֶת־נִמְרֹד הוּא
הֵחֵל לִהְיוֹת גִּבֹּר בָּאָרֶץ: 9 הוּא־הָיָה גִבֹּר־צַיִד לִפְנֵי יְהֹוָה עַל־כֵּן יֵאָמַר
כְּנִמְרֹד גִּבּוֹר צַיִד לִפְנֵי יְהֹוָה: 10 וַתְּהִי רֵאשִׁית מַמְלַכְתּוֹ בָּבֶל וְאֶרֶךְ וְאַכַּד

9 12 אשר ‎°1 [אשר V ‎°1 || L C3 יִהְיֶה [יְ || L C3 נ] V ‎°1 בעננִי 14 || L C3 V בעֲנָנִי 15 || L C3 יִהְיֶה
V C3 בַּחוּץ 22 || L C3 וָ] V ן ‎° || V הקימתי [L C3 הקמתי || V ויפת [L C3 ן ו 18 || V הַקֶּמֹתִי 17 || L
ב ַ V || 23 אחרנית ‎°1-2 [L C3 נ ‎°1-2 || V עשה ‎°1-2 [L C3 V עשׂה] L || 24 עשה C3 V [עשׂה L ||
10 3 אשכנז C3 S V [כּ ַ L || 7 רעמה ‎°1-2 [C3 L; ‎°1 S] מ ַ ‎°2 S; מ ַ ‎°1-2 V

10 12 רסן M S] דסן G (Δασεμ); graphic confusion (ד/ר), cf. Akkadian *risnu*

13   לודים M S] לודיים 1 Chron 1:11 (Mᴷ); dittography, cf Mᵠ לודים

15   חת M] החת S; החתי? G (τον Χετταιον) Syr Vg; harmonization with gentilics of v 16

19   מצידן . . . לשע M G (απο Σιδωνος . . . εως Λασα)] מנהר מצרים עד הנהר
      הגדול נהר פרת ועד הים האחרון S; harmonization with מנהר מצרים עד
      הנהר הגדול נהר פרת Gen 15:18, and עד הים האחרון Deut 11:24 = Deut
      34:2 (boundaries of promised land)

22   fin] + וקינן G (και Καιναν); editorial revision and harmonizing plus, cf
      קינן Gen 5:9–14, and below v 24 and 11:12 (G sim Jub 8:1)

23   ובני ארם M S G (και υιοι Αραμ)] om 1 Chron 1:17 (M); haplography by
      homoioteleuton (ארם ∩ ארם); note extensive haplography by homoio-
      teleuton in G of 1 Chron 1:17–24 (ארפכשד ∩ ארפכשד)

      מש M] משא S; משך G (Μοσοχ) 1 Chron 1:17; prps harmonizations; S: cf
      משא v 30 and Gen 25:14 (son of Ishmael); G and Chron: cf משך v 2

24   ילד M S G (εγεννησεν)] + את קינן וקינן ילד G (τον Καιναν, και Καιναν
      εγεννησεν); editoral revision and harmonizing plus, see above v 22

25   ילד M G (εγενηθησαν)] ילדו S; linguistic modernization (sg. → pl.)

27   אוזל M and 1 Chron 1:21] איזל S G (Αιζηλ)]; graphic confusion (י/ו)

28   עובל M] עיבל S Vg Gᵐˢˢ (Γεβαλ) 1 Chron 1:22] graphic confusion
      (י/ו), cf עיבל Gen 36:23; note haplography in G (ואת ∩ ואת)

32   נפרדו M S G (διεσπαρησαν)] + איי S G (νησοι); harmonizing plus with
      נפרדו איי הגוים v 5

11 1 fin] + לכל G (πασιν); harmonizing plus with שפה אחת לכלם v 6

8   העיר M] ואת העיר ואת המגדל S G (την πολιν και τον πυργον) Jub 10:24;
      harmonization with את העיר ואת המגדל v 5

וְכַלְנֶה בְּאֶרֶץ שִׁנְעָר: ¹¹ מִן־הָאָרֶץ הַהִוא יָצָא אַשּׁוּר וַיִּבֶן אֶת־נִינְוֵה
וְאֶת־רְחֹבֹת עִיר וְאֶת־כָּלַח: ¹² וְאֶת־רֶסֶן בֵּין נִינְוֵה וּבֵין כָּלַח הִוא הָעִיר
הַגְּדֹלָה: ¹³ וּמִצְרַיִם יָלַד אֶת־לוּדִים וְאֶת־עֲנָמִים וְאֶת־לְהָבִים וְאֶת־נַפְתֻּחִים:
¹⁴ וְאֶת־פַּתְרֻסִים וְאֶת־כַּסְלֻחִים אֲשֶׁר יָצְאוּ מִשָּׁם פְּלִשְׁתִּים וְאֶת־כַּפְתֹּרִים:
□□פ□□ ¹⁵ וּכְנַעַן יָלַד אֶת־צִידֹן בְּכֹרוֹ וְאֶת־חֵת: ¹⁶ וְאֶת־הַיְבוּסִי
וְאֶת־הָאֱמֹרִי וְאֵת הַגִּרְגָּשִׁי: ¹⁷ וְאֶת־הַחִוִּי וְאֶת־הַעַרְקִי וְאֶת־הַסִּינִי:
¹⁸ וְאֶת־הָאַרְוָדִי וְאֶת־הַצְּמָרִי וְאֶת־הַחֲמָתִי וְאַחַר נָפֹצוּ מִשְׁפְּחוֹת הַכְּנַעֲנִי:
¹⁹ וַיְהִי גְּבוּל הַכְּנַעֲנִי מִצִּידֹן בֹּאֲכָה גְרָרָה עַד־עַזָּה בֹּאֲכָה סְדֹמָה וַעֲמֹרָה
וְאַדְמָה וּצְבֹיִם עַד־לָשַׁע: ²⁰ אֵלֶּה בְנֵי־חָם לְמִשְׁפְּחֹתָם לִלְשֹׁנֹתָם בְּאַרְצֹתָם
בְּגוֹיֵהֶם: □□[ס]□□ ²¹ וּלְשֵׁם יֻלַּד גַּם־הוּא אֲבִי כָּל־בְּנֵי־עֵבֶר אֲחִי יֶפֶת
הַגָּדוֹל: ²² בְּנֵי שֵׁם עֵילָם וְאַשּׁוּר וְאַרְפַּכְשַׁד וְלוּד וַאֲרָם: ²³ וּבְנֵי אֲרָם עוּץ
וְחוּל וְגֶתֶר וָמַשׁ: ²⁴ וְאַרְפַּכְשַׁד יָלַד אֶת־שָׁלַח וְשֶׁלַח יָלַד אֶת־עֵבֶר:
²⁵ וּלְעֵבֶר יֻלַּד שְׁנֵי בָנִים שֵׁם הָאֶחָד פֶּלֶג כִּי בְיָמָיו נִפְלְגָה הָאָרֶץ וְשֵׁם אָחִיו
יָקְטָן: ²⁶ וְיָקְטָן יָלַד אֶת־אַלְמוֹדָד וְאֶת־שָׁלֶף וְאֶת־חֲצַרְמָוֶת וְאֶת־יָרַח:
²⁷ וְאֶת־הֲדוֹרָם וְאֶת־אוּזָל וְאֶת־דִּקְלָה: ²⁸ וְאֶת־עוֹבָל וְאֶת־אֲבִימָאֵל
וְאֶת־שְׁבָא: ²⁹ וְאֶת־אוֹפִר וְאֶת־חֲוִילָה וְאֶת־יוֹבָב כָּל־אֵלֶּה בְּנֵי יָקְטָן: ³⁰ וַיְהִי
מוֹשָׁבָם מִמֵּשָׁא בֹּאֲכָה סְפָרָה הַר הַקֶּדֶם: ³¹ אֵלֶּה בְנֵי־שֵׁם לְמִשְׁפְּחֹתָם
לִלְשֹׁנֹתָם בְּאַרְצֹתָם לְגוֹיֵהֶם: ³² אֵלֶּה מִשְׁפְּחֹת בְּנֵי־נֹחַ לְתוֹלְדֹתָם בְּגוֹיֵהֶם
וּמֵאֵלֶּה נִפְרְדוּ הַגּוֹיִם בָּאָרֶץ אַחַר הַמַּבּוּל: □□[פ]□□
¹¹ ¹ וַיְהִי כָל־הָאָרֶץ שָׂפָה אֶחָת וּדְבָרִים אֲחָדִים: ² וַיְהִי בְּנָסְעָם
מִקֶּדֶם וַיִּמְצְאוּ בִקְעָה בְּאֶרֶץ שִׁנְעָר וַיֵּשְׁבוּ שָׁם: ³ וַיֹּאמְרוּ אִישׁ אֶל־רֵעֵהוּ
הָבָה נִלְבְּנָה לְבֵנִים וְנִשְׂרְפָה לִשְׂרֵפָה וַתְּהִי לָהֶם הַלְּבֵנָה לְאָבֶן וְהַחֵמָר הָיָה
לָהֶם לַחֹמֶר: ⁴ וַיֹּאמְרוּ הָבָה נִבְנֶה־לָּנוּ עִיר וּמִגְדָּל וְרֹאשׁוֹ בַשָּׁמַיִם
וְנַעֲשֶׂה־לָּנוּ שֵׁם פֶּן־נָפוּץ עַל־פְּנֵי כָל־הָאָרֶץ: ⁵ וַיֵּרֶד יְהוָה לִרְאֹת אֶת־הָעִיר
וְאֶת־הַמִּגְדָּל אֲשֶׁר בָּנוּ בְּנֵי הָאָדָם: ⁶ וַיֹּאמֶר יְהוָה הֵן עַם אֶחָד וְשָׂפָה אַחַת
לְכֻלָּם וְזֶה הַחִלָּם לַעֲשׂוֹת וְעַתָּה לֹא־יִבָּצֵר מֵהֶם כֹּל אֲשֶׁר יָזְמוּ לַעֲשׂוֹת:
⁷ הָבָה נֵרְדָה וְנָבְלָה שָׁם שְׂפָתָם אֲשֶׁר לֹא יִשְׁמְעוּ אִישׁ שְׂפַת רֵעֵהוּ: ⁸ וַיָּפֶץ
יְהוָה אֹתָם מִשָּׁם עַל־פְּנֵי כָל־הָאָרֶץ וַיַּחְדְּלוּ לִבְנֹת הָעִיר: ⁹ עַל־כֵּן קָרָא
שְׁמָהּ בָּבֶל כִּי־שָׁם בָּלַל יְהוָה שְׂפַת כָּל־הָאָרֶץ וּמִשָּׁם הֱפִיצָם יְהוָה עַל־פְּנֵי

גַּ] C3 L S ‖ גְרָרָה 19 ‖ הַ] C3 L S ‖ V הַעַרְקִי 17 ‖ C3 L S] גְּבוֹר־ V ‖ גְּבוֹר 9
V ‖ בְּנֵי 29 ‖ C3 L S] בְּ V ‖ הַקֶּדֶם 30 C3 L S] קְ V

11 11–25   fin] + וימת מאות שנה (#) (PN) ויהיו כל ימי S; + וימת G (καὶ

ἀπεθανεν); (mult S and G); S: harmonizing plus with (PN) ויהיו כל ימי

מאות שנה וימת (#) Gen 5:8, 11, 14, 17, 20, 27, 31, sim 5:5, 23, sim

11:32; G: harmonizing plus with וימת in same vv of Gen 5; these formu-

laic pluses recur in S and G in vv 13 (2× in G), 15, 17, 19, 21, 23, 25

12   35 M] 135 S G; revision of chronology

      שלח M S] קינן G (Καιναν) Jub 8:1; editoral revision, cf קינן Gen 5:9–

      14, see 10:22 and following entries

13   שלח M S] קינן G (Καιναν); see previous entry

      403 M] 303 S; 430 G; S: revision of chronology; G: *403 → 430 by

      reminiscence or anticipation of שלשים, vv 12, 14

      ויחי קינן שלשים שנה ומאת שנה ויולד את שלח ויחי קינן אחרי הולידו + [fin

      את שלח שלשים שנה ויולד בנים ובנות וימת G (καὶ εζησεν Καιναν ετη

      εκατον τριακοντα και εγεννησεν τον Σαλα. Και εζησεν Καιναν μετα το

      γεννησαι αυτον τον Σαλα ετη τριακοσια τριακοντα, και εγεννησεν υιους

      και θυγατερος, και απεθανεν) sim Jub 8:5; editorial revision, cf number

      of antediluvian patriarchs in Genesis 5 (10 total); Kainan's ages (130,

      330) harmonized from Shelah's (130, 330) vv 14–15

14   ושלח חי M] ויחי שלח S; harmonization with clause-initial word order vv

      15–26 (12 times)

      30 M] 130 S G; revision of chronology

15   403 M] 303 S; 330 G; S: revision of chronology; G: *403 → 330 by

      reminiscence or anticipation of שלשים, vv 14, 16, and anticipation of

      ושלש מאות v 17 (G)

16   34 M] 134 S G; revision of chronology

17   370 G] 430 M; 270 S; S: revision of chronology; M: *370 → 430 by

      reminiscence of ארבע ושלשים שנה, v 16

18   30 M] 130 S G; revision of chronology

19   209 M G] 109 S; revision of chronology

20   32 M] 132 S G; revision of chronology

21   207 M G] 107 S; revision of chronology

22   30 M] 130 S G; revision of chronology

23   200 M G] 100 S; revision of chronology

24   29 M] 79 S G; revision of chronology

25   119 M] 69 S; 129 G; S: revision of chronology; G: *119 → 129, prps

      עשרם → עשרה by graphic confusion (ה/ם)

כָּל־הָאָֽרֶץ: ☐☐[פ]☐☐ 10 אֵ֚לֶּה תּוֹלְדֹ֣ת שֵׁ֔ם שֵׁ֚ם בֶּן־מְאַ֣ת שָׁנָ֔ה וַיּ֖וֹלֶד

אֶת־אַרְפַּכְשָׁ֑ד שְׁנָתַ֖יִם אַחַ֥ר הַמַּבּֽוּל: 11 וַֽיְחִי־שֵׁ֗ם אַֽחֲרֵי֙ הוֹלִיד֣וֹ אֶת־אַרְפַּכְשָׁ֔ד

חֲמֵ֥שׁ מֵא֖וֹת שָׁנָ֑ה וַיּ֥וֹלֶד בָּנִ֖ים וּבָנֽוֹת: ☐☐[פ]☐☐ 12 וְאַרְפַּכְשַׁ֣ד חַ֔י

חָמֵ֥שׁ וּשְׁלֹשִׁ֖ים שָׁנָ֑ה וַיּ֖וֹלֶד אֶת־שָֽׁלַח: 13 וַֽיְחִ֣י אַרְפַּכְשַׁ֗ד אַֽחֲרֵי֙ הוֹלִיד֣וֹ

אֶת־שֶׁ֔לַח שָׁלֹ֣שׁ שָׁנִ֔ים וְאַרְבַּ֥ע מֵא֖וֹת שָׁנָ֑ה וַיּ֥וֹלֶד בָּנִ֖ים וּבָנֽוֹת: ☐☐[פ]☐☐

14 וְשֶׁ֥לַח חַ֖י שְׁלֹשִׁ֣ים שָׁנָ֑ה וַיּ֖וֹלֶד אֶת־עֵֽבֶר: 15 וַֽיְחִי־שֶׁ֗לַח אַֽחֲרֵי֙ הוֹלִיד֣וֹ

אֶת־עֵ֔בֶר שָׁלֹ֣שׁ שָׁנִ֔ים וְאַרְבַּ֥ע מֵא֖וֹת שָׁנָ֑ה וַיּ֥וֹלֶד בָּנִ֖ים וּבָנֽוֹת: ☐☐[ס]☐☐

16 וַֽיְחִי־עֵ֕בֶר אַרְבַּ֥ע וּשְׁלֹשִׁ֖ים שָׁנָ֑ה וַיּ֖וֹלֶד אֶת־פָּֽלֶג: 17 וַֽיְחִי־עֵ֗בֶר אַֽחֲרֵי֙

הוֹלִיד֣וֹ אֶת־פֶּ֔לֶג שְׁלֹשִׁ֣ים שָׁנָ֔ה וּשְׁלֹ֥שׁ מֵא֖וֹת שָׁנָ֑ה וַיּ֥וֹלֶד בָּנִ֖ים וּבָנֽוֹת:

18 וַֽיְחִי־פֶ֖לֶג שְׁלֹשִׁ֣ים שָׁנָ֑ה וַיּ֖וֹלֶד אֶת־רְעֽוּ: 19 וַֽיְחִי־פֶ֗לֶג אַֽחֲרֵי֙ ☐☐[ס]☐☐

הוֹלִיד֣וֹ אֶת־רְע֔וּ תֵּ֥שַׁע שָׁנִ֖ים וּמָאתַ֣יִם שָׁנָ֑ה וַיּ֥וֹלֶד בָּנִ֖ים וּבָנֽוֹת:

20 וַיְחִ֣י רְע֔וּ שְׁתַּ֥יִם וּשְׁלֹשִׁ֖ים שָׁנָ֑ה וַיּ֖וֹלֶד אֶת־שְׂרֽוּג: 21 וַיְחִ֣י ☐☐[פ]☐☐

רְע֗וּ אַֽחֲרֵי֙ הוֹלִיד֣וֹ אֶת־שְׂר֔וּג שֶׁ֥בַע שָׁנִ֖ים וּמָאתַ֣יִם שָׁנָ֑ה וַיּ֥וֹלֶד בָּנִ֖ים וּבָנֽוֹת:

22 וַיְחִ֣י שְׂר֔וּג שְׁלֹשִׁ֖ים שָׁנָ֑ה וַיּ֖וֹלֶד אֶת־נָחֽוֹר: 23 וַיְחִ֣י שְׂר֗וּג ☐☐[ס]☐☐

אַֽחֲרֵי֙ הוֹלִיד֣וֹ אֶת־נָח֔וֹר מָאתַ֖יִם שָׁנָ֑ה וַיּ֥וֹלֶד בָּנִ֖ים וּבָנֽוֹת: ☐☐[ס]☐☐

24 וַיְחִ֣י נָח֔וֹר תֵּ֥שַׁע וְעֶשְׂרִ֖ים שָׁנָ֑ה וַיּ֖וֹלֶד אֶת־תָּֽרַח: 25 וַיְחִ֣י נָח֗וֹר אַֽחֲרֵי֙

הוֹלִיד֣וֹ אֶת־תֶּ֔רַח תְּשַֽׁע־עֶשְׂרֵ֥ה שָׁנָ֖ה וּמְאַ֣ת שָׁנָ֑ה וַיּ֥וֹלֶד בָּנִ֖ים וּבָנֽוֹת:

26 וַֽיְחִי־תֶ֖רַח שִׁבְעִ֣ים שָׁנָ֑ה וַיּ֨וֹלֶד֙ אֶת־אַבְרָ֔ם אֶת־נָח֖וֹר ☐☐[ס]☐☐

וְאֶת־הָרָֽן: 27 וְאֵ֨לֶּה֙ תּוֹלְדֹ֣ת תֶּ֔רַח תֶּ֣רַח הוֹלִ֣יד אֶת־אַבְרָ֔ם אֶת־נָח֖וֹר וְאֶת־הָרָ֑ן

11 28 באור M S] בארץ G (εν τη χωρα); reminiscence of בארץ v 28, cf v 31, 15:7, Neh 9:7 (all G)

30 לה ילד S [לה ולד M; ר(י)להול G (ετεκνοποιει); M: graphic confusion (ו/י); G: graphic confusion (ו/י) with word misdivision

31 שרי M S G (Σαραν)] + ואת מלכה S; harmonizing plus with . . . שרי מלכה v 29

כלתו M G (την νυμφην αυτου)] כלותו S; harmonization of number, see previous entry

אברם M S G (Αβραμ)] + ונחור S; harmonizing plus with אברם ונחור v 29

בנו M G (του υιου αυτου)] בניו S; harmonization of number, see previous entry

ויצא אתם S (ויוציא) G (εξηγαγεν αυτους) Vg] ויצאו אתם M; parablepsis; note linguistic modernization in S (jussive form → imperfect form, frequent in S)

מאור M S 4QCommGen^a] מארץ G (εκ της χωρας); reminiscence or harmonization with בארץ כשדים v 28 (G)

ויבאו M S] ויבוא G (και ηλθεν) sim 4QCommGen^a (ויבוא); metathesis (או) or exegetical revision

וישבו M S] וישב G (και κατωκησεν); see previous entry

32 תרח 1° M S G (Θαρα)] + בחרן G (εν Χαρραν); anticipation or harmonizing plus with תרח בחרן v 32

205 M G] 145 S cf Acts 7:4 and Philo, *Mig.* 177; revision of chronology

וְהָרָן הוֹלִיד אֶת־לֽוֹט: ‏28 וַיָּ֣מָת הָרָ֗ן עַל־פְּנֵ֛י תֶּ֥רַח אָבִ֖יו בְּאֶ֣רֶץ מֽוֹלַדְתּ֑וֹ בְּא֖וּר

כַּשְׂדִּֽים: ‏29 וַיִּקַּ֨ח אַבְרָ֧ם וְנָח֛וֹר לָהֶ֖ם נָשִׁ֑ים שֵׁ֤ם אֵֽשֶׁת־אַבְרָם֙ שָׂרָ֔י וְשֵׁ֤ם

אֵֽשֶׁת־נָחוֹר֙ מִלְכָּ֔ה בַּת־הָרָ֥ן אֲבִֽי־מִלְכָּ֖ה וַֽאֲבִ֥י יִסְכָּֽה: ‏30 וַתְּהִ֥י שָׂרַ֖י עֲקָרָ֑ה אֵ֥ין

לָ֖הּ וָלָֽד: ‏31 וַיִּקַּ֨ח תֶּ֜רַח אֶת־אַבְרָ֣ם בְּנ֗וֹ וְאֶת־ל֤וֹט בֶּן־הָרָן֙ בֶּן־בְּנ֔וֹ וְאֵת֙ שָׂרַ֣י

כַּלָּת֔וֹ אֵ֖שֶׁת אַבְרָ֣ם בְּנ֑וֹ וַיֵּצְא֨וּ אִתָּ֜ם מֵא֣וּר כַּשְׂדִּ֗ים לָלֶ֨כֶת֙ אַ֣רְצָה כְּנַ֔עַן וַיָּבֹ֥אוּ

עַד־חָרָ֖ן וַיֵּ֥שְׁבוּ שָֽׁם: ‏32 וַיִּֽהְי֣וּ יְמֵי־תֶ֔רַח חָמֵ֥שׁ שָׁנִ֖ים וּמָאתַ֣יִם שָׁנָ֑ה וַיָּ֥מָת תֶּ֖רַח

בְּחָרָֽן: ‏   □□[פ]□□

Bibliography

Aejmelaeus, A. 1987. "What Can We Know about the Hebrew *Vorlage* of the Septuagint?" *ZAW* 99: 58–89 = Pp. 77–115 in Aejmelaeus, *On the Trail of the Septuagint Translators: Collected Essays*. Kampen: Kok Pharos, 1993.

Albrektson, B. 1978. "Reflections on the Emergence of a Standard Text of the Hebrew Bible." Pp. 49–65 in J. A. Emerton, ed., *Congress Volume: Göttingen 1977*. VTSup 29. Leiden: Brill.

_____. 1994. "Translation and Emendation." Pp. 27–39 in S. E. Balentine and J. Barton, eds., *Language, Theology, and the Bible: Essays in Honour of James Barr*. Oxford: Clarendon.

Alexander, P. S. 1988a. "Jewish Aramaic Translations of Hebrew Scriptures." Pp. 217–53 in Mulder 1988b.

_____. 1988b. "Retelling the Old Testament." Pp. 99–121 in D. A. Carson and H. G. M. Williamson, eds., *It Is Written: Scripture Citing Scripture. Essays in Honour of Barnabas Lindars*. Cambridge: Cambridge University Press.

Andersen, F. I., and Forbes, A. D. 1986. *Spelling in the Hebrew Bible*. BibOr 41. Rome: Pontifical Biblical Institute.

Bacher, W. 1891. "A Contribution to the History of the Term 'Massorah.'" *JQR* 3: 785–90 = Pp. 600–5 in Leiman 1974.

Barr, J. 1979. *The Typology of Literalism in Ancient Biblical Translations*. MSU 15. Göttingen: Vandenhoeck & Ruprecht.

_____. 1989a. *The Variable Spellings of the Hebrew Bible*. Oxford: Oxford University Press.

_____. 1989b. "Hebrew, Aramaic and Greek in the Hellenistic Age." Pp. 79–114 in W. D. Davies and L. Finkelstein, eds., *The Cambridge History of Judaism. Vol. 2: The Hellenistic Age*. Cambridge: Cambridge University Press.

Barré, M. L. 1995. "Rabiṣu." Cols. 1287–90 in K. van der Toorn, B. Becking, and P. W. van der Horst, eds., *Dictionary of Deities and Demons in the Bible*. Leiden: Brill.

Barthélemy, D., ed. 1973. *Preliminary and Interim Report on the Hebrew Old Testament Text Project. Vol. 1: Pentateuch*. New York: United Bible Societies.

_____. 1982. *Critique textuelle de l'Ancien Testament. Tome 1: Josué, Juges, Ruth, Samuel, Rois, Chroniques, Esdras, Néhémie, Esther*. OBO 50/1. Fribourg/Göttingen: Éditions Universitaires/Vandenhoeck & Ruprecht.

_____. 1992. *Critique textuelle de l'Ancien Testament. Tome 3: Ézéchiel, Daniel et les 12 Prophètes*. OBO 50/3. Fribourg/Göttingen: Éditions Universitaires/Vandenhoeck & Ruprecht.

Ben-Ḥayyim, Z. 1965. "Traditions in the Hebrew Language, with Special Reference to the Dead Sea Scrolls." Pp. 200–14 in C. Rabin and Y. Yadin, eds., *Aspects of the Dead Sea Scrolls*. ScrHier 4. Jerusalem: Magnes.

Bernstein, M. J. 1994. "4Q252 i 2 לא ידור רוחי באדם לעולם: Biblical Text or Biblical Interpretation?" *RevQ* 16: 421–27.

Borbone, P. G. 1990. *Il libro del Profeta Osea: Edizione critica del testo ebraico*. QH 2. Torino: Zamorani.

Breuer, M. 1976. *The Aleppo Codex and the Received Text of the Bible* [Hebrew]. Jerusalem: Kook.

Brock, S. P. 1972. "The Phenomenon of the Septuagint." Pp. 11–36 in A. S. van der Woude, ed., *The Witness of Tradition*. OTS 17. Leiden: Brill.

_____. 1979. "Jewish Traditions in Syriac Sources." *JJS* 30: 212–32.

_____. 1992a. "To Revise or Not to Revise: Attitudes to Jewish Biblical Translation." Pp. 301–38 in Brooke and Lindars 1992.

_____. 1992b. "Versions, Ancient: Syriac Versions." *ABD* 6. 794–99.

Brooke, G. J., and Lindars, B., eds. 1992. *Septuagint, Scrolls and Cognate Writings*. SCS 33. Atlanta: Scholars.

Brown, W. P. 1993. *Structure, Role, and Ideology in the Hebrew and Greek Texts of Genesis 1:1–2:3*. SBLDS 132. Atlanta: Scholars.

Budde, K. 1883. *Die Biblische Urgeschichte*. Giessen: Ricker'sche.

Burchard, C. 1966. "Gen 35,6–10 und 36,5–12 MT aus der Wüste Juda." *ZAW* 78: 71–75.

Carr, D. M. 1996. *Reading the Fractures of Genesis: Historical and Literary Approaches*. Louisville: Westminster John Knox.

Cassuto, U. 1961–64. *A Commentary on the Book of Genesis*. 2 vols. Trans. I. Abrahams. Jerusalem: Magnes.

Chiesa, B. 1992a. "Textual History and Textual Criticism of the Hebrew Old Testament." Pp. 257–72 in Trebolle Barrera and Vegas Montaner 1992.

_____. 1992b. "Some Remarks on Textual Criticism and the Editing of Hebrew Texts." *Manuscripts of the Middle East* 6: 138–44.

Cohen, S. J. D. 1987. *From the Maccabees to the Mishnah*. Philadelphia: Westminster.

Cook, J. 1982. "Genesis 1 in the Septuagint as an Example of the Problem: Text and Tradition." *JNSL* 10: 25–36.

_____. 1985. "The Translator of the Greek Genesis." Pp. 169–82 in N. Fernández Marcos, ed., *La Septuaginta en la investigación contemporánea*. TE 34. Madrid: Instituto Arias Montano.

_____. 1987. "The Exegesis of the Greek Genesis." Pp. 91–125 in C. E. Cox, ed., *VI Congress of the International Organization for Septuagint and Cognate Studies*. SCS 23. Atlanta: Scholars.

Cross, F. M. 1953. "A New Qumran Biblical Fragment related to the Original Hebrew underlying the Septuagint." *BASOR* 132: 15–26.

_____. 1955. "The Oldest Manuscripts from Qumran." *JBL* 74: 147–72 = Pp. 147–76 in Cross and Talmon 1975.

_____. 1964. "The History of the Biblical Text in the Light of Discoveries in the Judaean Desert." *HTR* 57: 281–99 = Pp. 177–95 in Cross and Talmon 1975.

_____. 1966. "The Contribution of the Qumran Discoveries to the Study of the Biblical Text." *IEJ* 16: 81-95 = Pp. 278-92 in Cross and Talmon 1975.

_____. 1973. *Canaanite Myth and Hebrew Epic: Essays in the History of the Religion of Israel*. Cambridge: Harvard University Press.

_____. 1979. "Problems of Method in the Textual Criticism of the Hebrew Bible." Pp. 31-54 in W. D. O'Flaherty, ed., *The Critical Study of Sacred Texts*. Berkeley: Graduate Theological Union.

_____. 1985. "The Text behind the Text of the Hebrew Bible." *BR* 1: 12-25 = Pp. 139-55 in H. Shanks, ed., *Understanding the Dead Sea Scrolls*. New York: Random House, 1992.

_____. 1992. "Some Notes on a Generation of Qumran Studies." Pp. 1-14 in Trebolle Barrera and Vegas Montaner 1992 = Pp. 171-91 in Cross 1995.

_____. 1995. *The Ancient Library of Qumran*. 3d ed. Minneapolis: Fortress.

Cross, F. M., and Talmon, S., eds. 1975. *Qumran and the History of the Biblical Text*. Cambridge: Harvard University Press.

Davila, J. R. 1989. *Unpublished Pentateuchal Manuscripts from Cave IV, Qumran: 4QGenEx[a], 4QGen[b–h,j–k]*. Ann Arbor: University Microfilms.

_____. 1990. "New Qumran Readings for Genesis One." Pp. 3-11 in H. W. Attridge, J. J. Collins, and T. H. Tobin, eds., *Of Scribes and Scrolls: Studies on the Hebrew Bible, Intertestamental Judaism, and Christian Origins Presented to John Strugnell*. CTS 5. Lanham: University Press of America.

_____. 1991. "The Name of God at Moriah: An Unpublished Fragment from 4QGenExod[a]." *JBL* 110: 577-82.

_____. 1992. "New Qumran Readings for the Joseph Story (Genesis 37–50)." Pp. 167-75 in Trebolle Barrera and Vegas Montaner 1992.

_____. 1993. "Text–Type and Terminology: Genesis and Exodus as Test Cases. *RevQ* 16: 3-37.

Deist, F. E. 1988. *Witnesses to the Old Testament: Introducing Old Testament Textual Criticism*. Pretoria: Kerkboekhandel.

Delitzsch, F. 1920. *Die Lese- und Schreibfehler im Alten Testament*. Berlin: de Gruyter.

Dillmann, A. 1897. *Genesis*. 2 vols. Trans. W. B. Stevenson. Edinburgh: Clark. (= *Die Genesis*, 6th ed., 1892.) Citations are from vol. 1.

Dirksen, P. B. 1992. "The Peshiṭta and Textual Criticism of the Old Testament." *VT* 42: 376-90.

Dotan, A. 1971. "Masorah." *EJ* 16: 1401-82.

―――, ed. 1973. תורה נביאים וכתובים. Tel Aviv: Adi.

Driver, G. R. 1946. "Theological and Philological Problems in the Old Testament." *JTS* 47: 156-66.

Driver, S. R. 1905. *The Book of Genesis*. WC. 4th ed. London: Methuen.

Eichhorn, J. G. 1888. *Introduction to the Study of the Old Testament*. Trans. G. T. Gollop. London: Spottiswoode. (= *Einleitung ins Alte Testament*, chs. 1-3, 3rd ed., 1803.)

Emerton, J. A. 1994. "When Did Terah Die? (Genesis 11:32)." Pp. 170-81 in S. E. Balentine and J. Barton, eds., *Language, Theology, and the Bible: Essays in Honour of James Barr*. Oxford: Clarendon.

Etz, D. V. 1993. "The Numbers of Genesis V 3–31: A Suggested Conversion and Its Implications." *VT* 43: 171–89.

Ewald, H. 1869. *The History of Israel.* Vol. 1. Trans. R. Martineau. London: Spottiswoode. (= *Geschichte des Volkes Israel,* 3d ed., 1864.)

Fishbane, M. 1985. *Biblical Interpretation in Ancient Israel.* Oxford: Clarendon.

Fraenkel, D. 1984. "Die Überlieferung der Genealogien Gen 5:3–28 und Gen 11:10–26 in den 'Antiquitates Iudaicae' des Flavius Josephus." Pp. 175–200 in A. Pietersma and C. Cox, eds., *De Septuaginta: Studies in Honour of John William Wevers.* Mississauga: Benben.

Frankel, Z. 1841. *Vorstudien zu der Septuaginta.* Leipzig: Vogel.

Freedman, D. N. 1952. "Notes on Genesis." *ZAW* 64: 190–94 = Pp. 3–7 in Freedman 1997, vol. 1.

_____. 1962. "The Massoretic Text and the Qumran Scrolls: A Study in Orthography." *Textus* 2: 87–102 = Pp. 13–28 in Freedman 1997, vol. 2.

_____. 1987. "The Earliest Bible." Pp. 29–37 in M. P. O'Connor and D. N. Freedman, eds., *Backgrounds for the Bible.* Winona Lake: Eisenbrauns = Pp. 341–49 in Freedman 1997, vol. 1.

_____. 1997. *Divine Commitment and Human Obligation: Selected Writings of David Noel Freedman,* ed. J. R. Huddlestun. 2 vols. Grand Rapids: Eerdmans.

Ginsburg, C. D. 1897. *Introduction to the Massoretico-Critical Edition of the Hebrew Bible.* London: Trinitarian Bible Society. Reprint, New York: Ktav, 1966.

_____, ed. 1908. חמשה חומשי תורה. London: British and Foreign Bible Society.

Goshen-Gottstein, M. H. 1957. "The History of the Bible-Text and Comparative Semitics: A Methodological Problem." *VT* 7: 195–201.

_____. 1963. "The Rise of the Tiberian Bible Text." Pp. 79–122 in A. Altmann, ed., *Biblical and Other Studies.* Cambridge: Harvard University Press = Pp. 666–709 in Leiman 1974.

_____. 1965. *The Book of Isaiah: Sample Edition with Introduction.* HUBP. Jerusalem: Magnes.

_____. 1967. "Hebrew Biblical Manuscripts: Their History and Their Place in the HUBP Edition." *Bib* 48: 243–90 = Pp. 42–89 in Cross and Talmon 1975.

_____. 1983. "The Textual Criticism of the Old Testament: Rise, Decline, Rebirth." *JBL* 102: 365–99.

_____. 1992a. "Editions of the Hebrew Bible: Past and Future." Pp. 221–42 in M. Fishbane and E. Tov, eds., *'Sha'arei Talmon': Studies in the Bible, Qumran, and the Ancient Near East Presented to Shemaryahu Talmon.* Winona Lake: Eisenbrauns.

_____. 1992b. "The Development of the Hebrew Text of the Bible: Theories and Practice of Textual Criticism." *VT* 42: 204–13.

Greenberg, M. 1983a. *Ezekiel 1–20.* AB 22. New York: Doubleday.

_____. 1983b. "MSRT HBRYT, 'The Obligation of the Covenant,' in Ezekiel 20:37." Pp. 37–46 in C. L. Meyers and M. O'Connor, eds., *The Word of the Lord Shall Go Forth: Essays in Honor of David Noel Freedman.* Winona Lake: Eisenbrauns.

Greenspahn, F. E. 1987. "Biblical Scholars, Medieval and Modern." Pp. 245–58 in J. Neusner, B. A. Levine, and E. S. Frerichs, eds., *Judaic Perspectives on Ancient Israel.* Philadelphia: Fortress.

Grossfeld, B. 1988. *The Targum Onqelos to Genesis: Translated, with a Critical Introduction, Apparatus, and Notes.* ArB 6. Wilmington: Glazier.

Gunkel, H. 1910. *Genesis.* HKAT. 3d ed. Göttingen: Vandenhoeck & Ruprecht.

Hall, B. 1963. "Biblical Scholarship: Editions and Commentaries." Pp. 38–93 in S. L. Greenslade, ed., *The Cambridge History of the Bible. Vol. 3: The West from the Reformation to the Present Day.* Cambridge: Cambridge University Press.

Hanhart, R. 1992. "The Translation of the Septuagint in Light of Earlier Tradition and Subsequent Influences." Pp. 339–79 in Brooke and Lindars 1992.

Harl, M. 1986. *La Bible d'Alexandrie: La Genèse.* Paris: Cerf.

Harrington, D. J. 1971. "The Biblical Text of Pseudo-Philo's *Liber Antiquitatum Biblicarum.*" *CBQ* 33: 1–17.

Hartman, L. F., ed. 1970. *Textual Notes on the New American Bible.* Paterson: St. Anthony's Guild.

Hayward, C. T. R. 1995. *Saint Jerome's Hebrew Questions on Genesis: Translated with Introduction and Commentary.* OECS. Oxford: Clarendon.

Hendel, R. S. 1994. Review of Brown 1993. *JR* 74: 596.

———. 1995a. Review of Wevers 1993. *JR* 75: 103–4.

———. 1995b. "4Q252 and the Flood Chronology of Genesis 7–8: A Text-Critical Solution." *DSD* 2: 72–79.

———. In press. "Scriptures: Translations." In L. H. Schiffman and J. C. VanderKam, eds., *Encyclopedia of the Dead Sea Scrolls.* New York: Oxford University Press.

Hess, R. S. 1993. *Studies in the Personal Names of Genesis 1–11.* AOAT 234. Neukirchen-Vluyn: Neukirchener.

Horowitz, W. 1990. "The Isles of the Nations: Genesis X and Babylonian Geography." Pp. 35–43 in J. A. Emerton, ed., *Studies in the Pentateuch.* VTSup 41. Leiden: Brill.

Housman, A. E. 1961a. "Preface to Juvenal." Pp. 53–62 in Housman, *Selected Prose,* ed. J. Carter. Cambridge: Cambridge University Press. Originally published in 1905.

———. 1961b. "The Application of Thought to Textual Criticism." Pp. 131–50 in *Selected Prose.* Originally published in 1921.

Huehnergard, J. 1992. "Languages: Introductory Survey." *ABD* 4. 155–70.

Hughes, J. 1990. *Secrets of the Times: Myth and History in Biblical Chronology.* JSOTSup 66. Sheffield: JSOT.

Isenberg, S. R. 1971. "On the Jewish-Palestinian Origins of the Peshitta to the Pentateuch." *JBL* 90: 69–81.

Jastram, N. 1992. "The Text of 4QNum[b]." Pp. 177–98 in Trebolle Barrera and Vegas Montaner 1992.

Kamesar, A. 1993. *Jerome, Greek Scholarship, and the Hebrew Bible.* OECS. Oxford: Clarendon.

Kaufman, S. A. 1994. "Dating the Language of the Palestinian Targums and Their Use in the Study of First Century CE Texts." Pp. 118–41 in D. R. G. Beattie and M. J. McNamara, eds., *The Aramaic Bible: Targums in Their Historical Context.* JSOTSup 166. Sheffield: JSOT.

Kedar, B. 1988. "The Latin Translations." Pp. 299–338 in Mulder 1988b.

Kenney, E. J. 1974. *The Classical Text: Aspects of Editing in the Age of the Printed Book*. Berkeley: University of California Press.

———. 1992. "Textual Criticism." *EB* 20: 614–20.

Klein, R. W. 1974a. "Archaic Chronologies and the Textual History of the Old Testament." *HTR* 67: 255–63.

———. 1974b. *Textual Criticism of the Old Testament: The Septuagint after Qumran*. Philadelphia: Fortress.

Komlosh, Y. 1973. *The Bible in the Light of the Aramaic Translations* [Hebrew]. Tel Aviv: Dvir.

Koster, M. D. 1993. "Peshiṭta Revisited: A Reassessment of Its Value as a Version." *JSS* 38: 235–68.

Kuenen, A. 1884. "Bijdragen tot de critiek van Pentateuch en Jozua: De geboorteges-chiedenis van Genesis Hoofdstuk I–XI."*TT* 18: 121–71.

Lambdin, T. O. 1971. *Introduction to Biblical Hebrew*. New York: Scribner's.

Larsson, G. 1983. "The Chronology of the Pentateuch: A Comparison of the MT and LXX." *JBL* 102: 401–9.

Layton, S. C. 1997. "Remarks on the Canaanite Origin of Eve." *CBQ* 59: 22–32.

Leiman, S. Z., ed. 1974. *The Canon and Masorah of the Hebrew Bible: An Introductory Reader*. New York: Ktav.

Lewis, J. P. 1968. *A Study of the Interpretation of Noah and the Flood in Jewish and Christian Literature*. Leiden: Brill.

Lim, T. H. 1992. "The Chronology of the Flood Story in a Qumran Text (4Q252)." *JJS* 43: 288–98.

———. 1993. "Notes on 4Q252 fr. 1, cols. i–ii." *JJS* 44: 121–26.

Lipiński, É. 1990. "Les Japhétites selon Gen 10,2–4 et 1 Chr 1,5–7." *ZAH* 3: 40–53.

Lipschütz, L., ed. 1962. *"Kitāb al-Khilaf*: Mishael Ben Uzziel's Treatise on the Differences between Ben Asher and Ben Naphtali" [Hebrew and Arabic]. *Textus* 2: -א יב.

Lust, J. 1991. "'For Man Shall His Blood Be Shed': Gen 9:6 in Hebrew and in Greek." Pp. 91–102 in G. J. Norton and S. Pisano, eds., *Tradition of the Text: Studies Offered to Dominique Barthélemy*. OBO 109. Freiburg/Göttingen: Universitäts-verlag/Vandenhoeck & Ruprecht.

Maas, P. 1958. *Textual Criticism*. Trans. B. Flower. Oxford: Clarendon.

Maher, M. 1992. *Targum Pseudo-Jonathan: Genesis. Translated, with Introduction and Notes*. ArB 1B. Collegeville: Glazier.

Maori, Y. 1992. "The Text of the Hebrew Bible in Rabbinic Writings in the Light of the Qumran Evidence." Pp. 283–89 in D. Dimant and U. Rappaport, eds., *The Dead Sea Scrolls: Forty Years of Research*. STDJ 10. Leiden: Brill.

———. 1995. *The Peshitta Version of the Pentateuch and Early Jewish Exegesis* [Hebrew]. Jerusalem: Magnes.

McCarter, P. K., Jr. 1986. *Textual Criticism: Recovering the Text of the Hebrew Bible*. Philadelphia: Fortress.

McEvenue, S. E. 1971. *The Narrative Style of the Priestly Writer*. AnBib 50. Rome: Pontifical Biblical Institute.

McGann, J. J. 1991. *The Textual Condition*. Princeton: Princeton University Press.

McNamara, M. 1992. *Targum Neofiti 1: Genesis. Translated, with Apparatus and Notes.* ArB 1A. Collegeville: Glazier.

Merton, R. K. 1965. *On the Shoulders of Giants: A Shandean Postscript.* San Diego: Harcourt Brace Jovanovich.

Metzger, B. 1992. *The Text of the New Testament: Its Transmission, Corruption, and Restoration.* 3d ed. Oxford: Oxford University Press.

Mulder, M. J. 1988a. "The Transmission of the Biblical Text." Pp. 87–135 in Mulder 1988b.

_____, ed. 1988b. *Mikra: Text, Translation, Reading and Interpretation in Ancient Judaism and Early Christianity.* CRINT 2/1. Philadelphia: Fortress.

Neusner, J. 1994. *Introduction to Rabbinic Literature.* New York: Doubleday.

Ofer, J. 1989. "M. D. Cassuto's Notes on the Aleppo Codex" [Hebrew]. *Sefunot* 19 (n.s. 4): 277–344.

Orlinsky, H. M. 1961. "The Textual Criticism of the Old Testament." Pp. 113–32 in G. E. Wright, ed., *The Bible and the Ancient Near East: Essays in Honor of William Foxwell Albright.* Garden City: Doubleday.

_____. 1966. "The Masoretic Text: A Critical Evaluation." Pp. i–xlv in 1966 Ktav reprint of Ginsburg 1897 = Pp. 833–77 in Leiman 1974.

Paradise, B. 1986. "Food for Thought: The Septuagint Translation of Genesis 1.11–12." Pp. 177–204 in J. D. Martin and P. R. Davies, eds., *A Word in Season: Essays in Honour of William McKane.* JSOTSup 42. Sheffield: JSOT.

Penkower, J. S. 1988. "A Tenth-Century Pentateuchal MS from Jerusalem (MS C3), Corrected by Mishael Ben Uzziel" [Hebrew]. *Tarbiz* 58: 49–74.

Polak, F. 1992. "Statistics and Textual Filiation: The Case of 4QSam^a/LXX (with a Note on the Text of the Pentateuch)." Pp. 215–76 in Brooke and Lindars 1992.

Puech, É. 1980. "Fragment d'un rouleau de la Genèse provenant du désert de Juda (Gen. 33,18–34,3)." *RevQ* 10: 163–66.

Purvis, J. D. 1968. *The Samaritan Pentateuch and the Origin of the Samaritan Sect.* HSM 2. Cambridge: Harvard University Press.

Qimron, E. 1986. *The Hebrew of the Dead Sea Scrolls.* HSS 29. Atlanta: Scholars.

Reynolds, L. D., and Wilson, N. G. 1974. *Scribes and Scholars: A Guide to the Transmission of Greek and Latin Literature.* 2d ed. Oxford: Clarendon.

Roberts, B. J. 1951. *The Old Testament Text and Versions.* Cardiff: University of Wales Press.

Rösel, M. 1991. "Die Übersetzung der Gottesbezeichnungen in der Genesis-Septuaginta." Pp. 357–78 in D. R. Daniels, U. Glessmer, and M. Rösel, eds., *Ernten, was Man sät: Festschrift für Klaus Koch.* Neukirchen-Vluyn: Neukirchener.

_____. 1994. *Übersetzung als Vollendung der Auslegung: Studien zur Genesis-Septuaginta.* BZAW 223. Berlin: de Gruyter.

Ṣadaqa, A., and Ṣadaqa, R., eds. 1962. *Jewish and Samaritan Versions of the Pentateuch: Genesis* [Hebrew]. Tel Aviv: Mass.

Sáenz-Badillos, A. 1993. *A History of the Hebrew Language.* Trans. J. Elwolde. Cambridge: Cambridge University Press.

Salvesen, A. 1991. *Symmachus in the Pentateuch*. JSSM 15. Manchester: University of Manchester Press.

Sanders, J. A. 1991. "Stability and Fluidity in Text and Canon." Pp. 203–17 in G. J. Norton and S. Pisano, eds., *Tradition of the Text: Studies Offered to Dominique Barthélemy*. OBO 109. Freiburg/Göttingen: Universitätsverlag/Vandenhoeck & Ruprecht.

Sanderson, J. E. 1986. *An Exodus Scroll from Qumran: 4QpaleoExod*[m] *and the Samaritan Tradition*. HSS 30. Atlanta: Scholars.

Schmidt, W. H. 1973. *Die Schöpfungsgeschichte der Priesterschrift*. WMANT 17. 3d ed. Neukirchen-Vluyn: Neukirchener.

Seebass H. 1986. "LXX und MT in Gen 31,44–53." *BN* 34: 30–38.

Siegel, J. P. 1975. *The Severus Scroll and 1QIs*[a]. MS 2. Missoula: Scholars.

Skehan, P. W. 1969. "The Scrolls and the Old Testament Text." Pp. 89–100 in D. N. Freedman and J. C. Greenfield, eds., *New Directions in Biblical Archaeology*. Garden City: Doubleday.

Skinner, J. 1914. *The Divine Names in Genesis*. London: Hodder and Stoughton.

_____. 1930. *A Critical and Exegetical Commentary on Genesis*. ICC. 2d ed. Edinburgh: Clark.

Sollamo, R. 1995. *Repetition of the Possessive Pronouns in the Septuagint*. SCS 40. Atlanta: Scholars.

Speiser, E. A. 1964. *Genesis*. AB 1. Garden City: Doubleday.

Spurrell, G. J. 1896. *Notes on the Text of the Book of Genesis*. Oxford: Clarendon.

Steiner, G. 1975. *After Babel: Aspects of Language and Translation*. London: Oxford University Press.

Strack, H. L. 1902. "Text of the Old Testament." *HDB* 4: 726–32.

Talmage, F. 1987. "Keep Your Sons from Scripture: The Bible in Medieval Jewish Scholarship and Spirituality." Pp. 81–101 in C. Thoma and M. Wyschogrod, eds., *Understanding Scripture: Explorations of Jewish and Christian Traditions of Interpretation*. New York: Paulist.

Talmon, S. 1970. "The Old Testament Text." Pp. 159–99 in P. R. Ackroyd and C. F. Evans, eds., *The Cambridge History of the Bible. Vol. 1: From the Beginnings to Jerome*. Cambridge: Cambridge University Press = Pp. 1–41 in Cross and Talmon 1975.

_____. 1975. "The Textual Study of the Bible: A New Outlook." Pp. 321–400 in Cross and Talmon 1975.

Tansell, G. T. 1989. *A Rationale of Textual Criticism*. Philadelphia: University of Pennsylvania Press.

ter Haar Romeny, R. B. 1995. "Techniques of Translation and Transmission in the Earliest Text Forms of the Syriac Version of Genesis." Pp. 177–85 in P. B. Dirksen and A. van der Kooij, eds., *The Peshitta as a Translation*. MPI 8. Leiden: Brill.

Tov E. 1981. *The Text-Critical Use of the Septuagint in Biblical Research*. Jerusalem: Simor.

_____. 1982. "A Modern Textual Outlook Based on the Qumran Scrolls. *HUCA* 53: 11–27.

_____. 1985. "The Nature and Background of Harmonizations in Biblical Manuscripts." *JSOT* 31: 3–29.

_____. 1988. "The Septuagint." Pp. 161–88 in Mulder 1988b.

_____. 1992a. *Textual Criticism of the Hebrew Bible*. Minneapolis: Fortress.

_____. 1992b. "The Contribution of the Qumran Scrolls to the Understanding of the LXX." Pp. 11–47 in Brooke and Lindars 1992.

_____. 1992c. "Some Notes on a Generation of Qumran Studies (by Frank M. Cross): A Reply." Pp. 15–21 in Trebolle Barrera and Vegas Montaner 1992.

_____. 1994a. "Glosses, Interpolations and Other Types of Scribal Additions in the Text of the Hebrew Bible." Pp. 40–66 in S. E. Balentine and J. Barton, eds., *Language, Theology, and the Bible: Essays in Honour of James Barr*. Oxford: Clarendon.

_____. 1994b. "Biblical Texts as Reworked in Some Qumran Manuscripts with Special Attention to 4QRP and 4QParaGen-Exod." Pp. 111–34 in E. Ulrich and J. Vander-Kam, eds., *The Community of the Renewed Covenant: The Notre Dame Symposium on the Dead Sea Scrolls*. Notre Dame: University of Notre Dame Press.

_____. 1995. "Groups of Biblical Texts Found at Qumran." Pp. 85–102 in D. Dimant and L. H. Schiffman, eds., *Time to Prepare the Way in the Wilderness: Papers on the Qumran Scrolls*. STDJ 16. Leiden: Brill.

Trebolle Barrera, J., and Vegas Montaner, L., eds. 1992. *The Madrid Qumran Congress*. 2 vols. STDJ 11. Leiden: Brill. Citations are from vol. 1.

Ulrich, E. 1992. "The Canonical Process, Textual Criticism, and the Latter Stages in the Composition of the Bible." Pp. 267–91 in M. Fishbane and E. Tov, eds., *'Shaʿarei Talmon': Studies in the Bible, Qumran, and the Ancient Near East Presented to Shemaryahu Talmon*. Winona Lake: Eisenbrauns.

VanderKam, J. C. 1977. *Textual and Historical Studies in the Book of Jubilees*. HSM 14. Missoula: Scholars.

_____. 1978. "The Textual Affinities of the Biblical Citations in the Genesis Apocryphon." *JBL* 97: 45–55.

_____. 1988. "Jubilees and Hebrew Texts of Genesis-Exodus." *Textus* 14: 71–85.

_____. 1995. "Das chronologische Konzept des Jubiläenbuches." *ZAW* 107: 80–100.

Wallace, H. N. 1990. "The Toledot of Adam." Pp. 17–33 in J. A. Emerton, ed., *Studies in the Pentateuch*. VTSup 41. Leiden: Brill.

Waltke, B. K. 1970. "The Samaritan Pentateuch and the Text of the Old Testament." Pp. 212–39 in J. B. Payne, ed., *New Perspectives on the Old Testament*. Waco: Word.

_____. 1992. "Samaritan Pentateuch." *ABD* 5. 932–40.

Waltke, B. K., and O'Connor, M. 1990. *An Introduction to Biblical Hebrew Syntax*. Winona Lake: Eisenbrauns.

Weinfeld, M. 1972. *Deuteronomy and the Deuteronomic School*. Oxford: Clarendon.

Weingreen, J. 1957. "Rabbinic-type Glosses in the Old Testament." *JSS* 2: 149–62 = Pp. 32–54 in Weingreen, *From Bible to Mishna: The Continuity of Tradition*. Manchester: Manchester University Press, 1976.

Wellhausen, J. 1899. *Die Composition des Hexateuchs und der historischen Bücher des Alten Testaments*. 3d ed. Berlin: Reimer. Reprint, Berlin: de Gruyter, 1963.

Wenham, G. J. 1987. *Genesis 1–15*. WBC 1. Waco: Word.

Wernberg-Møller, P. 1962. "Some Observations of the Relationship of the Peshitta Version of the Book of Genesis to the Palestinian Targum Fragments Published by Professor Kahle, and to Targum Onkelos. *ST* 15: 128–80.

West, M. L. 1973. *Textual Criticism and Editorial Technique*. Stuttgart: Teubner.

Westermann, C. 1984. *Genesis 1–11: A Commentary*. Trans. J. J. Scullion. Minneapolis: Augsburg.

Wevers, J. W. 1974. *Text History of the Greek Genesis*. MSU 11. Göttingen: Vandenhoeck & Ruprecht.

_____. 1985. "An Apologia for Septuagint Studies." *BIOSCS* 18: 16–38.

_____. 1993. *Notes on the Greek Text of Genesis*. SCS 35. Atlanta: Scholars.

Wickes, W. 1887. *A Treatise on the Accentuation of the Twenty-One So-Called Prose Books of the Old Testament. With a Facsimile of a Page of the Codex Assigned to Ben-Asher in Aleppo*. Oxford: Clarendon.

Williamson, H. G. M. 1987. *Ezra and Nehemiah*. Sheffield: JSOT.

Yeivin, I. 1968. *The Aleppo Codex of the Bible: A Study of Its Vocalization and Accentuation* [Hebrew]. HUBP 3. Jerusalem: Magnes.

_____. 1980. *Introduction to the Tiberian Masorah*. Trans. and ed. E. J. Revell. MS 5. Missoula: Scholars.

Author Index

Subject Index

anticipation 7, 25, 32–34, 41, 43, 48, 67, 92, 122, 128, 132, 134, 137, 142, 146, 148
Aquila 69, 104
Aramaic; see Targums
archetype 6, 8–9, 22, 35, 47–48, 52, 55–56, 63–68, 71–75, 78–80, 98, 100, 113–114
assimilation 9, 33–34, 41, 43, 47, 57, 66–67, 137, 142

Ben Asher xii, 4, 117–118
Ben Hayyim, Jacob xii, 4
Ben Naphtali xii, 117
Ben Uzziel, Mishael xii, 117
best manuscript 111

canonical form 114
chronology 8, 54–55, 61–80, 85, 97–99, 130, 132, 146, 148
conjecture 6, 109; see diagnostic conjecture
critical apparatus 4, 40, 115–118
critical edition xiii, 14, 109–112, 115
critical text 5, 8, 10, 110–116

diagnostic conjecture xiii, 6, 9–10, 48, 59, 113
dittography 30–31, 40–41, 43, 49, 55, 87, 120, 122, 124, 125, 132, 136, 137, 140, 144
divine names 34–39

editorial revision 41, 50–51, 59, 77, 92, 144, 146
exegesis 14, 17, 19, 33, 81
explication 23, 41, 44–45, 48, 51–53, 56–57, 120, 122, 124, 125, 128, 130, 132, 134, 136, 140, 142

gloss 28, 48, 51–52, 57, 75, 76, 113
graphic confusion 7, 24–25, 40–41, 43, 47–48, 50, 53–55, 57–60, 85, 91, 94, 120, 124, 125, 128, 130, 132, 134, 136, 137, 140, 142, 144, 146, 148
Greek; see Septuagint
Greek-Hebrew equivalents 18–20, 24, 26, 30

haplography xiii, 23, 27, 30, 40–46, 49–50, 54–56, 60, 76, 85, 120, 122, 124, 128, 130, 132, 136, 137, 140, 144
harmonization 20–24, 26–32, 34–35, 37–38, 41, 51–54, 56–57, 67, 81–92, 96–97, 101–102, 120, 122, 124, 125, 128, 130, 132, 134, 136, 137, 140, 142, 144, 146, 148
ḥaṭep vowels 116–118
Hebrew (language)
    Late Biblical Hebrew 26, 120
    Qumran Hebrew 103, 105
    Rabbinic Hebrew 59, 103, 105
homoioarkton 23, 27, 30, 41, 49, 120, 122, 130, 140
homoioteleuton 27, 41, 44, 120, 124, 140, 144
horizontal transmission 94–95, 97–100
hyparchetype 80, 97–101

indicative errors 94–98, 100

Jerome 14, 18, 61, 74, 101
Josephus xiii, 15, 61, 69–71, 76–77, 99, 116
Jubilees xiii, 14, 69–71, 74, 76–77, 100, 116

164

Index of Biblical Citations